MARY WARD
FIRST SISTER OF FEMINISM

For Omi

MARY WARD
FIRST SISTER OF FEMINISM

SYDNEY THORNE

PEN & SWORD
HISTORY

AN IMPRINT OF PEN & SWORD BOOKS LTD.
YORKSHIRE – PHILADELPHIA

First published in Great Britain in 2021 by
PEN AND SWORD HISTORY
An imprint of
Pen & Sword Books Ltd
Yorkshire – Philadelphia

ISBN 978 1 39900 523 4

A CIP catalogue record for this book is available from the British Library.

Typeset in Times New Roman 11.5/14 by
SJmagic DESIGN SERVICES, India.
Printed and bound by CPI Group (UK) Ltd, Croydon, CR0 4YY

Pen & Sword Books Limited incorporates the imprints of Atlas, Archaeology,
Aviation, Discovery, Family History, Fiction, History, Maritime, Military, Military
Classics, Politics, Select, Transport, True Crime, Air World, Frontline Publishing,
Leo Cooper, Remember When, Seaforth Publishing, The Praetorian Press,
Wharncliffe Local History, Wharncliffe Transport, Wharncliffe True Crime and
White Owl.

For a complete list of Pen & Sword titles please contact
PEN & SWORD BOOKS LIMITED
47 Church Street, Barnsley, South Yorkshire, S70 2AS, England
E-mail: enquiries@pen-and-sword.co.uk
Website: www.pen-and-sword.co.uk

Or
PEN AND SWORD BOOKS
1950 Lawrence Rd, Havertown, PA 19083, USA
E-mail: Uspen-and-sword@casematepublishers.com
Website: www.penandswordbooks.com

Contents

Acknowledgements

I would like to thank Mark-Peter Holbek, Dr. Gabriele Kliegl, Ursula Pachlatko-Zürcher, Patrick Scanlan, Andrew Thorne, Irmgard Thorne and Nicky Thorne for reading the manuscript and raising interesting questions which led to the improvement of the text.

My hearfelt thanks too to Theodora Hawksley and Sr. Patricia Harriss CJ for lively discussions about Mary Ward, for insights into her mission and for granting me access to the Bar Convent library in York, and to Dr. Danna Messer and all the team at Pen and Sword for publishing the book.

And thank you Irmgard, Miranda, Lara and Nicky for putting up for so many years with a husband and dad so obsessed with Mary Ward.

Cast of main characters

Mary's family

Parents: Marmaduke Ward, Ursula Wright
Siblings: Frances Ward, Barbara Ward, Elizabeth Ward

Mary's childhood guardians

Ursula and Robert Wright, the parents of Christopher and Robert Wright
Katherine Ardington
Sir Ralph and Lady Grace Babthorpe, the parents of Barbara Babthorpe

Mary's first companions

Barbara Babthorpe
Jane Browne
Mary Poyntz
Susannah Rookwood
Catherine Smith
Barbara Ward
Winefrid Wigmore

Mary's later companions

Frances Bedingfield
Frances Brookesby
Elizabeth Cotton
Catherine Dawson
Anne Gage

Margaret Genison
Margaret Horde
Elizabeth Keyes
Mary Ratcliffe
Anne Turner (nurse)
Joyce Vaux

Backers of Mary's Institute

Father John Gerard, English Jesuit priest, later rector of the Jesuit college in Liège
Father Roger Lee, English Jesuit priest in St Omer
Jacques Blaes, Bishop of St Omer
Albert and Isabella, Habsburg Archdukes in Brussels
Ferdinand of Wittelsbach, Prince-Archbishop of Liège and Cologne
Lothar von Metternich, Prince-Archbishop of Trier
Father Domenico di Gesu e Maria, Dominican monk
Antonio Albergati, papal nuncio in Cologne
Napoleone Comitoli, Bishop of Perugia
Peter Pazmany, Archbishop of Bratislava
Maximilian Wittelsbach, Duke of Bavaria
Ferdinand, Habsburg Holy Roman Emperor

In Rome

Pope Gregory XV
Pope Urban VIII
Juan Bautista Vives, Isabella's ambassador in Rome
Mutius Vitelleschi, Jesuit father general
Francesco Ingoli, secretary of *Propaganda Fide*
Francesco Barberini, nephew of Pope Urban VIII

Opponents of Mary's Institute

Melchior Klesl, Archbishop of Vienna
Ernst Adalbert von Harrach, Archbishop of Prague

Giovanni Pallotto, papal nuncio in Prague
Pier Luigi Carafa, papal nuncio in Liège and Cologne
Henry Silisdon, rector of the English Jesuit Novitiate in Liège
William Harrison, John Bennett, Thomas Rant: agents of the English
    clergy in Rome

1

Why Mary Ward?

Mary who?

Four hundred years ago – in October 1621 – a Yorkshire woman called Mary Ward set off on a long, long walk from Brussels to Rome. She walked across a Europe in the throes of the Thirty Years' War, made her way over the Alps in winter and completed her epic 1,500 mile journey in only eight weeks.

It was, of course, highly unusual for a woman to undertake such a journey in the early seventeenth century. But Mary's reason for travelling was, if anything, even more extraordinary than the journey itself. Her aim was to persuade one of the most powerful men in Europe, the pope, to grant her, a woman, some of the rights and freedoms enjoyed by men. It was rare indeed for a woman to seek an audience with the pope, rarer still for a petitioner of either sex to challenge the pope on a point of doctrine. But Mary Ward was confident of her case. She had chutzpah.

What moved Mary Ward was a passion that is surprisingly modern: she saw the crying need for girls to be educated to the same standard as boys, and was appalled by the almost total absence of girls' schools. Within the previous century the Jesuits had established schools for boys across Europe and as far afield as Persia, Florida, Brazil and Japan. Very well, then: if the Jesuits could achieve this for boys, she would do the same for girls. It was a given that the teachers in boys' schools were male, so the teachers of girls must be women. But that meant that Mary and her female teachers must enjoy the same freedom of organisation as the Jesuit teachers. Hence her journey to Rome to see the pope. Her appeal for more freedoms for women was born from the practical realisation that if a network of girls' schools was to be set up across Europe and the world, then women must be given the freedom of action to achieve this. If Mary Ward was a visionary, she was a strictly practical one. Not a dreamer, but a do-er with big dreams.

Mary certainly had experience of fighting against the system. Born into an English Catholic family a few years before the Spanish Armada, she knew what it was like to grow up within a persecuted minority. Against a background of hideous executions of Catholic priests and those who harboured them, and a ban on celebrating Catholic Mass, most English Catholics – recusants,[1] they were called – were at any moment subject to house searches, punitive fines and imprisonment.

Thwarted by the penal laws that imposed restrictions and fines on anyone who did not toe the Church of England line, Mary Ward slipped out of the country and, within a few years, set up four girls' schools in four different European cities. And they were free. Indeed, they were among Europe's first ever free schools for girls.

What did Mary teach her girls? Sure, there was reading, arithmetic and needlework, as we may expect, but also Latin, modern languages and drama, subjects which were traditionally reserved for boys. In an age when female roles in Elizabethan theatre were still taken by men, this makes Mary Ward one of the first recorded people to put English girls on stage. And over and above setting up the schools themselves, Mary had to recruit women with the ability to teach in the schools and organise their training – as there was no existing system she could tap into. Not bad for a woman who was only 36 years old.

Back home in England, opening a Catholic school was illegal, so Mary operated clandestinely and established a secret network of women who went about in disguise and taught girls within their own homes. Mary Ward had pluck and initiative, but she soon faced the hostility of a more formidable power than the English government with its spies and pursuivants[2]: the mighty Catholic Church.

As a loyal Catholic, Mary adhered to the time-honoured Christian tradition of organising her teachers as a religious order of nuns. The trouble was, the Catholic Church did not accord nuns the same rights and freedoms as monks. Nuns were subject to strict enclosure. That is to say, they were forbidden to go out into society and obliged, instead, to spend their whole lives enclosed within the walls of their convent. There were no exceptions – not to teach, not even to look after the sick. These restrictions derived from the prevailing view that women were weaker creatures, prone to sin and incapable of taking responsibility for themselves. It was, in consequence, the duty of men to take charge of women, whether in convents where women were enclosed for their own good, or in marriage, where husbands had the duty to impose their will, if necessary, by force.

Mary Ward strove with all her being against this negative, defeatist view of women. 'There is no such difference between men and women that women may not do great things,' she asserted. It was a remarkably bold claim in the early seventeenth century.

What Mary Ward saw very clearly was that the problem lay not with women, but in the restrictions put upon them. That was the reason for her walk across Europe to petition the pope. Mary sought a dispensation from enclosure for herself and her teachers, a dispensation that would kick-start the effective teaching of girls. Given the benefits that would result, not least for the Catholic Church itself, it did not seem much to ask.

But the men in Rome had no intention of loosening the rules that gave them a grip on the lives of women. To begin with, they played for time. Then, when it became clear that Mary would not back down, all the force of the Vatican was brought down on her: muck-raking rumours, interception of letters, school closures, hearings before the Inquisition, orders restricting her freedom of movement, a papal bull, excommunication, prison. These men were ruthless. They were the very cardinals who, two years later, would force Galileo to recant.

So, on one level, Mary Ward's story is a classic tale of an individual's struggle for justice in the face of impossible odds. How will Mary respond to the pressure brought to bear on her? Will she compromise? Will she, like Galileo, recant? The fact that Mary Ward schools exist today in some thirty-eight countries is proof that victory of sorts was won in the end. Mother Teresa was a Mary Ward sister before she founded her own order. Africa's first female Nobel Peace Prize winner, Professor Wangari Maathai, was a student at a Mary Ward school in Kenya and Pope Benedict XVI attended a Mary Ward kindergarten in Germany. But what kind of victory was it? And how was it achieved against such odds?

Mary Ward's is also the story of an exceptional leader. Through setback after setback, Mary sustained an astonishing morale among her companions – the women who opted to join what she called her Institute. She had a gift for recognising leaders among them and for delegating authority to them, and they proved themselves exceptionally loyal, competent and resilient. They survived years of poverty and isolation and maintained the highest ethical and religious standards while Mary fought their corner in Rome. An order of teaching monks, founded at much the same time as Mary's Institute, was closed down for gross sexual misconduct.[3] Oh, how Mary's opponents would have crowed had they been able to uncover similar scandal among her companions! But though spies were set on them and their letters intercepted and opened, no evidence of untoward behaviour was ever unearthed. That speaks volumes about the calibre of the women that Mary appointed as superiors.

Mary led by trust, love, and – here's the surprising one – good humour. Her reaction when a priest thanked God he was not a woman because, said he, women cannot understand God? 'I answered nothing,' said she, 'but only smiled.' Her greatest comfort when negotiations in Rome were particularly tough? 'Mirth at this time is next to grace,' she wrote. Cheerfulness was so much part of Mary's nature that when her companions grew morbid around her deathbed, she led them in song. And paraphrasing Saint Paul's famous line about faith, hope and love she wrote, 'In our calling, a cheerful mind, a good understanding, and a great desire after virtue are necessary, but of all three a cheerful mind is the most so.' A cheerful mind rated higher than a great desire after virtue! It's a rare motto for an age in which rules were generally applied against the threat of punishment. It makes Mary Ward appealingly human, ordinary and modern.

As a Catholic in England, an Englishwoman in Flanders, and a woman in the Vatican, Mary Ward was the eternal outsider and her life offers fascinating glimpses into the societies on whose peripheries she existed. We meet the Gunpowder Plotters on their desperate flight from London. We see priests emerging from secret priest holes and cardinals at work in the Roman Inquisition. We find out what it was like to cross the Channel by boat, the Alps on foot, and Europe during the Thirty Years' War. We peek inside two of the most flamboyant courts in Europe, witness life inside a nunnery, and discover how prisoners use lemon juice to sneak messages past their gaolers. We meet a bishop raising the standard of education in his diocese and a prince bishop spending time with his mistress. We smell the decaying corpses of Catholic priests hung out on

London Bridge and hear the screams of a family executed for witchcraft in Munich. We narrowly miss the plague in Bologna, a siege in Mantua, and an earthquake in Naples, then shelter from the hand-made bombs lobbed by the Parliamentary forces besieging York.

And because we see all this through the eyes of an outsider, history as we thought we knew it is, as it were, pulled inside out. The Gunpowder Plotters are the cuddly uncles that Mary played with as a child, while Queen Elizabeth morphs from Good Queen Bess into a vindictive queen of the night. We meet English Catholics who, far from being potential traitors as they are still often portrayed, swore allegiance to, and fought for, their Protestant monarch. And while Catholic narratives would often have you think that English Catholics universally suffered persecution during this period, we shall meet Catholics who resided in fine houses, served as magistrates and were proud to see their sons knighted by the king. What's more, as we follow Mary on her travels across Europe, we shall be able to see the plight of Catholics in England in the light of the treatment of Protestant and Jewish minorities in Catholic Flanders, Bavaria and Austria – not, of course, to excuse or justify persecution on either side, but as a gentle reminder that religious persecution was not the one-way traffic that is sometimes implied.

Indeed, the very life and work of Mary Ward is a paradox. Her mission was to serve the Catholic Church by setting up a network of girls' schools across Europe. But in pursuit of that mission, by plucking women from their sheltered backgrounds, empowering them and launching them into the world as confident, active, responsible human beings, she carved out a modern role for women – the role of the professional woman free to go about town on her business.[4] It is the reason why, in a further delicious paradox, Mary the Catholic nun has been hailed as 'the first known English feminist.'[5]

The poignant tragedy is that had this pioneer of female education been allowed to achieve her dream back in the early seventeenth century, the benefits of education for humankind – male and female – would have come so much earlier.

I first heard of Mary Ward in Germany, from my mother-in-law-to-be. On my first visit to her flat, she dropped the name of Mary Ward as one would mention Shakespeare, in evident expectation that the name needed no further explanation. I was taken aback, for I had never heard the name before. It transpired that my mother-in-law had, as a child, attended a school in Bavaria run by Mary Ward sisters who, some 300 years after Mary Ward died in England, were still called the *Englische Fräulein* (English women). This Mary Ward had, apparently, lived in Yorkshire, in Brussels and in Munich – all places in which, by coincidence, I too had lived. In Canterbury she had found lodging in the house behind that oddly dilapidated brick gateway that I passed on my way into town. Later, my children's comprehensive school in York turned out to have evolved from England's first convent since the Reformation – yes, set up by those ubiquitous Mary Ward sisters. And then, when I discovered that Mary was buried in the village next door to where I live, I felt our paths had crossed so often that I really had to unearth her story.

So there you have it. I am not a historian, and I have no religious axe to grind. Nor is this an exhaustive history of Mary Ward in the tradition of Mary Chambers, Henriette Peters, Immolata Wetter and Margaret Mary Littlehales.[6] My motivation is solely to bring to a wider audience a story which I have stumbled into, and which has increasingly fascinated me the more I have delved into it.

England, indeed, has an unofficial pantheon of great women who fought for justice and reform in various fields of life: think Florence Nightingale, Elizabeth Fry, Edith Cavell, Mary Wollstonecraft, Elizabeth Gaskell. They are the women who, to put it flippantly, feature on postage stamps and banknotes. Their motivation often sprang from a deeply-held commitment to one particular religious denomination, but their contributions are now seen to transcend religious and regional divides and we are proud to acknowledge them as giants of our national heritage. As yet, these national female icons are still all white Anglo-Saxon Protestants, and the time has surely come for them to be joined by women from a wider cross-section of society. Arise, then, Mary Prince, Mary Seacole, and others championed by the ethnic minorities, and, from the Roman Catholic corner, step forward Mary Ward, in the words of Gemma Simmonds 'one of the most attractive figures in English history: joyful, fearless, deeply human and firm in her belief in the greatness of the ordinary.'[7]

Recusant: Twenty unsettled years (1585–1605)

The story is as old and as universal as civilisation itself.

A father has brought up his daughter with love and a firm hand, and now he has found her an eminently suitable match. The youth is rich, he is noble, he is willing – and, of course, marriage to the young man's family would be very much in the father's own interests. The daughter dotes on her father and has hitherto obeyed him in all things, but now, to his intense irritation, she refuses the husband he has found for her. Her reason is the simplest reason of all: she loves another.

There have been words, and tears, and pleadings, but the father is determined to exercise his prerogative as head of the family. And he has hit on a plan. Not very original, but it is a plan. So father and daughter are travelling together by coach to seek the advice of a wise man, trusted by both sides, who shall decide between them. Of course, while setting up the meeting, the father has made sure that the wise man will take the father's part.

In our version of this age-old story, the year is 1605, the location is Yorkshire, and the father goes by the wonderful name of Marmaduke Ward. A member of the gentry, he owns farmland near Ripon and manages the Newby estate alongside his manor house in Mulwith. His rank is important in our story, but even more so his religion. For Marmaduke is a recusant, one of that small, tenacious number of Roman Catholics who, despite King Henry VIII's break with Rome, have held true to what they still regard as England's traditional religion. His wife Ursula is of impeccable Roman Catholic stock.[1] Her mother, also called Ursula, had even been shut up in prison for her faith. And not for a short sharp shock. Grandma Ursula spent an awesome fourteen years in gaol. Fourteen years – think about it! I for one find it hard to get my head round that figure. Small wonder that her two boys John and Christopher – we shall meet them again soon – harboured a passionate hatred for the government in London.

Marmaduke's religion gave him access to a remarkable number of ancient, wealthy Yorkshire families who had kept the faith of their ancestors, many of them much above him in rank. Since Catholics married Catholics, and the number of eligible Catholics in Yorkshire was limited, Marmaduke was related to the Mallorys of Studley Royal, the Inglebys of Ripley Castle, the Vavasours of Hazlewood Castle near York, the Gascoignes of Parlington near Leeds, the Babthorpes of Osgodby near Selby, to name but a few. Some seventy years after Henry VIII put himself at the head of the Church of England, and despite a litany of laws and edicts enacted against recusants, these Catholic families still commanded wealth and power in the north of England.

And the match that Marmaduke now intended for his eldest daughter would connect the Wards with perhaps the very grandest Catholic families of them all. With luck, it might one day also become one of the richest.

The Nevilles, earls of Westmorland, had amassed eye-watering amounts of land, wealth and power in the north of England when, in 1569, Charles Neville led an armed uprising against Queen Elizabeth I. The Rising of the North, as it came to be called, clamoured among other things for the rights of Catholics and the release of Mary Queen of Scots. Release? Or was the intention more sinister – to remove Elizabeth from the throne and install Mary in her place? The pope certainly gave credence to this interpretation by choosing this moment to excommunicate Elizabeth and relieve English Catholics of their duty to obey her.

The rebels seized Durham in November 1569 and marched on York, the kingdom's most important city in the north. But Catholic families were, in fact, divided in their allegiance. Two Catholics related to Mary, Francis and David Ingleby, joined the rebels, while their father, Sir William Ingleby, fought for Elizabeth. The Rising picked up less support than expected, and when the earl of Essex marched against them, the rebels fled in disarray. Some 600 of them were arrested and executed. Charles Neville fled into exile, his assets were seized, his title made null and void.

Edmund Neville, the man chosen by Marmaduke in 1605 as his daughter's suitor, might not therefore seem an ideal choice as a son-in-law. But Charles had died childless, and Edmund was seen by Catholics as the rightful heir to Charles Neville's fortune. Moreover the death of Elizabeth in 1603 had given Catholics new hope. Her successor, James I of England, was after all the son of Mary Queen of Scots for whom Charles Neville and his supporters had risked their all. English Catholics had high hopes that, in return, James would restore the lands and titles taken from them. If so, Edmund Neville might become wondrously wealthy yet. Not that Marmaduke valued wealth for its own sake. Marmaduke had no doubt that Edmund would use any fortune that came his way to further the Catholic cause in England. That was his chief interest.

Well, there was another interest too, of course, thought Marmaduke as he glanced at his daughter sitting opposite him in the carriage: a brood of Catholic children. Children! Children were vital for the survival of Catholicism, but there was a dearth of them, not least because so many Catholic sons and daughters were choosing to become priests and nuns in monasteries and convents in France and Flanders. Of course, Marmaduke could hardly object to this flowering of faith in the younger generation. It was very laudable, very noble. But Marmaduke was not the only one to ask himself where, if so many of their offspring chose a virtuous future of celibacy, the next generations of Catholics would come from? Without children, Catholic families would die out. The sufferings of recusants in England would have been in vain; the Protestants would win by default. Marmaduke shifted in his seat. He was all the more resolved to ensure that his daughter married as he wished.

So much for Marmaduke, the father in the carriage trundling southward down the rutted London Road through Selby where the noble abbey church stood disused and stripped of its altar – a ghastly symbol, in Marmaduke's eyes, of an England stripped of its Catholic soul.[2]

But what of the daughter sitting opposite him?

Born in January 1585, Mary Ward was now 20 years old – and twenty unsettled years they had been. For the first ten, the earl of Huntingdon, president of the Council of the North, was particularly assiduous in sending his agents into Catholic homes to search for rosary beads, crucifixes or other evidence of Catholic practice. In response, Catholic families moved from house to house to evade the pursuivants, often sending their children to be brought up in the safety of another home. The result was that little Mary spent fully half her childhood separated from her brothers and sisters and her family home at Mulwith.

Mary was only 4 when she was sent to live with her maternal grandmother, the fearless Ursula Wright, she who had spent fourteen years in gaol for her faith. Grandma Ursula and her husband Robert Wright lived in Holderness, the flat tract of land that pokes out into the sea south-east of Hull. It was an ideal landing-place for many of the 800 Catholic priests who are estimated to have returned to England before 1603. They landed on the deserted beaches, celebrated Mass in secret in the Wright household, and departed, heavily disguised, to take the sacraments to other safe houses.

Imprisonment, then, had not persuaded Ursula to renounce her faith. Far from it. She spent hours of the day and night in prayer and sent food and money to Catholic prisoners in gaol. Little Mary, who slept in her grandmother's room, was deeply impressed by this combination of prayer and contemplation on the one hand, and direct practical action on the other.

Mary was fascinated, too, by the priests who arrived at dead of night and slipped away as suddenly as they appeared. No distant dignitaries who stood on protocol, these men arrived hungry and put their lives in the hands of the women of the house. They talked with reverence about men called bishops, and with awe and love about the pope in Rome who prayed for all his children, even those in faraway England. How could the little girl, separated from her own father, fail to idealise such a fount of all-embracing love? It was a deep, unshakeable, child-like view of the pope which Mary Ward would never lose, not even when she was condemned as a heretic – by a pope.

Mary duly learned to say her prayers and recite the rosary. She learned to read and write. She mastered basic arithmetic and Latin,[3] gave alms to the poor and fasted on days prescribed in the banned Catholic calendar. Not that fasting was the preserve of the religious. Many in the country were still swayed by folklore and superstition, and believed, for example, that girls who fasted on St Agnes Day (21 January) would that same night see their future bridegroom in their dreams. It makes Mary Ward all the more human to read that she too – encouraged, perhaps, by her aunt Alice – secretly began fasting one St Agnes Day. Alas, Mary's pangs of hunger were too great, she broke her fast, and no young man appeared in her sleep.

We may smile, but Mary's conclusion from this experience is significant: it was not hunger, but God who had protected her from the temptation of paganism. Or, if you like, God had provoked her hunger. The mechanics were immaterial. Modelling herself on her grandmother, Mary was already interpreting events in her life in terms of God's protective intervention on her behalf.

Mary was less influenced by her grandfather Robert because he conformed to the religious laws of the land enough to keep the family out of trouble, and to send his sons John and Christopher to St Peter's School in York. It was a common pattern in recusant households: husbands toed the line, while the women guarded the flame of the true faith at home. The law, for example, imposed a fine for failing to attend church on Sundays – so the head of the family attended church, while his wife, children and servants secretly celebrated Mass at home. Another law deemed guilty any recusant who failed to appear when summoned before the president and commissioners (as was Robert Wright in 1592) – so the head of the family would appear in court, but would first put his property in the hands of his wife or a friend, so that the court could not confiscate it.

It was the age-old game of cat and mouse, played at all times and in all places by all communities persecuted for their faith, race or political beliefs. The authorities clamp down on what they claim is a dangerous minority, the members of that minority develop strategies to outwit the worst excesses of the law. More than 200 executions of Catholics are recorded in Mary Ward's lifetime; but for most recusants the dominant feature of daily life was their sheer vulnerability to the whims of the monarch, local authorities, and even neighbours.

When Grandpa Robert died in July 1594, Mary, now aged 9, returned to Mulwith and to three new baby sisters: Frances, Elizabeth and Barbara. Given how little time Mary spent with her brothers and sisters, it strikes me that she developed remarkably strong bonds with them. During this particular stay, Mary was home for less than two years, and even this short period saw mighty upheaval. One night early in February 1595 a fire broke out in the house: flames consumed the furniture, the ceilings, the polished wooden floors and the dark wooden wall panelling, and in the thick smoke all was terror, noise and confusion. With Marmaduke busy organising help to put the fire out, it was a while before anyone realised that three of the children were unaccounted for. Were they, God forbid, still inside the burning building?

What happened next, according to the earliest biography of Mary Ward, is the stuff of legends: Marmaduke strode into the very flames and stumbled through the heat and smoke till he found Mary and

11

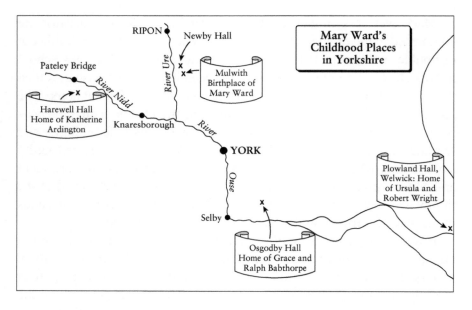

her sisters Barbara and Elizabeth, calm and composed in one room, reciting the rosary and praying for deliverance from the fire. Legend? Mary herself would not have thought so. As with her deliverance from pagan superstition on St Agnes Day, Mary saw the Hand of God in her miraculous escape. She had no doubt about it.

But I am a child of a less credulous age, and I have to admit that such stories make me feel vaguely uncomfortable. Rightly or wrongly, I am unable, unwilling, to see rescue from the fire as a personal intervention by God. My instinct is to rationalise what I am told. Was Mary perhaps in a part of the house that was not threatened by the flames? Was the bit about Mary saying the rosary maybe added later, to foreshadow her subsequent religious life? Well, it could be: we can never know, because what we are touching here are matters of faith. And unused to being confronted by such unquestioning faith, maybe I do not know how to deal with it. I am not persuaded by stories of miraculous rescue, but nor, I suppose, need I be. The stories are there to shed light on Mary Ward and *her* unshakeable faith in God, a faith as high as mountains and as deep as the sea, and the source of her energy, courage and audacity. Not that it gave her an easy life. His ways and His will are, God knows, mysterious, and Mary's understanding of them would bring her into conflict with the Church that claimed to know them best.

Soon after the fire at the manor house in Mulwith, Marmaduke moved his family to Alnwick in Northumberland. All except Mary, who was sent off again in 1596, this time to a widowed relative, Katherine Ardington, *née* Ingleby, in Harewell Hall, deep in the Yorkshire Pennines. The reason, we are told, was that Mary's health was frail. Marmaduke feared that the raw climate of Northumberland would be bad for her – an understandable concern in an era when between a third and a half of all children died before they reached the age of 16.

And yet the given reason does not quite ring true. Yes, Upper Nidderdale is glorious on a sunny morning when the dew is luminous and lambs gambol in the lush green meadows with all the joy of burgeoning life, but these can be bleak, windswept places, and when I walked to Aunt Katherine's house beneath the craggy rocks of Guise Cliff, it did not strike me as a particularly suitable refuge for a sickly child in winter. Nor was Harewell even safely remote: the house was just off the road to the lead mines near Pateley Bridge, and in 1586 pursuivants had come to the house, arrested Katherine Ardington and thrown her into prison in York. And the house had been searched again as recently as 1594. Perhaps, then, it was rather the character of Lady Ardington that persuaded Marmaduke to send Mary to Harewell Hall, for she was a woman of the same grit as Ursula Wright. She too emerged from prison with her faith strengthened, and she now became Mary's second feisty female role model. When Mary turned 12, Aunt Katherine had a priest smuggled into Harewell Hall for Mary to take her first communion.

Twelve years old. At a time when the average life expectancy in England was about 35, girls of Mary's age were coming into their marriageable years. Mary had indeed already had more than one proposal, but the youths had either disappeared (led away by the Hand of God?) or been turned down. A Catholic Northumbrian named Ralph Eldrington, for example, had proposed to Mary, and Marmaduke had urged her to accept the lad, but Mary would have none of him and Ralph faded from the scene.

But Marmaduke was more tenacious. His oldest daughter was growing up, the need to see her married was becoming more pressing, and Harewell Hall was not best placed for meeting eligible young men. So Marmaduke re-located his daughter once more in 1600, this time to Mary's Babthorpe relatives at Osgodby, near Selby. If Holderness had nurtured, and Harewell deepened Mary's devotion to her Catholic faith, Osgodby would see it blossom.

Low lies the land around Osgodby. The ploughed earth is black and heavy, the draining ditches are deep, and puddles stretch like necklaces along the muddy tracks long after it has stopped raining. To the north, a large area of unworked, water-logged land now known as Skipwith Common formed a barrier between Osgodby and York. When, in 1603 and 1604, 3,500 people died of the plague in York – a horrific proportion of the total population of some 11,000 – Osgodby escaped unscathed, even though twenty-four people perished in the hamlet of Monk Fryston less than 10 miles away. A barrier as effective as this offered a measure of protection for an isolated cluster of recusant families. And as the penal laws applied to those over the age of 16, as from January 1601 Mary was now a recusant in her own right.

In this flat country – as unlike the steep-sided valley at Harewell as can be imagined – the human eye yearns for a vertical feature and focuses gratefully on the soaring spire of Hemingbrough Minster, the church where generations of Babthorpes had worshipped. Indeed, they had paid for a chantry chapel which housed a life-sized stone carving of a corpse – a symbol of man's mortality. But all that changed in 1534, when the Minster was dissolved and the building became an Anglican parish church. No Babthorpe had set foot in there since.

Oh yes, the Babthorpes of Osgodby were another fervently Catholic family, and I am by now not surprised to discover that the redoubtable Lady Grace Babthorpe had served her time in gaol when the earl of Huntingdon summoned her in 1592. How often, he challenged her, had she attended Anglican worship as prescribed by the law? 'Never!,' she answered. And how many Masses had she heard during this time, asked Huntingdon. 'So many that I cannot count them,' she flung back at him. Grace Babthorpe received two years in gaol at Sheriff Hutton Castle for her temerity.

The Babthorpes maintained a seriously large household. Among the seven Babthorpe children, Mary found a special friend in Barbara, some six years her junior. Two chaplains and a Catholic schoolmaster ministered to the family and to neighbours in this recusant hotspot. And hiding-places were prepared for Mary's confessors Father John

Mush and Father Richard Holtby, and for visiting priests like Father John Gerard. The latter was a living legend: after years of evading the pursuivants in priest holes up and down the country, he had been captured and hung by his hands in the Tower of London till he fainted from the excruciating pain in his hands, arms, chest and belly. He was then revived, and made to hang again. But to the delight of the recusant community, Father Gerard had managed to throw a rope across the moat and stage a dramatic escape. We shall meet Father Gerard again, later.

The servants were hand-picked from loyal Catholic families, for a disloyal servant could betray the secrets of the house and send the men to the gallows. Even carelessness could be fatal. Just five years before, servants of the Watkinsons at Menthorpe, a few miles from Osgodby, were seen gathering large leaves on the day before Palm Sunday. The leaves, reasoned a peeping tom, were big enough to serve as palms for a Palm Sunday Mass, and (sniff, sniff) where there was a Mass, there must be a priest. The local justice of the peace was tipped off, and when his men stormed the house by night, they were rewarded with the discovery of Father Robert Thorp in the Watkinson household. In line with the macabre hierarchy of executions at the time, Thorp was hanged, drawn and quartered, Watkinson 'only' hanged.[4]

Elizabeth I died in March 1603. Were Mary Ward and the Babthorpes among the Catholics who cheered the new king, James, on his way to London? If so, they will have returned home disappointed for James excluded papists and wilful murderers from the list of prisoners freed in York.[5] The message was not lost on the recusant community, and some of the more impatient young men concluded that there was now nothing for it but to resort to violence.

Mary, meanwhile, spent her time devouring the religious books in the Babthorpe library. Marmaduke had brought Mary to Osgodby so that she might find a suitor, but it was not long before the suitor to whom Mary chose to dedicate her life was Christ himself.

Now, in Catholic countries young women who dedicated their lives to Christ became nuns. But Mary had never seen a nun. Her role models were Ursula Wright, Katherine Ardington and Grace Babthorpe, women who publicly stood up for their beliefs. And Catholic women who died for their faith. Margaret Clitherow, for instance, the York mother of three who, for hiding Catholic priests, was laid on the ground and had heavy stones thrown onto her till a sharp stone placed under her back snapped her spine. Similarly, Anne Line, who, for 'entertaining' a Catholic priest, was hanged in 1601, boldly declaring on the scaffold: 'So far I am from repenting for having so done, that I wish, with all my soul, that where I have entertained one, I could have entertained a thousand.' Or Margaret Ward, who, for helping Father Watson escape from Bridewell Prison, was hung by her hands and whipped before being hanged at Tyburn. Soon, Mary Ward began fantasising about dying a martyr's death herself.

By good fortune, however (or, as Mary Ward saw it, by God's will), there was in the Babthorpe household a maid, one Margaret Garrett, who was old enough to remember convent life in England, and who liked to chatter about it. A scene in the *Painted Life* shows Mary and her cousin Barbara listening, spellbound, to Margaret's tales.[6] And Margaret's tales evidently had their effect, for Mary's dream of martyrdom morphed after all into an aching desire to take the veil and become a nun.

A nun! The very outcome that Marmaduke had feared! He had entrusted his daughter to three women who anchored their Catholic faith in family life – and here she was, wishing to go abroad and join a convent. But from his eldest daughter Marmaduke expected marriage into a Catholic family, he would settle for no less. He required children – heirs to take the fight for the Catholic cause into the next generation. And that is why he had taken Mary away from Osgodby, and was now travelling with her to London.

The plan was to travel to Lapworth, in the Midlands, where they would meet Mary's uncle John Wright and his wife Dorothy in the house of friends called the Catesbys. After a few days' rest, Marmaduke and Mary would continue to London, where they had a rendezvous with Father Richard Holtby, one of Mary's Jesuit confessors in Osgodby. And Marmaduke was confident that Father Holtby would use his authority as a priest to change his daughter's mind.

So, in late October 1605, Marmaduke and Mary, each lost in their own thoughts, jolted their way southward towards Warwickshire. But, knowing it will be a while before Mary returns to Yorkshire, I linger a little longer in the area where she spent five formative years. Babthorpe Manor is no more, but Hemingbrough Minster's proud spire still soars 191 feet into the sky, etched now not only against the clouds but against the enormous cooling towers of Drax power station. The columns, the vaulting, the windows and the font inside the minster all survive from the pre-Reformation days when the Babthorpes worshipped here. And, amazingly, I find a faint echo of Mary's stay in the area in the chapel north of the chancel – for it is still called the Babthorpe Chantry.

High on the chancel wall there now hangs a painting of the Madonna and Child. The Babthorpes would have approved of it, their immediate successors would have considered it idolatrous. So we have come full circle. And one man in the minster has seen all these changes come and go with equanimity. No longer in the Babthorpe Chantry but in the north transept lies the life-sized stone carving of a cadaver which the Babthorpes knew very well – a symbol of man's mortality.

1621: The long road to Rome

Walking, walking, walking.
Walking, wading, fording.

The tracks are dusty, stony or muddy, depending on the weather. In places, bundles of matted reeds and twigs have been laid over the ruts to prevent feet from sinking in, but real paving is rare. Signposts are even rarer.

Tolls are levied on vehicles, cattle and merchandise. France alone has 5,688 tolls in the early seventeenth century.

Rivers are usually forded. The Po has only one bridge below Turin, the Danube no bridges below Regensburg, the Rhine no bridges below Strasburg. Paris has only two bridges in 1613. Bridges bring trade and prosperity, as in Frankfurt, whose bridge over the Main channels much of the north-south trade in Germany. But they can also bring destruction, by allowing enemies to invade. So the bridges over the Rhine at Basel and Strasburg have wooden planks that can be quickly taken up if an army approaches.

Wolves are still a danger in many European countries. As late as 1773 the authorities in Grandfontaine, between Nancy and Strasbourg, will reward a forester for killing forty-one wolves.

Stage coaches with cushioned seating inside and cheaper seating out on the roof have yet to make their appearance.

So, apart from short stretches by boat, Mary Ward walks. And walks.

3

Rebellion: A frightening sequence of events (1605)

The Gunpowder Plot of November 1605 is surely the most celebrated attempted act of terrorism in British history. Tamed as it now is with fireworks, bonfires and those irresistible grilled sausages, it is easy to lose sight of the scale of the atrocity that was planned – the murder of the monarch and the assembled houses of parliament in one single, horrific explosion. The famous engraving of the plotters with their wizard-like hats and beards has bequeathed us a deceptively romantic cloak-and-dagger picture of a plot which might easily have plunged the country into civil war. A far less violent act in 1618, when three representatives of the Austrian emperor Ferdinand were thrown out of a palace window in Prague, unleashed thirty years of war across Europe.

The extraordinary point about the events of November 1605 from the perspective of our story is that our Mary was related, in one way or another, to nearly all of the plotters.

Mary had spent five years in the home of her uncles John and Christopher Wright, while Thomas Percy was the husband of her Aunt Martha. A complicated web of family connections connected her to Thomas and Robert Wintour, Ambrose Rookwood and Thomas Keyes. And the house in which Mary and her father Marmaduke were staying at the time of the plot belonged to the leader of the conspiracy, Robert Catesby. One cannot but wonder: was it by chance that Marmaduke was in Catesby's house at the time of the plot, or by design? It has never been alleged that Marmaduke was party to the actual plot. But whether he was wittingly or unwittingly involved in the plotters' escape is another matter.

We now know, of course, that the kegs of gunpowder in the cellars of the House of Lords never exploded. Lord Monteagle received an anonymous letter warning him to avoid the state opening of parliament on 5 November. Monteagle passed the letter on to King James's chief minister, Robert Cecil, and when Cecil ordered Sir Thomas Knyvett to search the cellars, Knyvett discovered Guy Fawkes as he was about to light the first fuse.

Fawkes was arrested, questioned and gruesomely tortured until he betrayed the names of his fellow conspirators, who by this time had fled to the very part of the country which Marmaduke had chosen for the break in his journey. Clearly, what the plotters needed most desperately on that day was fresh horses for their flight – and what was Marmaduke doing on the afternoon of 5 November but leading a fresh horse to the very house at which the conspirators had arranged to convene. No wonder he was arrested when the authorities got wind of the foiled plot in London. 'Marmaduke Ward, gentleman, of Newbie, in the county of York,' we are told, was 'taken ... on November 6, 1605, at Beauchamp's Court, Warwickshire.'

Marmaduke's story was that John Wright's wife Dorothy had 'entreated him ... to go to Mr. Winter with a horse to Huddenton [Huddington], when as [he] past by Alcester an hour after the troops past, [he] was apprehended ... He further saith he knew not of the companies passing that way until they came to Alcester, nor of their purpose anything at all.'[1]

Coincidence? Or had it been arranged that Marmaduke would have a horse that day for the plotters – the companies passing?

Frustratingly, we shall probably never know. It is just one more of the many mysteries that surround the story of the Gunpowder Plot, including who wrote the giveaway letter to Monteagle. That question may touch on Marmaduke as well, for one version is that the fateful letter was handed to Monteagle by a member of household called Thomas (*wait for it!*) ... Ward. Of course, Ward is a common enough name; but the historian Henry Spink traced Thomas Ward back to Mulwith and speculates that Thomas Ward was none other than Marmaduke's brother. Might Thomas have got wind of the plot? And, fearing the reprisals that would follow, had Thomas maybe begged Marmaduke to come to Warwickshire to plead with his brother-in-law John Wright to call it all off?

But enough speculation! Marmaduke is arrested on his way to Huddington, the house where the conspirators regroup on that grim afternoon of 5 November. Most of the conspirators ride on from Huddington to Holbeach House, where they are surrounded by 200 men sent by the sheriff of Worcestershire. Catesby, Thomas Wintour, John

Grant and both Wright brothers are killed outright in the shoot-out that ensues. Thomas Percy dies from his wounds, Ambrose Rookwood is arrested. The remaining conspirators are rounded up, and early in 1606 they are condemned to be drawn with their feet tied to a horse, and then hanged. They will be taken down while still alive and have their genitals cut off and burnt before their eyes. Their bowels and heart will be gouged out, and they will then – finally – be decapitated. The cruelty of the punishments meted out by the authorities forms a backdrop to Mary Ward's life that always threatened those who rebelled against the system.

What, meanwhile, of Mary herself? On her first ever journey to London, steeling herself for a meeting that will decide whether she must marry a man against her wishes, she finds herself confronted, out of the blue, with a bewildering and frightening sequence of events. Rumours fly to and fro, and when the facts emerge, they are as grim as they can be. Her father has been arrested. Three uncles have been slain. Her aunts Dorothy, Margaret and Martha have been taken into custody. Warrants of arrest have been issued against Father Gerard and other priests. We can imagine Mary's anguish. What will happen to her father? And what should *she* do? Should she stay put or return to Yorkshire? All we can know for sure is that she will have sought comfort in prayer.

In the event, the Catholic families in Warwickshire take the abandoned Mary Ward under their wings and lie low. It does not take a genius to work out that retribution will follow: indeed, that is why most English Catholics adamantly oppose violent uprisings in the first place. They know they will be their principal victims.

After an agonising wait, Mary learns that Marmaduke has been taken to London on suspicion of high treason. Things look bleak indeed. But then the astonishing news comes through that far from being charged, Marmaduke has been set free. It is hardly believable – and some have wondered whether Marmaduke was protected by a person at court, maybe by Lord Monteagle himself?[2] But whatever the reasons, the plan that was so abruptly cancelled is just as suddenly back on track. Father and daughter, both no doubt badly shaken, re-unite and return to their plan to meet Father Holtby. And that is how, for the first time in her life, Mary arrives in London.

It was a larger city than Mary could possibly imagine.[3] Most of its tall, narrow wooden houses still clustered within the city walls, and Mary will have been bewildered by the bustle – one [could] scarcely pass along the streets, on account of the throng, wrote one visitor.[4] Looming in the east was the Tower of London; towering in the centre was the old Gothic cathedral of St Paul's, whose spire, which had once soared as gracefully as Hemingbrough's, had been struck by lightning in 1561 and never rebuilt. Odd, that at a time when men were at each other's throats across Europe in the name of religion, a capital city lacked the fervour and resolve to repair its cathedral. Nor, we shall discover, was London unique in this respect.

Such a crowded medieval city was, of course, an ideal hiding-place for Marmaduke and Mary to meet Father Holtby – so it comes as a surprise that they did not take cover here at all. Instead Marmaduke and Mary put up in Baldwin's Gardens, a road that had been laid out in 1589 for rich Londoners looking for desirable residences in what had until recently been empty land between London and Westminster.[5] One of Marmaduke's Catholic friends was clearly wealthy and confident enough to have set up home in this fashionable street. It was a strangely prominent location in which to set up a meeting with a Catholic priest in the weeks following the Gunpowder Plot, but Marmaduke was bent on settling the issue of his daughter's marriage once and for all. Having come this far, he was not going to turn back.

Father Richard Holtby commanded respect. At 53 years old, he had been active as a priest in England since 1579, successfully dodging the authorities in safe houses like the Babthorpes' home in Osgodby. He listened as Marmaduke explained why his daughter could best serve the Catholic cause by marrying the likely heir to the Westmorland estate – and to Mary's chagrin, he sided with her father.[6] As Mary tells it, 'My confessor, to whom I had confessed for seven years ... was also of opinion that in no way ought I to leave England nor to make myself a religious.'[7] Even if she were a novice (a nun who had not yet taken her public vows of poverty, obedience and chastity), said Richard Holtby, he would advise that she should leave the convent and marry as her father desired. His words, we may well understand, caused Mary inexpressible distress.

Well, that was that. The father had got his way. Or had he? It is typical of Mary Ward that she showed all the humility and obedience due to male authority, while making it irritatingly clear that she put her trust in God, not in men. Of course, neither Marmaduke nor Father Holtby could object to her trust in God, but her stance fell just short – frustratingly short – of the total, unconditional obedience these male authorities were accustomed to.

Father Holtby now prepared a Mass to bring the meeting to an end. But all was not as it seemed, for the priest was clearly upset. His hands were shaking, and when it came to Communion his hands shook so much that he knocked over the chalice and spilt the wine. Was this a sign of God's displeasure? That, having sided with Marmaduke, he was now no longer worthy to hold the blood of Christ? This is certainly how Father Holtby took it, for he abruptly turned to Mary and said, 'I will never more hinder your religious design and holy resolution, but further you all I can and assist you to effect it as much as possible.'[8] It was a remarkable volte face. Mary's confidence that God would direct things for the best, even when men in authority over her had decided otherwise, had been vindicated. It was a lesson she would never forget.

As for poor Marmaduke – well, I imagine he must have been astonished beyond measure. All his well-laid plans suddenly lay in tatters. But he was a man of his word: he had said he would abide by Father Holtby's decision, and so he did. This dominating character now recedes from our story – leaving Mary free to travel abroad and join a convent.

She finally set off around Whitsun 1606. Her first stop was Canterbury, where Mary took a right turn at St Dunstan's Church, and then turned left through a step-gabled, red-brick Tudor archway to arrive at Place House, once the home of Margaret Roper, the eldest daughter of Sir Thomas More.[9] It was Margaret Roper's daughter-in-law Lucy who now lived there. Lucy had inherited her grandfather's and mother's Catholicism, but far from suffering from persecution, as we might expect, Lucy was wealthy enough to own both Place House and Well Hall in Eltham, and her eldest son William was knighted by James in July 1603, along with two of his cousins.

And yet Lucy was fully involved in the people-smuggling trade of the day – the illicit smuggling of Catholic girls to convents in Flanders. The law forbade young women from going overseas to join a convent, and government spies kept a look-out for women who might be trying to do so. But Lucy's cousin Catherine Bentley specialised in escorting young Catholic women abroad, passing them off as her daughters or nieces – and it was now arranged that this is how Mary Ward would leave her native England.

The authorities already had their eyes on Catherine Bentley, and she would one day herself have to flee to Flanders. That, however, was in the future.

In May 1606 Catherine Bentley and Mary Ward set sail for Calais.

1621: The long road to Rome

Walking, walking, walking.
Walking, stopping, resting.

You have to find shelter well before the shadows lengthen, for town gates are shut fast at dusk. In Protestant cities, they are locked during sermons too.

Inns are often of dubious cleanliness. Some travellers carry their own bedding, for fear of fleas. Many sleep in their own clothes for the same reason. Some prefer to sleep on tables to avoid the vermin in beds. The lucky ones get the nice warm benches around the stove. There may be several beds in one room, and in German lands several travellers may share a bed, so there is no privacy as we would understand it today. Italy offers the luxury of one traveller per bed.

The evening meal is often shared, too. All sit at one big table – all except the hangman, whose company is shunned. Food is usually served in wooden dishes. Germans often drink from pewter or stone, Venetians from glass. In England, guests often save part of their evening meal for use as breakfast. In German-speaking lands breakfast is often not taken at the inn, but at the town gate.

And then the next day's walking begins.

4

Religious: A Poor Clare in St Omer (1606–1607)

The miniscule port of Dover receded into the distance, and for the first time on her event-filled journey from Osgodby, Mary Ward suffered a crisis of confidence. 'A great obscurity darkened my mind,' Mary wrote in her account of her life, 'and doubts rose up within me.'[1]

It is hardly surprising. She found herself for the first time in her life in the middle of the sea, and she was in what we would consider a ridiculously small boat.

Back in the early 1600s the crossing from Dover to Calais took four hours or so in good conditions, but sea crossings could be bedevilled with dangers and delays that would seem extraordinary today. Two ambassadors travelling to Dover in 1610 had to wait two weeks in Calais before they could even make a start. The writer John Chamberlain set out from Rotterdam in 1611 and was blown back into the same port twenty-four hours later. On his second attempt, his boat was blown hopelessly off course during two days of storms, and when it finally ran aground at the mouth of Yarmouth harbour, some passengers drowned before the rest could be brought ashore in boats.[2]

But what travellers feared even more than the weather were pirates such as those who boarded the earl of Worcester's boat in 1573, killed eleven people and seized property worth £500. The French blamed English pirates for plundering French boats to the tune of 100,000 crowns a year. The English in turn blamed the *Dunkirkers* – 'scarce one bark in five' escaped them, complained the mayor of Exeter in 1600. The *Dunkirkers* were, in fact, usually Spanish vessels trying to intercept Dutch shipping as part of Spain's attempt to quell the Dutch struggle for independence. If they had the opportunity to plunder an English ship or two on the way, so much the better.

These local raiders were joined in the early seventeenth century by fellow 'pirates' from an unexpected country: forty 'Turkish' ships were said to be operating in waters off the southern coast of England by 1630, with six English ships lost to the 'Turks' as far west as Bristol. Most of these ships set off from what was then called the Barbary Coast of North Africa (present day Algeria), and by 1627 they were striking as far afield as Iceland. In a raid in 1631 they kidnapped more than 100 men, women and children in Baltimore in Ireland, taking them to be sold into slavery in North Africa. Piracy and kidnap were such real and ubiquitous dangers that people travelling from Flanders to Italy would rather risk the land route over the Alps than putting out to sea. Mary Ward would do so herself.

Nor were harbours necessarily safe havens. Channel ports were repeatedly besieged, taken and retaken by warring armies. Calais had been in English hands for over a hundred years before the French took it back in 1558; in 1596 they lost it to Spain – for Spain laid claim to the Low Countries from Calais to the German border. By the time Mary Ward arrived in 1606, the French had grabbed Calais back again. Further north the Dutch, fighting for independence from Spain, took Ostend in 1600, temporarily making it safe for Protestant boats, but they lost it to Spain in 1604. In English ports, meanwhile, boatmen were suspected of smuggling Catholic priests into England and ferrying Catholics abroad – as many 5,000 English Catholics are estimated to have crossed the Channel to begin life in a religious house abroad between 1598 and 1642. Woe betide a ship that was blown back into a British port and found to be carrying rosaries, prayer books, Bibles, or any other evidence of Catholic activity.

The boats that plied the Channel were not, of course, ferries in any sense that we would recognise. Mary Ward and her 'mother' Catherine Bentley, having each paid their 5 shillings for the journey, would have had to find floor space among the sixty or so passengers on the deck of the 60-foot long wooden boat, or might have sought shelter below among the crates and sacks of cargo. Fires were out of the question for obvious safety reasons, so passengers made do with cold food. On Protestant boats, passengers sang psalms and were fined for swearing – and garlands of flowers were draped from the mast if the captain was engaged to be married.

On arrival in Calais, the boat stayed out at sea, obliging Catherine and Mary to transfer onto a smaller landing vessel which charged them a further fee. Never mind! The crossing had been safely made. It was time for Mary Ward to part with Catherine Bentley, to find the coach to St Omer, to cross from France into Spanish Flanders – and to *arrive*.

For the first time in her life, Mary Ward was in a country where Catholicism was practised freely, a fact that will have been visible all around her. The names of the streets resounded with the names of monastic orders – the street of the Dominicans, Benedictines, Carmelites, Franciscans, Augustinians. Statuettes of saints and the Madonna graced alcoves at street corners. Bells called the faithful to Mass and people crossed themselves in public. Priests and monks walked in the streets and town square as openly as merchants and builders.

Priests and monks, yes – but no nuns. For centuries it had been the rule that nuns were enclosed: once they had taken their full vows, they were not allowed to leave their convent. It is true that this rule had often been disregarded, but following the shock of the Reformation a conference of Catholic bishops in the northern Italian city of Trento had taken steps to eliminate some of the loose practice for which the Church had been attacked – and one of the decrees of the Council of Trento was that full enclosure of nuns must now be rigorously observed. As Pius V put it in his papal bull (or decree) Circa Pastoralis of 1566: 'We command … that all nuns, now and in the future, regardless of their order, whether they have taken their vows secretly or in public, whatever name they give themselves, even if their own order does not explicitly ordain enclosure, and even if enclosure has never been observed in their order before, live in enclosure from now on and for ever.'[3] A treatise on the enclosure of women written as late as 1681 gives the reasoning: 'A nun out of enclosure is like a tree wrenched out of the earth, like a fish out of water, like a lamb out of its pen and in danger of being devoured by wolves, like a bird out of its nest or a frog out of its marsh, like a corpse out of its tomb that can infect anyone who comes near … .'[4]

This enclosed existence was the life that Mary Ward was now intending to lead. She would have one year as a novice during which period the superior of her convent would be allowed to dismiss her, and Mary would be entitled to abandon her novitiate if she felt it did not suit her. If successful, she would profess, or qualify for full nun-hood, and take the three public vows of obedience, poverty and chastity. She would then be a full member – or a choir sister – of the convent. She would live according to the particular rule of the convent's order (Benedictine, Cistercian, Poor Clares, etc., each had their own Rule), would sing the Divine Office in choir (hence choir sister), partake in all the activities in the convent, and vote in its affairs. From that point on she would no longer be allowed to set foot beyond the convent's walls.

But which convent was Mary to join? Mary had been agonising about this. Not that there was a shortage of choice in St Omer. Thanks to the trade brought by its sea canal, the town was one of the biggest in the Netherlands. Its church of Notre-Dame had recently been raised to cathedral status when Emperor Charles V destroyed the nearby cathedral town of Thérouanne, and its very rare astrological clock was an impressive symbol of the city's new-found pride. As a cathedral city, St Omer now sported its own bishop, established in his own palace – and the bishop in Mary Ward's day was Bishop Jacques Blaes.

He was aptly named. Bishop Blaes blazed with a passion for raising the standard of education in his diocese. And not only for boys: Bishop Blaes provided funds to enable Marie Aubrun and Agnes de Mailly to run two girls' schools. But boys had the better deal, for their schools were run by the religious orders that Blaes actively welcomed to St Omer. Religious orders were a great catch for a town. They had their own sources of funding, and they brought status through their links with powerful men. In the case of the Spanish Netherlands, the connections were to a powerful man and woman, for the rulers, Albert and Isabella, were both archdukes in their own right.

Recently an organisation of – if the pun may be forgiven – quite a different order had arrived in St Omer. These were the Jesuits, and as the Jesuits will play a big part in our story, it is worth taking a moment to consider who they were and what they stood for. Ignatius of Loyola had founded the Society of Jesus for men who trained extremely hard in order to dedicate themselves to a life of mission for the Catholic

Church. The Jesuits studied theology, philosophy and the humanities for ten (!) years, were rigorously trained in logic, and carried out 'spiritual exercises' designed to help them love and serve Christ. Ignatius had obtained special concessions from the pope to give his followers the flexibility to carry out their missionary work. In particular, while all other orders answered to local bishops, the Jesuits were exempted from this local control and answered directly to the pope.

As part of their missionary work, the Jesuits provided first-class education to the sons of important families in as many countries as possible, and the results spoke for themselves. Their school in Billom, Puy de Dome (1535) was followed by schools in Leuven in Spanish Flanders in 1542, Mainz and Ingolstadt in Germany in 1542 and 1549, and in Vienna in 1551. They arrived in Poland in 1558, in Sweden in 1577, and in Moscow in 1581. The schools gave the Jesuits enormous influence over the next generation – by 1600 the bishops of Salzburg, Breslau, Olmütz, Augsburg, Trieste, Würzburg and Passau were all Jesuit-educated. By 1627, some 40,000 boys were receiving a Jesuit education in France. And the growth of the Jesuits outside Europe was just as phenomenal. Jesuits started preaching in India in 1541, in Brazil in 1549, in Japan in 1563, in Florida in 1566, and in Angola in 1579 – one year before they began work in England.

The Jesuits who arrived in St Omer in 1566 from Wallonia (what would be southern Belgium today) were joined in 1593 by Jesuits from England. Banned from running schools and training priests at home, English Catholics responded by setting up colleges abroad, and the English Jesuits chose St Omer for theirs. The English Jesuits were teaching some 100 boys when Mary Ward arrived in town, providing an education that included the arts, drama and colourful processions.[5] The college ran its own printing press and owned a valuable collection of books, including a first folio of Shakespeare's plays that was rediscovered in St Omer in 2014.

It was to these English Jesuits that Mary Ward had a letter of recommendation from Father Holtby.

So, taking her courage in both her hands, Mary knocked at their heavy front door.

Mary found, to her relief, that she was expected. And not only expected. Without consulting her, the Jesuits had arranged for Mary to join the convent of the Poor Clares, a female order with a particular emphasis on poverty. So far so good – that sounded like the sort of order that Mary would wish to join. But the convent apparently had no more spaces for choir sisters, so Mary was to be accepted as a novice lay sister.

This was a shock – for in the seventeenth century convents were organised on class lines. The choir sisters – the full members of the convent who sang the Divine Office in choir, partook in the full life of the convent, voted in convent affairs and lived within enclosure – were educated young women drawn from wealthy families. They were admitted only if they brought a large dowry as a financial contribution to the institution, making convents, in the words of Eileen Power, 'essentially aristocratic institutions, the refuge of the gently born.'[6]

The daughters of poorer families were admitted as lay sisters. These women, who usually spoke no Latin, did not sing the Divine Office, had no vote in convent affairs, did not take the same vows and were therefore not enclosed. More to the point, they did the meaner, heavier work of the convent – the work that would have roughened the smooth, delicate hands of the choir sisters. And one of their chief activities was begging for alms.

Mary Ward, a gentlewoman fluent in Latin, would have expected by right to be admitted as a novice choir sister, but she now faced years of walking the streets of St Omer and surrounding villages, begging alms in her halting French and Flemish. As a lay sister, she would have no contact with the English choir sisters, and few in the sizeable English Catholic ex-pat population in St Omer would deign to associate with a woman begging in the streets. But Mary accepted her lot, trusting that God would direct her life for the best. And I like to think that while walking in St Omer, Mary sometimes sought comfort within the cathedral at the shrine of Saint Erkembode, who, as bishop, had walked his diocese so extensively that he developed a bad limp. When he died Erkembode became the patron saint of children with disabilities, and pilgrims to his shrine traditionally placed a shoe on his grave. A saint revered for his walking – it would be hard to think of a saint more fitting for Mary Ward.

The one man who had contact with Mary at the convent was her Jesuit confessor, Father Keynes – and it did not take him long to realise that Mary Ward was not best suited to being an external lay sister. So he recommended a change. But instead of trying to get Mary accepted as a choir sister, Father Keynes advised Mary to leave the Poor Clares convent altogether.

Mary was thrown into total confusion. Should she follow her confessor's advice? Or would this be yielding to temptation and taking the easy way out? Should she remain with the Poor Clares, as her abbess advised? Mary hesitated for several months, praying for guidance.

Guidance came in the form of a 'visit', or inspection, to the Poor Clares by Andres de Soto, the grandly-named Franciscan Commissary General of the Provinces of Strasbourg, Cologne, Ireland, England, Flanders, and Lower Germany. The visitor was akin to a seventeenth-century Ofsted inspector, although as confessor to Archduke Isabella Andres de Soto wielded even more influence. He was the first of the many powerful men that Mary Ward would have dealings with in her life, and the encounter gives us a fascinating glimpse of Mary's strategy for dealing with them. As she had done with her father and Father Richard Holtby, she showed de Soto all the obedience due to his male authority, but combined her humility with an assertion of female independence that took the great man by surprise.

On this occasion, De Soto agreed with Father Keynes that Mary should leave the Poor Clares: 'My daughter,' he said, 'this life is not for you; choose another way, and I shall help you to the best of my power.' So Mary Ward followed the great man's advice and left the Poor Clares. But then, far from leaning on the great man for help as he expected, Mary used her new-found liberty to decide, by herself, on a project that dumbfounded de Soto and all St Omer with him. She would, she announced, set up her own Poor Clares convent in Flanders. One that would cater specifically for English women.

A convent for English women! It was typical of the age that while English men had a choice of several English religious houses in Flanders, there was only one small convent specifically for English women: an English Benedictine Convent in Brussels founded in 1599 by Mary Percy. Yet English women had just as much need of their own national institutions as English men. It was not just a matter of language: the English women were in exile and, lacking any models of convent life in their native country, their expectations of convent life were often unrealistic.

It was a daring project indeed for an unknown 22-year-old novice. She needed finance, and used some 10,000 florins of her dowry money (retrieved, I wonder, from the Walloon sisters? Or had it never been paid?) to purchase a suitable property in the quaintly named village of Ekelsbeke in the diocese of Ypres.[7] She needed the permission of the local bishop, and Bishop Blaes promised to put in a good word for her with the bishop of Ypres. And she needed a confessor who, at Mary's request, should be from the English Jesuit college. A confessor who spoke the language of the convent sisters? That sounded reasonable enough.

But Mary had not reckoned with the quagmire of Church politics. The bishop of Ypres was a Franciscan who resented the increasing influence of the upstart Jesuits, and he wanted a Franciscan confessor to be appointed – not a Jesuit. And he imposed three conditions. The first condition, that the English sisters must not go begging in the streets, deprived the budding convent of a principal source of income. The second condition, that the new convent must be within a fortified town, undermined Mary's project because the house she had found for her new convent was in a village. And the third condition, that the new convent must be put under his sole authority as a bishop and a Franciscan, torpedoed Mary's wish for a Jesuit confessor. And then the bishop produced his trump card: these conditions were supported by none less than Commissary General Andres de Soto himself.

However, if the bishop and the Commissary General thought they could brow-beat Mary Ward, they had underestimated her. Mary dealt with the bishop's conditions with characteristic energy and aplomb.

To address the first point, Mary shored up her convent's finances with a donation from Edward Gage, the father of Anne Gage, a fellow English nun in St Omer. To satisfy the second, she exchanged the property she had purchased in Ekelsbeke for a plot of land in the walled city of Gravelines. And to counter the third, she sought powerful allies of her own. She would go over the bishop's head and go to the very top: she would petition Archdukes Albert and Isabella. If they backed her choice of confessor, she reasoned, would the bishop dare object?

A petition presented in person would of course have more effect than one written in a letter.

So, undaunted by the prospect of appearing at the court of two of the most powerful sovereigns in Europe, Mary Ward set off for Brussels.

1621: The long road to Rome

Walking, walking, walking.
Walking, praying, venerating.

Mary and her small band of followers are not the only pilgrims on the road. Some head for local shrines like that of St Erkembode in St Omer, others are on their way to Rome or to the tomb of St James at Santiago de Compostella. Like Mary, they wear a broad-brimmed hat to shield their eyes from the sun. The pilgrim's hat and cloak afford a degree of protection, even in Protestant territories.

Pilgrims spend the night at monasteries and hospices. And they venerate relics in churches along their way: in Liège the relics of St Lambert, in Arras manna fallen from heaven, in Milan the shrines of St Ambrose and St Charles Borromeo. Turin is famous for its shroud with the imprint of the face of Christ, Cologne boasts the magnificent golden shrine of the Three Magi, and Paris the Crown of Thorns. Trier outshines them all, claiming as many bodies of saints as there are days in the year, and the very loincloth worn by Christ on the Cross.

Relics raise the status of Catholic towns. When Charles of Lorraine wants Europe to take note of his capital, Nancy, he first secures the relics of St Sigisbert for its cathedral.

And relics strengthen the resolve of the Catholic faithful. Mary Ward will make the pilgrimage to Loreto to pray for strength at the House of the Virgin Mary. And both the great scientist Galileo Galilei and the great mathematician and rationalist philosopher René Descartes will do the same.

5

Revelation: 'Some other thing' (1607–1609)

Brussels was a prosperous, thriving city in Mary Ward's day, and its court one of the most flamboyant in the whole of Europe. In what would turn out to be a five month stay in Brussels, Mary Ward was to get to know both.

Mary may have entered the city through a gate such as the massive Porte de Hal that still stands in Brussels today, or by boat through a water-gate, for Brussels was connected to the sea by a canal. And what a canal! Begun in 1550, 17 miles long and 30 metres wide, the Willebroek Canal linked Brussels via the river Scheldt to Antwerp. When Mary Ward arrived in 1607, the canalside quays were still being built. One crane erected in 1573 was so powerful that it would be used 250 years later to hoist Belgium's first locomotive when it arrived from England.[1] People as well as freight arrived at the quayside because in an age when roads were frequently virtually impassable, water transport was often faster and cheaper. The Low Countries offered the best passenger service in Europe.[2]

Many of the buildings and monuments familiar to me from growing up in Brussels existed when Mary Ward arrived. There on the Grand' Place stood the beautifully intricate, asymmetrical town hall with its lace-like stone work and its perfect soaring spire, although the guild-houses marshalled around it were the half-timbered predecessors of the ornate buildings we see today. There on the hill behind the Grand' Place rose the graceful twin towers of Sainte Gudule, yet to be raised to the status of cathedral, and there to the right was the beautiful Gothic church of Notre Dame du Sablon. And between the Grand Place and the Sablon was – yes, even then! – the Manneken Pis: a stone statue, replaced by a bronze version in 1619.

But in 1607 Brussels was perhaps most famous for a majestic building that, alas, can no longer be seen or admired, for it burnt to the ground in 1731: the magnificent Coudenberg Palace, one of the great palaces of Europe. Here Archdukes Albert and Isabella held court with all the pomp and ceremony they had brought with them from the Spanish Court in Madrid. They had commissioned Jan Breughel, Pieter Paul Rubens and other great artists of the age to decorate it, and had laid out ornamental gardens behind it – and this was where Mary Ward would meet and petition two of Europe's most powerful sovereigns.

Mary did not travel alone. With her came her half-sister Frances who, on hearing that Mary was planning a new English convent, had promptly asked to join it as a novice. In Brussels, the two Ward sisters put up at the convent of the English Benedictines: its founder Mary Percy was (of course!) a distant relative of theirs. She enjoyed cordial relations with Archdukes Albert and Isabella, so was in a good position to prime the young Mary Ward on court etiquette.

The English Benedictines resided in a narrow street below St Gudule,[3] not far from the Sablon district where noble families had built fine mansions for themselves, houses like the *Hôtel de Thurn et Taxis*, the residence of the family that had created Europe's first international postal system. The current master of the house, Leonard of Taxis, had set up a relay service from Brussels via Liège and Trier to Augsburg, Munich and Rome: this service would play its part at pivotal moments in Mary's life. Letters from Brussels to Innsbruck (570 miles) took five days in summer and six days in winter, from Brussels to Paris a mere forty-four hours.

Mary may have snatched a first glance of the archdukes during one of the flamboyant processions which they loved to stage through the streets of Brussels. They had begun their reign with a series of magnificent ceremonial *cortèges* in Brussels, Ghent, Tournai, and other cities; in Antwerp they were greeted with a motet by local composer Cornelius Verdonck, maybe the only piece of music ever written for performance on an elephant. The grand processions combined religious symbolism with royal patronage. The monastic orders and the powerful guilds of the city took part, wagons were decorated to depict legendary scenes, there were giants to scare the crowds and exotic animals to fascinate them, and at the climax of it all came the archdukes themselves in full array. Albert and Isabella perfectly understood the powerful, dramatic effect of such stage-managed symbolism.

In contrast, Brussels had no public theatres like the *Rose* or the *Globe* in London for other than Passion or Mystery plays put on by students in the Jesuit colleges, theatre plays were banned. Theatres were less easy to control than the elaborate processions and could be misused, the archdukes feared, to foment protest against the Spanish. Nor were their fears misplaced. Resentment against the Spanish was omnipresent, and found expression in the only public stages that remained – the puppet theatres. To get a good idea of what the Spaniards feared, pop along to Brussels' wonderful surviving *Toone* puppet theatre where all performances, no matter whether *Hamlet, Cyrano de Bergerac* or the *Life of Christ*, have one thing in common: the 'baddie' is an evil-looking black-haired Spaniard. And he usually gets his head chopped off.

What figure did Mary cut with the archdukes when she was finally granted an audience with them? They will have seen at once that Mary was devout, honest, and passionate about her convent, but they will have been concerned about the financial under-pinning of the project. Who would finance the convent now that this young English woman had already sunk much of her dowry into the purchase of a house? Mary brought impressive recommendations from Bishop Blaes of St Omer, but was it not strange that a novice lay sister (albeit a gentlewoman) was petitioning for the project, and not one of the choir sisters? And why accede to the additional request for Jesuit confessors? It would ruffle the feathers of the local Church authorities. All this did not bode well.

On the other hand, some factors played in Mary's favour. It was a good moment politically because a temporary armistice secured with the Dutch (April 1607) had bought the archdukes some respite. And there was no doubting the archdukes' fervent desire to support new monasteries and convents. In the previous century, the Catholic Church had sometimes sided with the citizens of Brussels against their predecessor Charles V, but in these troubled times following the Reformation, Catholic monarchs and the clergy closed ranks. The archdukes needed the Catholic Church's unquestioning support, and in return they lavished funds on church buildings and monastic orders – 25 Jesuit houses and 300 Jesuit colleges sprang up in the Low Countries during their reign.[4] And the archdukes dutifully funded large numbers of English exiles in Flanders as their contribution to Rome's effort against Protestant England. To this extent, Mary was tapping at an open door.

But there must have been more. The archdukes would not have entertained Mary Ward at court if they had not been deeply impressed by the mettle of her character. They were wily rulers, and recognised a fighter when they saw one. Isabella, in particular, must have recognised in Mary a kindred spirit. Yes, she will have admired Mary's zeal and passion, but over and above this she will have appreciated that she and Mary Ward were each of them women asserting themselves in a world of men. Isabella was to prove a loyal, long-standing supporter.

Mary's first coup was to win over the chief English Jesuit in Brussels to the idea of having a Jesuit confessor for her convent. Father William Baldwin had himself indeed set a precedent, as he was confessor to the English Benedictine nuns with whom Mary was staying. And Baldwin's support clinched the deal as far as the archdukes were concerned: in September 1608 they gave the go-ahead for the new convent – with Jesuit confessors as Mary had requested.

This was extraordinary. Mary Ward, an inexperienced 22-year-old, had got her way – for as she had anticipated, once Albert and Isabella had given their support, the bishop of Ypres backed down. This remarkable achievement was secured, as Chambers puts it, 'to the great astonishment of the two parties, and to the admiration of both those who had so powerfully resisted her as well as of friends, and this in the space of six months.'[5] It was important enough to be noted by the beady eye of Thomas Edmondes, London's agent in Brussels who reported back on the activities of exiled English Catholics. 'Mrs. Ward,' he wrote on 29 June 1608, 'hath been set in hand by the Jesuits to sue for leave to erect near unto Gravelines a house of Poor Clares for English nuns … .' He took it for granted that Mary's plan had been instigated by the Jesuits: it was inconceivable to men on either side of the Catholic/ Protestant divide that a visionary project might be the initiative of a woman.

And Mary and Frances were met with more good news when they returned to St Omer: a number of English choir sisters at the Walloon Poor Clares were asking to join Mary's new community. So Mary and Frances set to work decking out a house that Bishop Blaes had found for them in St Omer while the new convent in Gravelines was being built. It is a strangely modern image: two sisters furnishing their first house, deciding what use to make of each room, making do on a limited budget, even if their dishes were 'earthenware crocks', their underwear made of 'coarse linen' and their clothes of 'rough frieze'.

At last the house was ready, and all could move into their temporary lodgings in St Omer: Mary, Frances, the English choir sisters from the Walloon Poor Clares, the first novices from England, and some Walloon sisters. And the English Poor Clares at once set a radical tone. Rejecting the pomp of the English Benedictines in Brussels who, Chambers tells us, 'were most bravely apparelled, and adorned with rich jewels like brides', they opted to live by the original Rule of St. Clare, one of the most austere in the Catholic Church.

They also had to elect a superior. Well, after all she had done to found the new convent, that would surely be Mary, wouldn't it? But no. Mary had long dreamed of being just a normal sister in a convent, so in her stead the members elected Mary Gough who had experience of managing the novices at the previous convent. Bishop Blaes and Father Roger Lee, the new community's Jesuit confessor, urged Mary to take her full vows and profess at once, but she insisted on starting out as a novice alongside the other sisters, with no special favours. This decision was to have unforeseen consequences.

The sisters now led a life of quiet prayer and contemplation, the life that Mary had desired so fervently. Father Lee took the women through 'spiritual exercises' in the Jesuit tradition. They ate little, wore coarse cloth as a sign of penance, and slept on a rough straw mattress from which they arose at midnight to say the long Divine Office – and yet Chambers is surely right to claim that, after all her efforts to become a choir sister, Mary Ward now experienced 'a great tranquillity of mind.' All was set for Mary to live out her dream as a Clare sister, enclosed within the walls of her convent for the rest of her life.

It did not, however, turn out that way.

At 10.00 am on 2 May 1608, Mary Ward had a dream, an inspiration, a transcendental experience, a revelation – call it what you will: the biographies of Mary Ward call it a 'vision'. The word is surely unimportant, as Mary herself rightly said, it was 'a thing of such a nature that I know not, and never did know, how to explain it.' It was, in her words, of such 'violence' that it caused her 'suffering'; she felt 'annihilated' and 'reduced to nothing.' At the same time, she felt so utterly convinced that God was speaking to and through her that she felt an overpowering sense of 'consolation'. All she could do was try to understand the message that this experience was communicating to her, a message as direct as it was baffling: 'it was shown to me that I was not to be of the Order of St. Clare; some other thing I was to do, what or of what nature I did not see, nor could I guess, only that it was to be a good thing, and what God willed.'

What?! After all Mary's efforts to found her Poor Clares convent, after her negotiations in St Omer and her petition in Brussels, was it God's will that she should not profess as a Poor Clare at all? Was she to walk out on the institution she had only just founded, before it had even moved to its permanent home in Gravelines?

Shaken to the core, Mary told Mary Gough about her vision – and the superior was not impressed. The devil, she warned, tempted young maidens with illusions and other figments of overactive imaginations. The community's confessor Roger Lee also advised Mary to ignore her 'vision' and complete her novitiate. So for nearly a year Mary tried to put the vision behind her and to focus on her coming profession as a Poor Clare. But the experience had been too powerful: the more she tried to shrug it off, the more convinced she was that God wished her to leave the convent and, as she put it, 'live in the world.' She could not, in all conscience, take the vow of obedience to the Poor Clares, so in the end there was, no other option but for her to leave. As a novice, she had the right to do this – had Bishop Blaes and Father

Lee prevailed upon her to profess at the outset, she would have been trapped.

Such is the story as handed down to us. But one detail niggles. Mary did not leave the English Poor Clares on her own – her sister Frances quit too. As a novice, Frances was of course entitled to leave – but why should *she* wish to leave? Frances had had no vision. It was not a question of loyalty to Mary, because the two sisters were about to go very different ways. Nor was Frances abandoning religious life as such, for in 1611 she would profess as a Carmelite – only the third English woman ever to do so. Clearly, then, Frances had not found fulfilment in the convent in Gravelines. Was this maybe the case with Mary too?

Whatever the reasons, Mary Ward was under no illusion as to what people would now say about her. This was the second time she was walking away from convent life. Her fellow sisters would have every right to reproach her for disloyalty. The clergy and, she feared, her friends and acquaintances would see her as weak willed, wayward, inconsistent – the very stereotype of what the seventeenth century considered a woman to be.

There was no turning back, however. Mary made a vow of chastity as a sign of her commitment to God, then in September 1609 she and Frances bid adieu to their sisters in the convent. It must have been a tearful parting, and it is hard not to feel considerable sympathy for the sisters who must have felt bewildered and betrayed.

And that was the end of Mary Ward's career as a Poor Clare. It was not, however, the end of the convent. The community moved into its new premises in Gravelines, Mary donated more of her dowry to enable it to thrive, and in time the convent founded offshoots in Rouen, in Dunkirk and in Ireland. At the French Revolution, the nuns were forced to leave Gravelines and find refuge – ironically – back in England. They were based in Darlington until 2007, and now lead their life of prayer – with solar powered electricity and hot water, but still enclosed – at Much Birch, south of Hereford.

For Mary, however, things were not so straightforward. Her vision had told her to leave the convent, but it had not told her what to do after that. She was no longer a novice, and the seventeenth century offered no role for unmarried women outside the family home or the walls of a convent.

What on earth could she do now?

1621: The long road to Rome

Walking, walking, walking.
Walking, resting, eating.

Cookery books, such as one published in Louvain in 1612, have introduced upper class families in Northern Europe to Mediterranean herbs and vegetables, and even to Parmesan and ricotta cheese. But most people live hand to mouth on the food that they grow themselves, and famine threatens when harvests fail.

Bread is most people's source of calories, but the price of wheat, oats and barley fluctuates wildly depending on the quality of the harvest. Beans, cauliflower, peas, onions and spinach are grown. Broccoli and Brussels sprouts are common in France and Flanders, less so in England. Yellow tomatoes are cultivated in Spain and Italy; in England they are considered poisonous. Potatoes, celery and runner beans are still widely unknown.

Soup might be eaten three times a day. The cauldron hangs over the fire all day, with vegetables and hunks of pork fat thrown in at intervals. Milk and eggs are luxuries to be sold in town rather than eaten at home. Most people only taste meat on feast days: the Catholic Church's injunction not to eat meat on Fridays only impacts on those rich enough to afford meat in the first place. Spices are the preserve of the rich.

It's a diet weak in calories. In northern France, 'meat was almost unknown, fruit rare, vegetables poor, and the staple was normally bread, soup, gruel, peas and beans ... It may be argued that undernourishment ... was constant.'[6] The same applied to much of Europe.

No wonder our travellers are weary after a long day of walking.

6

Reinforcements: A formidable group of women (1609)

Poor Bishop Blaes! He had staked his reputation on the young English woman and her unconventional ideas for an English Poor Clares convent – and look what happened!

Here she now was, a loose cannon in St Omer, far from her family, outside the protective walls of a convent, and a potential source of scandal. No wonder the bishop advised her warmly to enter the convent of the English Benedictine nuns in Brussels. The Jesuits, too, recommended the convent in Brussels, or else the Carmelite convent in Mons, where her sister Frances was heading. Mary Ward appeared amenable, and vowed before her confessor Father Lee that she would become a nun, and indeed a Carmelite if Father Lee insisted on this.

Well, that was a relief. The religious authorities wanted to see Mary inside the walls of a convent as soon as possible. But they had hardly begun to relax when Mary dropped her next bombshell. Her immediate plan, she announced, was to return to England – where there was of course not the faintest possibility of her entering a religious house. As Mary Ward later put it in a letter to Nuncio Albergati: 'I made a third vow, to spend some months in England to do all the little I could for God, and the good of those there … .' The wording is tantalising – for it hints that Mary's ideas about what she could achieve as a woman were developing in what was – back in the seventeenth century – a radical direction.

The commonly held view back then was that women were *weaker vessels* (1 Peter 3:7) in need of protection by men – either by husbands who were legally responsible for them, or by the Catholic Church which protected them by enclosing them within convents. Women were active in some trades, but men took almost all decisions, and the generally accepted view was that femininity was incompatible with a position of authority.[1]

And there was more. Women were not only considered intellectually inferior to men, but more vulnerable to sin. This warped view of women derived from a strand of Greek philosophy that distinguished between the realm of eternal, unchanging ideas grasped by the *mind*, and the transient, material world inhabited by the *body*. Early Christian writers associated the former with self-denial and a state of holiness, and the latter with the snares of the flesh. Building on the story of Adam and the temptress Eve, it was then only a small step for the spiritual, intellectual world of the *mind* to be associated with the male, and the carnal, material world of the *body* to be associated with the female.[2]

Men who wished to attain spiritual purity strove to be celibate, but women had to renounce not only sexual intercourse but womanhood itself. 'As long as a woman is for birth and children,' wrote St Jerome, 'she is as different from man as body from soul. But when she wishes to serve Christ more than the world, then she will cease to be a woman, and will be called man.'[3]

Or, as Albertus Magnus put it, 'woman is less qualified [than man] for moral behaviour. For the woman contains more liquid than the man, and it is a property of liquid to take things up easily and to hold onto them poorly ... Woman is a misbegotten man and has a faulty and defective nature in comparison with his ... she is unsure in herself. What she herself cannot get, she seeks to obtain through lying and diabolical deceptions. And so, to put it briefly, one must be on one's guard with every woman, as if she were a poisonous snake and the horned devil ... Her feelings drive woman towards every evil, just as reason impels man towards all good.'[4]

One consequence of this distorted, negative view of womanhood was the assumption that '[women's] prayers were somehow less effective than those of men',[5] and that women were therefore unable to give people spiritual help. Women nurtured children, of course, and offered their menfolk comforts of the flesh, but – so the argument went – they were incapable of healing other people's souls. That role was reserved for men. Had not Jesus picked only men to serve as his apostles?

The logical consequence was to limit the role of women in church. They were banned from celebrating Mass or giving Communion, even from preaching. St Paul, after all, had written, 'Let your women keep silence in the churches, for it is not permitted unto them to speak; but they are commanded to be under obedience, as also saith the law. And if they will learn anything, let them ask their husbands at home: for it is a shame for women to speak in the church.'[6]

Most Protestant churches, for all their reforms in some areas, swallowed the Catholic line on women. 'To promote a woman to bear rule, superiority, dominion, or empire above any realm, nation, or city,' wrote John Knox, the Presbyterian reformer, in 1558, 'is repugnant to nature; contumely to God, a thing most contrary to his revealed will and approved ordinance; and finally, it is the subversion of good order, or all equity and justice.' The title of his book, *The First Blast of the Trumpet against the Monstrous Regiment of Women* made its contents abundantly clear. There were not many points on which John Knox and the pope agreed, but this was one of them. It would be left to Margaret Fell, a Quaker, to refute the misogynist interpretation of Saint Paul's words in her pamphlet *Women's Speaking Justified* in 1666.

From the point of view of our story, the interesting question is where Mary Ward stood on this issue. Mary had, of course, begun by accepting the Catholic Church's line on enclosure, and had written 'Inclosure and observance of poverty were the two especial points I aimed at.' And she had assumed that women were indeed unable to heal other people's souls: 'I saw not how a religious woman could do good to more than herself alone.' Indeed, as late as 1606 Mary had written, 'A religious person of the female gender cannot exercise good works on anyone's behalf except her own.'

So far so clear.

But fast-forward to 1609, and instead of aiming for 'inclosure', Mary is travelling to England where no convents exist. And far from accepting that she could not 'do good to more than herself alone', she was, in her own words, going to England 'for the good of those there.' We know she visited the sick and the imprisoned, and Painting 17 in the *Painted Life* series shows us Mary converting a woman to Catholicism. Painting 18 shows Mary back in London, converting her cousin Anne Grey. Mary, it seems, was edging towards a realisation that women *could* serve God outside the enclosed world of the convent. As yet, this work was ad hoc, not yet institutionalised. Mary was perhaps herself not fully conscious of the significance of the step she was taking, but she was undeniably offering spiritual support to others.

Where, I wonder, did Mary find the inspiration for striking out in this way?

Mary would not have understood the question. For her it was crystal clear that her inspiration came from God in her vision. But God often works through human agencies, like her childhood role models such as her grandmother Ursula.

And I like to think that there was another possible source of inspiration. Throughout her years in St Omer, Mary Ward was surrounded by evidence in bricks and mortar – very beautiful bricks and mortar – of religious women who had not always kowtowed to the rules of men. Every town in Flanders had at least one *béguinage*, a collection of prim houses, often around a well-tended green, which had been built for béguines: women who had opted to live in groups that followed no recognised monastic Rule.[7] Unlike the public vows taken by choir sisters, béguines took private vows that could not be enforced by law. The women were therefore free to leave the community if they wished, to marry, and to own and inherit property. And a key feature of béguine communities was that they were organised and run by women.

The Church responded to this anarchic female movement with a policy of carrot and stick. Béguine communities were offered land and protection if they subjected themselves to a rule approved by the Catholic Church; others however were persecuted,[8] and two béguines, Aleydis and Marguerite Porete, were executed as heretics in 1236 and 1310. The Council of Vienne of 1311 declared béguines to be heretical, and in 1421 Pope Martin V suppressed 'any small convents of persons living under the cloak of religion without a definite Rule.'

This barrage of hostility by the Catholic Church finally reduced the béguines to a shadow of their former selves, but their independent spirit lingered in Flanders, and it is, I think, legitimate to speculate that Mary Ward inhaled something of it in the streets of St Omer, and from the Walloon nuns in her Poor Clares convent.

However, as her friends and acquaintances might have said to her, it was fine to have an independent spirit, but how was Mary to organise her life? She was living with (and off) friends and acquaintances in England, and this could not go on for ever. What direction should she follow? Should she join the Carmelites? Or some other order? But if she was not suited for the Poor Clares, why should she be suited to any other particular order? Only one thing was certain. Having taken a vow to be a nun, she could not return to life back home in Mulwith.

The answer – or part of the answer – to this string of questions came as Mary Ward was standing in front of a mirror one morning, getting dressed. Suddenly she had a second supernatural experience, similar to the vision she had had in St Omer commanding her to leave the Poor Clares. This second revelation struck her, she later wrote, even more violently than the first. 'I was abstracted from out of my whole being,' she wrote,

> and it was shown to me with clearness and inexpressible certainty that I was not to be of the Order of St. Teresa [i.e. the Carmelites], but that some other thing was determined for me ... I did not see what the assured good thing would be, but the glory to God which was to come through it, showed itself inexplicably and so abundantly as to fill my soul in such a way that I remained for a good space without feeling or hearing anything but the sound, 'Glory, Glory, Glory.' ... a good space of time passed before I recovered ... .

The scene is depicted in Painting 21 of the *Painted Life*.

Mary, then, was not destined to become a Carmelite: 'some other thing' was destined for her. Whether this insight came in a flash as Mary here describes it, or whether it was the culmination of months of thought and prayer, Mary was unassailably convinced that God had reserved some other, as yet undefined religious project for her, and this belief gave her immense joy, strength, energy and inspiration. Her mission, she believed, was to set up some 'other' community. How exactly it would be 'other' had not yet been revealed to her, but that would not prevent her from getting started. She would go back to St Omer, where she had friends and supporters, and she would set up a new community. Completely re-invigorated, Mary began to seek companions for her new venture.

But wait a minute! For anyone listening to Mary in the cold light of day, there was precious little to go on. Based on a voice she had heard in a trance, this 24-year-old who had blown most of her dowry on her Poor Clares convent in Gravelines was proposing to set up a religious community whose aims were unknown, in a city where she had already aggravated the religious authorities and had a track record for walking out on institutions within months of setting them up. Who in their right minds would take part in such a precarious venture? More to the point, bearing in mind the role of the male head of the family in the early seventeenth century, how many fathers in their right minds would allow their daughters to join?

Astonishingly, there were several.

The way Mary Ward now travelled around the country inspiring friends and relations to drop what they were doing and follow her, cannot but recall Jesus gathering his disciples in Galilee. And indeed the leap of faith required of each woman was similar to that made by each disciple: it would be a leap into the unknown, far from home, with no assurance but the word of their 'shepherd'. Yet within a few months Mary had gathered around her a group of women that were able, self-reliant, tenacious, devout, intelligent, multi-skilled, gutsy, self-effacing and loyal – one of the most formidable groups of women the world has ever seen.

There was Winefrid Wigmore: fearless, effervescent and fluent in five languages, a true friend whom Mary could confide in at moments of crisis. Direct novices in Naples? Open a school in Paris? Cross war-torn Europe or dodge warring armies in England's Civil War? Survive solitary confinement in prison? Winefrid would take it all in her stride, and never waiver in her fierce loyalty to Mary.

There was Susanna Rookwood: 'Doll' Rookwood as she was affectionately called by Mary Ward, but Susanna was no weakling. Imprisoned five times during her long stint as superior of the clandestine house in England, Susanna had all the courage of her brother Ambrose, the Gunpowder Plot conspirator. She would serve inspirationally in Liège, Rome and Naples.

There was Catherine Smith, the quiet one, always there at your side when you needed her most. She was at Mary Ward's bedside when she died, and after Mary's death, Catherine was one of those who kept the flame alive, taking charge of the pupils at the school in Paris in the 1650s.

There was Jane, or Joanna, Browne who at the age of 28 was, amazingly, the oldest of the group. She plunged into the covert work in

England with Susanna Rookwood, and held the reins in Naples when Susanna suddenly died there in 1624. And she was with Mary in Munich when Mary's Institute was suppressed.

And there was Mary Poyntz, who was only 16 when she first met Mary Ward.[9] What moved Edward Poyntz, her father, to allow a daughter so young to leave the family home and embark on such a madcap enterprise is unclear, but give his blessing he did. Mary Poyntz would author Mary's biography in an age when biographies written by women were rare indeed, and she would one day re-launch Mary's Institute by founding a new house in Augsburg.

Mary's five companions in England would be joined by two more in St Omer. One was Mary Ward's own sister, Barbara, who with her ready wit raised the sisters' spirits when times were bleak. Educated and able, Barbara served Mary loyally and never challenged her authority. One detractor would accuse Barbara of frequenting prostitutes with the purpose of winning back their souls. What an accolade!

And, bringing the number of 'first companions' to the heavenly number seven was a cheerful childhood friend we have met before: Barbara Babthorpe, Mary's cousin from Osgodby. Once a novice at Mary Percy's English Benedictines in Brussels, a defect in Barbara's throat prevented her from singing and therefore from professing as a choir sister there. The Benedictines' loss was Mary Ward's gain. Barbara would prove herself to be a reliable and able leader of Mary's houses in St Omer, Vienna and Bratislava, and Mary would appoint Barbara as her successor.

All these young women came from impeccable Catholic families.[10] And looking at Picture 22 of the *Painted Life* series, which depicts Mary and her five companions setting off from England, I see something else that they had in common: they are all wearing vivid blue, red and pink gowns. Now, colour was the preserve of the rich because alum, the product that fixed colours in garments, was exorbitantly expensive.[11] So the painting reminds us that the young women were all from privileged, wealthy families.

Their wealthy, sheltered background might easily mislead us into thinking of the companions as shy, docile and squeamish. Not a bit of it. They did not yet know it, but these women would travel foreign countries, rub shoulders with the poor, administer religious houses, give lessons to street urchins, outwit their gaolers, stand up to the Vatican's prelates, negotiate with some of the most powerful rulers in Europe and stand firm in the bleakest moments of despair – and in so doing they would challenge the Church's and society's perception of womanhood, and create a wholly new profession for unmarried women: that of the trained, professional female teacher.

Littlehales compares the little group of women who set off for France with Ignatius of Loyola and his first small band of followers.[12] Yet the Jesuits triumphed for their faith with full papal backing. Mary Ward and her companions would triumph despite the lack of it.

1621: The long road to Rome

Walking, walking, walking.
Walking, venturing, taking chances.

Few women travel before the late seventeenth century – though there are exceptions, of course. The Wife of Bath goes on pilgrimages. Anne of Cleves travels from Germany to England meet her bridegroom, Henry VIII. Elizabeth Stuart, the daughter of James I, travels in the other direction to join her husband Frederick in Heidelberg in 1613. And Luisa Carvajal travels from Spain in 1605 to carry out Catholic mission work in London.

One reason women rarely travel is that the roads are unsafe. In England the age of the highwayman is getting under way: Gamaliel Ratsey is one of the first highwaymen to be executed, in 1605. Mary Frith, born a year before Mary Ward, becomes a successful 'lady highwayman' and lives to a ripe old age.

In France and Germany, groups of bandits – often disbanded soldiers – infest the countryside The German lands are notorious for their roadside gallows on which victims are left to rot. With the outbreak of the Thirty Years' War in 1618, travellers in whole regions of central Europe can suddenly find themselves at the mercy of entire marauding armies.

It takes faith to walk across Europe at this time. But the wrong faith can land you in trouble. Catholic priests are arrested and hanged, drawn and quartered if they are caught in England. In 1658 the Quakers Katherine Evans and Sarah Cheevers are arrested and imprisoned in Malta by the Inquisition. They languish for three years in a hot and airless gaol.

7

Remit: 'The same of the Society' (1610–1612)

It was a party of some considerable size, then, that travelled with Mary Ward on her second journey to St Omer.

What a contrast with Mary's journey only three years before! Back then, Mary had been in the care of Catherine Bentley; now five women were in *her* care. Back then a Jesuit father had placed her in a convent of his choice; now she was setting up her own community on her own terms. Back then she had been just another girl from a wealthy English Catholic family; now she had a reputation for courage and initiative, and commanded the respect due to a protégée of Albert and Isabella's.

In St Omer there was an emotional parting, when Mary's half-sister Frances travelled on to join the Carmelite Convent in Mons. Frances had been at Mary's side during the turbulent events in Brussels and St Omer, but once she professed as a Carmelite, she would no longer be allowed to leave the walls of her convent. Would the two sisters ever see each other again?

However, Mary was not one dwell on sadness. Her little community needed a home, a vocation and an income – and Mary solved all three by declaring her intention to open a school for girls. Typical Mary Ward! Without yet knowing exactly what direction God was intending her community to take, without having decided which monastic rule the community would live by, she addressed the practicalities of her situation. There were girls in St Omer who needed teaching. Well then! She and her companions would teach, trusting that God would give them more guidance in His own good time.

Bishop Blaes was delighted, of course. He quickly found Mary a suitable house in the Grosse Rue, and Mary opened a free day-school for girls, which included the daughters of exiled English Catholic families. This was followed by a boarding-school for the daughters of English Catholic families still in England or elsewhere in Flanders. The boarding fees, together with the dowry money of new companions, would help to keep the community financially afloat. But only just. Mary and her companions began by sleeping on straw and surviving on one meal a day.[1]

Mary's school was a larger, more formal institution than the schools run by Marie Aubrun and Agnes de Mailly, and the people of St Omer welcomed it with open arms. She even won over some Jesuit fathers in the English college, who recognised and welcomed a practical, militant spirit similar to their own. In the Jesuit college's annual letter of 1610 we find 'There are in this city certain virgins, ladies of high rank and education, who with heart and soul embrace every opportunity of doing good works required of them at home and abroad. They are assisted spiritually by our Fathers.'

But not everyone shared this enthusiasm. The Church authorities had a duty to ensure that religious communities conformed to religious standards, and they were by no means as laid-back about the status of this band of women as were Mary Ward and Bishop Blaes. What they wanted to know was: were Mary and her companions nuns or weren't they?

The women lived together in a community, led pious lives and had dedicated themselves to God. So far, so good – but the women had taken no public vows, were not novices, and lived by no acknowledged monastic rule. They wore clothes that Mary Poyntz, in her biography of Mary, describes as 'conformable, very grave and retired' but were 'not of the monastical.' And above all, far from being enclosed as the Church prescribed, Mary and her companions walked freely about town.

Now, throughout Catholic Europe there existed groups of women who were engaged in hospital work and looked after the needy. Such female congregations, as they were called, took no public vows, the women were not nuns, and were therefore not enclosed within convents: they enjoyed the freedom of movement that Mary and her companions wanted for themselves. However, the status of congregations was emphatically lower than that of fully-professed nuns. For Mary and her companions to assume the status of a congregation would give the community less clout, because congregations attracted less financial support than did nuns in fully-fledged convents.

If Mary and her companions wished to be nuns, however, Church authorities wanted to know how they intended to reconcile their teaching with their obligation of enclosure. The authorities would brook no shilly-shallying. They, the companions' families, and indeed the companions themselves were all looking to Mary to solve this conundrum.

Before she could do so, however, disaster struck. Mary succumbed to an epidemic of measles that swept through St Omer in 1611. Measles was a killer disease, and Mary fell dangerously ill. Her fever raged so ominously that she was given the last sacraments. It looked as if the history of her venture in St Omer might be a short one.

The response of Mary's companions is a first indication of the stuff they were made of – a characteristic blend of initiative, faith and fearlessness. They had heard talk of the most famous centre of pilgrimage in Flanders: the Scherpenheuvel at Sichem, some 50 kilometres the wrong side of Brussels.[2] In their crisis, the companions decided to send a delegation to pray to Our Lady of Sichem for Mary's recovery. Bearing in mind that the women had no experience of pilgrimages (banned in Protestant England), did not speak the local languages, and only had experience of travelling in England, one of the most peaceful countries in Europe, this was a bold venture. They had no idea what dangers they might have to face. And, ironically, travel was particularly perilous in 1611 precisely because Albert had finally managed to convert the ceasefire with the Dutch into a formal ten-year truce: hundreds of disbanded soldiers now preyed on travellers.

Miraculously, however, (I use the word advisedly) Mary's companions succeeded in their mission of mercy. They reached the Scherpenheuvel, they prayed at the shrine to the Virgin, and Mary Ward recovered.

And not only recovered: her illness was followed by a third vision.

This third spiritual experience finally gave Mary the direction she had been seeking, the course by which she would live her life. A great light, an extraordinary peace and a wonderful sense of comfort overwhelmed her, and she discerned an instruction which she had no doubt came from God: 'I heard distinctly,' she wrote, 'not by sound of voice, but intellectually understood, these words: Take the same of the Society.'[3]

These six most critical of words in the story of Mary Ward may sound cryptic to us, but Mary had no doubt as to what they meant. The

'Society' meant the Society of Jesus, the Jesuits, and Mary understood that God was calling on her community to become nothing less than the female equivalent of the Jesuits. They would imitate the Jesuits 'both in matter and manner' and dedicate themselves to mission work for Christ. As women they could not become priests, but in all other things they would assume the zeal, the organisation and the mission of the Jesuits. They must serve with Jesuit-like commitment wherever in the world God might send them and in whatever capacity. And for this to be possible, they must organise themselves not under local bishops as traditional religious orders did, but answer directly to the pope himself. This freedom would allow them, as it did the Jesuits, to respond wherever in the world the need might arise.

Mary's third vision was her key to how she and her companions could participate in active spiritual renewal.[4] But it was, in all senses of the word, an awesome mission. Throwing age-old traditions overboard, it envisaged a more independent role for women than the Catholic Church, or European society, had ever seen before. It presupposed that women were in fact capable of organising themselves on a worldwide footing, and as able as men to go out into the world and teach. It assumed that women had the mettle to go about their business and the capacity for a missionary role without yielding to temptation or provoking scandal. It assumed that family patriarchs would entrust their daughters to such free-roaming nuns. And it assumed that the pope would give his blessing to the project, as Pope Paul III had done to the Jesuits back in 1540.

The prospects were daunting indeed, but Mary was assailed not by fears but by an overwhelming feeling of relief. For almost ten years now she had been seeking the special role that she had felt that God had prepared for her. Now she was as one who, having been thrashing around in the dark, had finally found the light, for she now saw her teaching work as a part of her overall God-given mission. The way forward was clear at last – clear, if also strewn with difficulties. But, as Chambers notes, 'Mary was not one accustomed to pause and spend time in thinking or talking over difficulties.' Mary shared her insights with her companions, and set about with renewed gusto to give her community more clearly-defined contours.

Needing now to focus on obtaining official recognition for her Institute, Mary appointed her cousin Barbara Babthorpe as superior of the community in St Omer. Typical Mary Ward once again! Few leaders excel at delegation, but Mary had the necessary humility. And it was also a brilliant judgement of character, for Barbara Babthorpe – still not quite 20 years old! – would prove to be an inspirational leader, seeing to the sisters' welfare, integrating new arrivals from England and Flanders, keeping up the companions' morale and channelling their enthusiasm into practical teaching work. She would inspire the companions through their very structured day, which laid great emphasis on self-improvement:

4.00 am	awake
4.30 to 5.30	meditate for an hour
5.30 to 8.00	hear Mass, say prayers and listen to spiritual readings
8.00 to 9.45	daily work duties
9.45 to 10.00	self-examination of conscience
10.00	main meal of the day
10.00 to 12.30 pm	recreation
12.30 to 1.00	spiritual reading
1.00 to 5.00	daily work duties
5.00	prayer
6.00	supper and recreation
8.00	– gather for the Litanies of Our Lady and the Saints
	– listen to readings chosen by the superior
	– self-examination of conscience for 15 minutes
	– receive points of meditation for the following day
	– and then to bed

Mary also wrote a curriculum whose aim was to enable each of her girl pupils to become a good Catholic mother or nun. Hmm, what might that include, I wonder: a bit of reading, writing and religion, backed up by a bit of embroidery? But Mary is ahead of me again. Reading, writing and religion were of course included, as was needlework, but, taking her cue from the Jesuits, Mary included subjects that encouraged the girls to broaden their minds and think for themselves – subjects such as Latin, foreign languages, arithmetic and rhetoric.

If this was revolutionary, one further subject – drama – was dynamite. The Jesuits recognised the value of drama for practising elocution, nurturing self-confidence and encouraging creativity – which was all fine and good for boys who would one day occupy positions of authority in society and the Church. But to awaken such notions in *girls*? That might empower them, which was the last thing that a male-dominated society desired. It was the reason why, in London's south bank theatres, men played the female parts. But Mary Ward actively encouraged her girls to use drama to boost their feeling of self-worth. It was a courageous decision for which she would be attacked when the Catholic Church turned its vengeance on her.

With the affairs of the community now in Barbara's hands, Mary could devote her time to obtaining official recognition for what she came to call her Institute. She was not naïve. She knew very well that there would be a barrage of resistance to the very notion of a female order that was not enclosed, and to a curriculum that taught subjects deemed unsuitable for girls. How could she justify this? How could she win over a suspicious male hierarchy?

The argument that Mary used to justify the aims and organisation of her Institute was a brilliant one. Both Spain and the Vatican wished to bring England back into the Catholic family of nations. Very well! The objective of her Institute was to promote the Catholic cause in England by teaching English Catholic children their catechism, strengthening the resolve of Catholic families, and supporting the work of Catholic priests. Of course, in England it would be not be possible for her Institute to operate from within the walls of convents: the operation in England could only succeed if the members had both the status of nuns and the freedom to roam from house to house. It was an irrefutable argument. Only nuns who were not enclosed could further the Catholic cause in England; in turn, the Catholic cause in England justified Mary Ward's appeal for a female order that was not enclosed.[5]

But the need back home in England was more than a just useful rhetorical device to win over the Vatican. It was a mission close to Mary's heart. So some time before 1614, without waiting for permission or orders from anybody, she and a group of companions set off back to England.

They would be the first community of Catholic women in England since the Reformation.

1621: The long road to Rome

Walking, walking, walking.
Bargaining, buying, paying.

A journey across Europe means using a profusion of coins. The Cologne mark is accepted across the German-speaking lands, but its subdivisions might be kreutzer, stiver, kopstücke, seslinge, pfennige, or groschen, to which you have to add plapparts and finfers in Switzerland. Bates tells us that the poet John Taylor (1578–1653) found himself in Hamburg with thirteen different sorts of groschen in his pocket, each minted in a different city.

France originally used livres. One livre consists of 20 sols, a sol consists of 12 deniers. A livre is, in theory, worth one pound of silver – but in practice it has been devalued many times. And to complicate matters, there are no livre coins: instead, francs, doubles, ecus or Spanish pistoles are used.

All of which is simplicity itself in comparison with the coinage in the different Italian states, where coins such as the soldi, grossi, giuli, paoli, reali, quattrini, susine, denari, cavallotti, cavallucci, carlini, bagatini, bolignei, baocchi, and baelli sound like so many different sorts of pasta. Milan alone uses quattrini, trillini, sesini, parpagliole and soldi. No wonder Italy has just become the first European country to use bank notes.

For security, Mary and her companions carry their money as backpackers do today, sewn into their clothes. But as Mary's money is all coin, it adds weight to her heavy clothing.

8

Resilience: Covert mission in England (1612–1619)

So here they were, Mary Ward and a group of companions, back in England – plucked from the sheltered life of their community, and plunged back into a society in which most people had never seen a convent, not even from the outside; wrenched from a world which agonised over whether nuns should be enclosed behind walls or allowed to work out in society, and pitched into a country in which nuns were banned, period. In St Omer, priests took a prominent part in the town's flamboyant saint-day processions; in London, the bodies of tortured Catholic priests, the saints of the future, were exposed at the Southwark end of London Bridge.

Not that Catholics were the only innocent victims under Elizabeth I and James I. Three Dissenters were executed in 1593,[1] nine Gypsies were hanged in 1596, and Edward Wightman, an Anabaptist mercer, was burned at the stake in April 1612. Twelve women and three men were executed as witches in the same year. The cruelties that pepper Shakespeare's plays – eyes gouged out, heads on spikes – were not sadistic inventions: they reflected the world which both Shakespeare and Mary Ward lived in.[2] The audience that watched scenes of torture or execution at the Globe might have seen the slain victims of torture swinging from a gibbet on their way to the theatre. They knew the real thing when they saw it.

The relatively small number of English people who were still Catholics (one estimate is 40,000 out of a population of over 4 million[3]) were doubly afflicted when Mary and her companions arrived in 1612.

On the one hand they were still exposed to the penal laws enacted against Catholics. The hideous executions of priests accompanied Mary's work in England like a deep, melancholy drumbeat: George Napier, John Roberts and Thomas Somers in 1610, William Scott, Richard Newport and John Almond in 1612, John Ogilvie in 1615. Many more languished in gaols that were so filthy and disease-ridden that they died during their incarceration.[4]

And the effect of the penal laws on individual families could be extreme. Barbara Babthorpe's father, Sir Ralph Babthorpe, had been forced into exile in Flanders, and when her brother William inherited the estate two thirds of the rental income went on paying fines. William had to sell more and more of his inheritance: 366 acres in Brackenholme in 1620, 270 acres of Babthorpe Farm in 1621, Osgodby in 1622 and Flotmanby in 1633.[5] Some of these transactions may have been to baffle the authorities and reduce what might be seized as forfeit, but William was in time forced to follow his father to Flanders. In 1455 a Babthorpe father and son had fallen in the field fighting for Henry VI; two hundred years later religious division had driven this loyal family out of the country, and William died fighting for Spain against the French.

However, the penal laws were applied erratically, not least because twenty of the seventy-four peers in the 1606 Parliament were openly Catholic, with maybe another dozen secretly so. In Newcastle upon Tyne, for example, the priests Joseph Lampton and Edward Waterson were executed in 1592 and 1594; yet 'popery' was said to 'flourish' in Newcastle in 1616, and in 1632 crowds including local dignitaries flocked to the funeral of Dorothy Lawson, a Catholic who was well-known both for her charitable work and for sheltering Catholic priests. And alongside the extreme cases like the Babthorpes, many well-off Catholic families – such as the Ropers in Canterbury, or Marmaduke's friends in London – continued to live 'in a style to which they long had been accustomed, not only possessing vast estates, but also having the means to support them.'[6]

If the penal laws affected some families more than others, the Catholics' second affliction struck them all. This was the destructive in-fighting, a very civil war, between large sections of the English Catholic community on the one hand, and the English Jesuit priests and their supporters on the other.

One cause of this self-inflicted tragedy was the Jesuits' willingness, even desire, to die as martyrs. Many English Catholics feared that this zeal would only provoke the authorities to clamp down harder with house searches, fines and arrests – fines paid by Catholics, for example, leapt from £1,414 in the first year of the reign of James I to £7,000 in the year following the disaster of the Gunpowder Plot.[7] Most Catholics wanted, instead, to keep their heads down and compromise. But this, in Jesuit eyes, was selling out to the enemy.

Since 1606 the quarrel had crystallised around a new oath of allegiance that James I required from his subjects. The oath managed to mention the pope four times, and required Catholics to swear that they would be loyal to the king if the pope attempted to depose or excommunicate him. It therefore faced Catholics with their nightmare dilemma: were they ultimately English subjects, subject to the laws of the kingdom, who practised the Catholic faith? In that case, they could take the oath of loyalty to the king. Or were they first and foremost Catholics, bound to obey the pope in whatever he decided, who happened to reside in England? In that case they should refuse it. No wonder the issue polarised the English Catholic community.

Among those who took the oath was the head of the English Catholics, George Blackwell, nineteen of the twenty openly Catholic peers in parliament, and large numbers of Yorkshire Catholic families. Mary's kinsmen the Inglebys, for example, who had had split loyalties during the Rising of the North, all took the oath.

The Jesuits, as we might expect, led the campaign against it. They took their lead from Pope Paul V, who dismissed Blackwell for having taken it, and were vehemently supported by Cardinal Bellarmine and the Jesuit Francesco Suarez, whose treatises on the subject made such an extreme case for the right of popes to depose kings that the works were publicly burnt – not in Protestant London, but in Catholic Paris.

Whatever the rights and wrongs, the bitter quarrelling was a calamity for English Catholicism. As Chambers trenchantly puts it: 'It will perhaps be seen [one day] that the dissensions among the English

Catholics did more to prevent the restoration of the ancient faith in the country, than the Anglican Establishment and the persecuting Government ... .'[8]

And from the point of view of our story, the quarrelling was a disaster for Mary Ward. It is easy to see why. Her Institute was inspired and infused by the Jesuit example, and was therefore – wrongly – seen as a very arm of the Jesuit movement. No matter that the Jesuits specifically excluded the possibility of a female wing within their organisation. No matter that Mary had written: 'We are so far from desiring or seeking to be one body with the Society [of Jesuits], or any ways subordinate to them, that if they should offer it, we would never admit such dependence.'

People began to call her companions Jesuitesses, which made them vulnerable to attack from both sides of the Catholic divide. The majority who feared that the Jesuits were leading English Catholics to disaster saw Mary's Institute as an easy target through which to attack the Jesuits themselves. Meanwhile the Jesuits were enraged because Ignatius had warned that they should never to create a Jesuit order for women. Mary and her companions were left as piggy in the middle – easy prey for both sides.

Such was the sorry state of affairs when Mary Ward arrived in England. One of her tasks was to visit families who were considering sending their daughters to her school in St Omer. Another was to collect dowry money due to members of the Institute, or money owed to the Institute for boarding fees. Tapping sources of finance was hard, because families were often unwilling to give financial support before the Institute was officially approved by the pope. Mary and her companions also visited Catholic prisoners in gaols.

The main task, however, was to set up a 'school' in England – not an official school of course, but a secret network of companions living in Catholic households and promoting Catholicism within the family. Many English Catholics had stopped making confessions, others had children who needed teaching, some were genuinely unsure about Catholic doctrine. Mary and her companions helped them as best they could, ever close to that fine dividing line between helping (which was seen as the woman's remit), teaching (which was borderline) and what Mary's opponents alleged to be preaching (strictly off limits for women). Of course, the actual distinctions between helping, teaching and preaching appeared less clear – and, indeed, irrelevant – when you were working with distressed Catholics in their own homes.

We know about the Institute's secret work thanks to the almost miraculous survival of an account written by a companion who went by the alias of Dorothea and who worked in various houses in England between 1621 and 1623. With her true identity known only to Lady Timperley, the mother of a recusant Suffolk family, Dorothea taught Catholic children within their own homes, prayed with the families, encouraged lapsed Catholics to return to the fold, visited the sick, reconciled husbands and wives, and arranged for Catholic priests to give Communion.

Dorothea's work was secret and dangerous, because she risked imprisonment or even death. The authorities justified their harsh treatment of Catholics on the grounds that they had to protect the population from being converted back to Catholicism, but Dorothea's account shows that she rarely, if ever, worked with non-Catholics. Her work was with Catholic, or lapsed Catholic, families. Not for the last time, the government of the day exaggerated the perceived threat to security from a religious minority that was, in fact, less threatening than was made out.

By 1615 Mary's English mission was fully operational. Anne Gage, who had been with Mary since the Poor Clares in St Omer, was the first superior in England, leaving Mary free to travel backwards and forwards across the Channel as required. In Flanders she supported her companions in St Omer and pursued her campaign for official recognition of her Institute; in England she supported the covert mission.

Not surprisingly, Mary had several close shaves with the authorities. She tried to evade them by changing her addresses, her name (at one point she went by the name of Tirell), and her clothes – sometimes she was disguised as a servant, sometimes she went dressed 'in a bright taffeta gown and rich petticoats, trimmed of the newest fashion, and a deep yellow ruff', according to her sister Barbara.

And the authorities were confused because – amazingly – there was a Mary Ward look-alike operating in London in 1612. This was the extraordinary Dona Luisa de Carvajal who, at a time when English Catholics were streaming into exile, travelled in the opposite direction and came from Spain to assist Catholics in London. Like Mary, she was from a moneyed and well-connected family, and set up a school for Catholic girls. Like Mary she wanted her followers to be unenclosed. Dona Luisa's project was in fact so similar to Mary Ward's that when she was arrested in 1613, George Abbot, the archbishop of Canterbury, asked her 'Whence is it that you are in such black dresses, with veil and wimple? You have certainly been at one time at St. Omer.' Abbot was clearly confusing Luisa (who had never been to St Omer) with Mary Ward.

It was of course only a matter of time before the authorities closed in on a figure who, in the words of George Abbot, was doing more harm than six Jesuits together. In 1618, pursuivants appeared at a house where Mary was staying in Hungerford, but she had been tipped off, so her party (which may have included her brother George) 'dispersed suddenlie.' On another occasion Mary was staying in Knightsbridge – interestingly, in the house of a Protestant friend – when friends noticed that the house was being watched. Mary moved on – just in time again, for within half an hour of her leaving 'officers came, broke open the doors, searched, and seized upon all.' But on a third occasion she was not so lucky.

Mary had embarked on a boat returning to France, and had begun to cross the Channel when, as Mary Poyntz tells the story, a contrary wind blew the vessel back towards the English shore where it 'landed just in the officers' hands.' Mary was arrested, brought before the justices in London and thrown into prison.[9] Mary had once dreamed of dying a martyr's death: it looked as if her desire might come true. Mary's friends, however – Isabella in Brussels, the Spanish ambassador in London, wealthy English Catholic families – exerted their influence. Money almost certainly changed hands, whether as a bribe or a fine, and Mary was released.

One lesson that Mary drew from the experience was to confirm her belief that, as the commentary to Painting 30 in the *Painted Life* series puts it, 'to help souls to salvation is a far more excellent gift than cloistered life, yea, than martyrdom itself.' And a second lesson that Mary learned in prison was how to smuggle messages past gaolers by writing on paper with lemon juice. This would come in handy the next time she was imprisoned – on orders from Rome.

When Mary left England for the last time, she had new plans for Anne Gage, so she appointed Susanna Rookwood as second superior in London. And we know that Susanna extended the reach of the Institute in England from two sources that, ironically, were antagonistic towards it.

One source is *A Game at Chess*, the very popular play by Thomas Middleton staged at the Globe Theatre in 1624. It is an allegory of a chess match in which the white pieces (Protestants) play against the black pieces (Catholics). The pieces reference important characters on each side of the religious divide (e.g. the king and members of his family as the white pieces, King Philip of Spain, the Spanish ambassador and others as the black) and in the prologue we learn that the black queen's pawn represents Mary Ward:

Ignatius	Were any of my sons placed for the game?
Error	Yes, and a daughter too, a secular daughter
	That plays the Black Queen's Pawn

And to make quite sure the audience gets the point, she introduces herself in the first scene of the play:

| Black Queen's pawn: | I am myself a secular Jesuitess |
| | As many ladies are of wealth and worth … |

The fact that Mary Ward features so prominently in the play, and that Middleton clearly expected his audience to pick up the references, is a back-handed tribute to her work.[10]

The second source that alludes to the reach of the Institute is a letter from a Catholic father who feared that his daughter might wish to join it. So concerned was this Catholic head of the family that he risked writing a letter to a Jesuit priest, and the letter has fortunately survived:

'Very Reverend Father,' he wrote in Latin in 1619:

> I am not accustomed, on account of surrounding dangers, to transact even the least business with foreign parts by letter, but ... an affair of no small importance now ... impels me to write ... .
>
> There is a certain ... Society of Virgins, which for some years has been scattered through almost all this island ... In this kingdom these new Mothers ... journey hither and thither and entice and allure as many people as they can to enter upon this new work; they especially strive to attract to their cause the Fathers of the Society ... Now [a father of the Society, i.e. a Jesuit priest] has besought me several times to allow the only daughter whom I have at home to be admitted to this Sodality. I refused because these Virgins detained amongst them another female relation of mine, almost by force, and by urgent persuasions, so that I was obliged to use several artifices in order to get her back ... .

Such was ever the lot of a radical new organisation. The firebrands on the inside see it as a force for good that will ultimately triumph over the stick-in-the-muds who obstruct it; the defenders of the status quo, feeling threatened by its success, accuse the new sect of seeking adherents by urgent persuasions and almost by force, allege that it divides the community, and feel justified in blocking its growth by the use of artifices. Either way, the letter is clear testimony to the influence of Mary's Institute in England.

In 1619, with the English mission established, Mary travelled to the Continent for the last time. She was 34.

It would be twenty years before she returned to her native England. It would be almost 300 years before a pope would publicly acknowledge her achievement.

1621: The long road to Rome

Walking, walking, walking.
Walking, noticing, marvelling.

Flanders is famous for its doormats. Germans are said to have baths as often as once a week. Augsburg's Maximilianstrasse is reputed to be the finest street in Europe. Augsburg also boasts Europe's first skyscraper in its new six-storey town hall, and travellers are spooked by a town gate which lowers its drawbridge and raises its portcullis as if by magic.[11] Queen Elizabeth I sends spies to find out how it works, but they fail to spot the operators hidden inside.

Travellers admire the water mechanisms at the Villa di Pratolino in Florence and the Villa d'Este in Tivoli, Rome, and shriek with delight when they get soaked. The prince-bishop of Salzburg likes to show off the trick fountains outside his palace at Hellbrunn. In Strasbourg visitors to the cathedral gaze in wonder at the dials and moving statues on the famous astronomical clock. They love the golden cockerel which, at midday, flaps its wings, opens its beak, sticks out its tongue and crows. A flash of lightning will shut it up in 1640.

Florence has two zoos where travellers can stare in amazement at lions, tigers, ostriches and porcupines. And if animals as strange as porcupines can exist, why not unicorns? England has just introduced the unicorn into its coat of arms, and Dresden has the real thing – an actual unicorn's horn. Venice has three.

In Italy, it's the people that are strange. They use fans to cool themselves, umbrellas to shield themselves from the sun, and strange instruments called forks to pick food off their plates. The reason, notes Thomas Coryate,[12] is that Italians 'cannot by any means endure to have [their] dish touched with fingers, seeing' – he adds delicately – that 'all men's fingers are not alike cleane.'

But Italians are used to seeing travelling groups of pilgrims. So they probably hardly give Mary and her companions a second glance.

9

Resolutions: No such difference between men and women (1615–1619)

While Mary Ward was busy setting up the English mission, her house and school in St Omer flourished under the leadership of Barbara Babthorpe. This allowed Mary to cross and re-cross the Channel, as often as her health would allow.[1] In England her work was the cloak and dagger business of disseminating Catholic teaching and playing cat and mouse with the authorities. In St Omer her work was less dramatic, but no less important: supporting her companions, shoring up her own strength with the help of her confessor Roger Lee, and battling to secure formal approval of her Institute by the pope.

Is it surprising that the English sisters in St Omer needed her moral support? Hardly. Put yourself in their shoes. Young (many under 20), and from sheltered backgrounds in stately homes, they were in a foreign country, living an utterly new way of life. Their financial situation veered between the precarious and the catastrophic. Mary, their charismatic leader, was often away. Taking all this into account, I find it impressive that the women managed as well as they did, especially in view of the lukewarm support they received from their confessors.

The confessors, as we have seen before, played a crucial role in the lives of religious women. Mary Ward's companions in St Omer depended on the English Jesuit fathers for moral and spiritual guidance – yet they, at best, 'studiously ignored'[2] the women they supposedly served, and at worst, actively undermined the women's self-confidence with crushingly negative remarks. It often fell to Mary, then, to restore the women's faith in themselves – which she had to do without overtly contradicting the priests to whom she too was bound.

On one occasion in 1617, for example, Thomas Sackville,[3] a visitor returning from Rome, had just cheered the sisters in St Omer by reporting how cardinals in the Vatican had praised their work and fervour – when a Jesuit father who heard Sackville's remarks scornfully commented: 'It is true whilst they [i.e. the companions] are in their first fervour. But fervour will decay, and when all is done, they are but women!'

What?! Were women incapable of sustaining fervour and commitment? If so, they had thrown overboard their lives in England for no purpose. No wonder Mary, arriving back in St Omer, found the sisters bewildered and dejected, in sore need of having fire put back into their bellies. And she rose to the occasion, with words that have gone down in history as some of the most spirited assertions ever of the qualities of women: 'I would know what you all think [the father] meant by this speech of his,' she began. 'I would know what "but women" and what "fervour" is … It is true fervour doth many times grow cold, but what is the cause? Is it because we are women? No, but because we are imperfect women. There is no such difference between men and women.'

No such difference between men and women! It was a bold assertion in the early 1600s. Nor was she yet done, for she went on: 'The verity of our Lord remaineth for ever. It is not verity of men, nor verity of women, but verity of our Lord, and this verity women may have, as well as men. If we fail, it is for want of this verity, and not because we are women… .' And, looking her companions in the eye, she made the following prophecy: 'There is no such difference between men and women that women may not do great things … And I hope in God it will be seen that women in time to come will do much.'

It is a loveable feature of Mary Ward that she asserted the equal value of women with passion but no trace of bitterness. Instead, she deflated the monstrous arrogance of men with gentle humour. I imagine the sisters splitting their sides with laughter when Mary told them with studied under-statement and a twinkle in her eye:

> There was a father that came recently to England, whom I heard say that he would not for a thousand worlds be a woman, because he thought that a woman … [pregnant pause] could not comprehend God!
> I answered nothing but only smiled – although I could have answered him by the experience I have of the contrary.

Mary had a gift for delivering a good punch line. Having acknowledged the prerogative of men to be priests, she added: 'wherein are we so inferior to other creatures that they should term us "but women"? As if we were in all things inferior to some other creation, which I suppose to be,' she added facetiously, 'men!'

Again, I imagine the giggles. And laughter must have done the companions good.

Yet the gentle humour should not blind us to the radical modernity of Mary's words. As Sister Gemma Simmonds put it: '[Mary Ward] had a vision of the equality of men and women before God and a vision of the capacity of women to do good and to work for the kingdom of God. She had this at a time when universities were still discussing whether women had souls.[4]

Well! Mary was not only sure she had a soul, but was sure that women were in no way inferior to men. And this gave her the confidence to challenge the priest's absurd view of women in language that is refreshingly unambiguous: 'I dare be bold to say it is a lie, and, with respect to the good Father, may say it is an error.'

෬————෨

Mary, then, found the words to comfort her companions – but where, did Mary draw her own resources of strength and resolve? It is easy for a biography of Mary Ward to focus on her travels and adventures, and overlook the more private moments in her life, the moments when she withdrew, cleared her mind of extraneous matters and focussed very intimately on her relationship with God. But these moments of prayer and meditation were crucial to her life. She regularly carried out spiritual exercises on the Jesuit model, guided by her confessor Father Roger Lee, and from these prayers and meditations on the Scriptures she developed resolutions, some thirty-five of which have survived. Among them I find:

> 1. I will endeavour that no occurrent accidents change easily my inward composition nor external carriage, because freedom of mind and calmness of passions are so necessary both for my own profit in spirit and proceedings with others.

> 20. I will labour always to overcome my passions in the beginning.

24. Always when the clock strikes, I will lift up my mind to God, and ... I will beg grace for myself and all others, especially our company and the Society of Jesus.

To interpret these resolutions as a set of rules is to miss the point. The aim of disciplined meditation is, paradoxically, to free the mind. As former Mary Ward sister Mother Teresa put it to the United Nations in 1985, 'it is by forgetting self that one finds' – and it was indeed by firmly pushing back her own desires that Mary Ward found the serenity to focus with simple devotion and total clarity on what she believed God willed her to achieve.

And God knows Mary needed every ounce of strength and clarity, because her efforts to get her Institute formerly recognised by the pope were running into trouble.

At a local level the good work that Mary and her companions were doing was there for all to see. Archduchess Isabella urged Bishop Blaes to afford the Institute 'all possible assistance', and Blaes very willingly wrote the Institute a glowing reference:

Mrs. Mary Ward and her companions wishing to render to their country certain services which are more or less incompatible with the usual routine and strict enclosure of monastic rule, had resolved to devote themselves wholly to the teaching and education of girls ... They drew up in writing their plan of life and their Institute, which ... we attentively examined, approved, and warmly commended in the Lord.

'More or less incompatible with... strict enclosure'! In his efforts to give a boost to Mary's Institute, good Bishop Blaes was certainly sailing as close to the wind as he dared.

But Mary's Institute was in trouble further afield. Opposition was, of course, to be expected from William Trumbull, James I's agent – or spy – at the court in Brussels from 1609. In May 1613 Trumbull intercepted a letter from the archdukes to Mary, and passed on to London 'the copy of a letter written from these princes to the matron of certain brain-sick English gentlewomen at St. Omers.'

Brain-sick! Well, Mary could expect no more from the English Protestant establishment.

But it was the opposition from within the Catholic Church that caused Mary more heartache. It came both from those who identified her with the Jesuits, and from Jesuits who wanted to have nothing to do with her, and they began a campaign of slurs and slander aimed at undermining her project. An anonymous document in 1614, for example, claimed that the Institute increased its numbers by a policy of coercion: 'They strive to keep all the young maidens who come to them from England, persuading them in various ways to remain with them.'

It asserted that Mary and her companions in England 'gadded about hither and thither' and overstepped the limits laid down for women by 'working for the profit of souls.' This scandalous behaviour, it went on, had offended men of weight and authority who would now write 'complaints ... from England to the Prelates of the Church.'

Bishop Blaes did his best to put the picture straight. It was not true, he wrote, that the English virgins had ever assumed the role of priests: 'They have not set on foot apostolic missions, but ... if while at home they profit others by their good examples and godly conversation, who may blame them?'

Roger Lee, for his part, refuted the claim that the 'English Ladies' discouraged young women from joining other orders – and, for the record, we know that Mary did nothing to dissuade her sister Frances from leaving St Omer to join the Carmelites in Mons.

But mud sticks, and the slanders and complaints from the 'men of weight and authority' would wing their way to Rome and prejudice 'the Prelates of the Church' against the Institute. What could Mary do to counter the attacks?

Roger Lee, more versed than Mary in the ways of Rome, advised her to draw up a constitution, or rationale, for her foundation – the 'plan of life and their Institute', as Bishop Blaes put it in his reference. These plans went through various drafts and versions, as Mary, who was inexperienced in the art of drawing up formal documents, sharpened and clarified her ideas. But the key points remained the same:

– full status of nuns for the women, with exemption from
   enclosure
– a single female chief superior to head the organisation,
– dispensation from wearing religious dress (or 'habit')

– the right to be placed directly under the pope rather than under a bishop

Mary's plans defined the roles of novices, lay-assistants, mistresses and mothers, but we need not lose ourselves in the minutiae. The essential point is that her Institute represented a radical departure in the history of women's orders.

Roger Lee urged Mary to send her plan to the pope as soon as possible, because he knew that Pope Paul V was a supporter of new foundations. It was his last piece of advice, for he died two weeks later, waiting in Dunkirk for a boat to take him back to England – a poignant reminder of the home-sickness that was part and parcel of the lives of English exiles on the Continent.

Mary Ward was able to give her plan to Thomas Sackville when he passed through St Omer on his way to Rome in November 1615. Mary attached to it a heartfelt appeal to Paul V:

> We have laboured for seven years, more or less, in the diocese of the … Lord Bishop of St. Omer, where we now number sixty persons. Others of our Society … are likewise labouring in England …
>
> Everywhere indeed we find persons anxious to embrace our Institute, were but the state of life declared to be approved by the Apostolic See … Good God! what instruments will they not be in gaining souls, in bringing to the Faith their relations, connexions, friends and equals, in procuring dwellings, residences, and stipends for priests.

However, when the answer from Rome came in a letter dated 10 April, 1616, it was not from the pope but from Cardinal Lancellotti, writing not on behalf of the pope but of the congregation of the cardinals of the Council of Trent. Nor did Lancellotti offer approval of Mary's project. Instead, he commanded Bishop Blaes to take 'the said Virgins' under his protection so that 'they, by Divine help, be the more inflamed to religion and produce daily more abundant fruits of their labours.'

Their eminences the cardinals clearly wanted to see more evidence of what the Institute could achieve. In the meantime, Mary and her companions would have to put up with a politician's classic ploy – a promise not of action, but of future deliberation about possible action: 'And if as we trust, it shall so come to pass,' wrote Lancellotti, 'then the Apostolic See will also deliberate about confirming their Institute.'

It was the very epitome of a diplomat's answer, couched in the form of a conditional sentence, and an unbalanced one at that. The women were required to act; the men only held out the prospect of talking.

Was Mary Ward disappointed by the cardinal's reply? If so, in line with Resolution 1 cited above she kept her thoughts to herself. But a clue to her inner turmoil may lie in the fact that she fell ill again in the early summer of 1616. To recuperate, Mary travelled to Spa, a small town in a territory that was then outside Flanders and under the control of the prince-bishop of Liège. Already notorious as a meeting-point for English Catholics,[5] Spa was in 1616 notorious for a so-called witch trial as a result of which ten innocent women were burned or garrotted, while more died in prison. It was Mary Ward's first close shave with witch hunts, and not her last.

In Spa Mary Ward had time to decide how she would respond to Lancellotti's letter. Perhaps, as Chambers would have us believe, she was fired by the good news from Rome. Perhaps, instead, she determined to show Lancellotti and his congregation of cardinals what she was made of, just as she had shown Andres de Soto before. The cardinals wished to see 'more fruits of her labours'? Very well. She would show them – not out of anger, still less out of spite, but with a zeal for the Lord that could not fail to convince them. She would come out fighting. She would found a new house in a new territory.

There were good reasons for founding a new house. The community in St Omer had grown much larger than she had ever intended: the women would be able to do more good if they had a new base in a new town, and would be able to give the cardinals evidence of 'more abundant fruits of their labours.'

In 1616, at the age of 31, Mary Ward founded her second house on the Continent – in the prince-bishopric of Liège. She did not know it, but this was the beginning of an expansion eastwards that would take her as far as Prague, Vienna and Bratislava.

1621: The long road to Rome

Walking, walking, walking.
Walking, aching, limping.

Little is yet known about the human body. William Harvey has not yet proved that blood circulates round the body. Few people have ever heard of Ambroise Paré or his thesis that turpentine is an effective antiseptic for open wounds. So open wounds are cauterised with boiling elderberry oil.

Water is widely mistrusted as a spreader of disease. Louis XIII, born in 1601, is not bathed till he is almost 7. Elizabeth I takes a bath once a month but James I only washes his fingers. Public baths are associated with syphilis.

Disease is a fact of life. People live in fear of smallpox, cholera, typhus, diphtheria and measles, and are positively petrified of the plague. Around 38,000 Londoners succumb to the plague in 1603, more in proportion to the total population than in the Great Plague of 1665. It recurs and kills thousands more in 1609, in 1620 and in 1625. The plague will wipe out almost a third of the population of Venice in 1629 and 1630: the Church of Santa Maria Della Salute will be built to give thanks for deliverance from it. Death is such a fact of life that marriages often do not last long. It is common for people to marry twice during their lifetime.

Mary Ward's kidney and gallstones will cause her excruciating pain for most of her adult life. There is little she can do about it, except take medicinal waters – at Spa, at San Casciano in Italy, and at Eger (Cheb) in Bohemia.

10

Recognition: 'A cheerful mind' (1616–1619)

In 1616 – some 154 years before James Cook – *Concorde* landed in Australia. No, not the plane: the *Eendracht* (which translates as 'concord') was a wooden ship that had set out from Amsterdam and been blown across the Pacific by the Roaring Forties. Its crew of 200 made the second recorded visit by Europeans to Australia, and left an inscribed pewter plate which is the oldest European object ever found on the Continent. The first name on the plate – above even that of the captain Dirk Hartog – is that of Gilles Miebais of Liège. Gilles is described as the supercargo, or 'leading merchant' of the ship.

That a citizen of Liège was the leading merchant of a ship such as the *Eendracht* is indicative of the wealth and influence of the city in the era of Mary Ward. It occupied a strategically pivotal position in Northern Europe, with France to the south, the German states of the Holy Roman Empire to the east, Spanish Flanders to the west and the newly independent, economically blossoming states of the Netherlands to the north. When Mary Ward arrived in 1616 the city was beginning to specialise in the manufacture of guns and armaments – just in time to cash in on the massive demand for weapons generated by the Thirty Years' War (1618–1648). No wonder merchant and arms supplier Jean Curtius had just had a palace built on the banks of the Meuse which, with its white stripes across a vivid red façade, is still one of the iconic buildings of Liège today.

A bastion of Catholicism against the Protestant tide from the north and east, Liège appeared to be a perfect setting for Mary Ward's second house on the Continent. It was ruled by a rock-solid Catholic prince-bishop to whom Mary had letters of introduction from Isabella. It boasted a cathedral, a Walloon Jesuit college and eighteen béguinages. The English Jesuits had just moved their college and house for novices from Louvain to Liège, and the rector of the Jesuit novitiate and college was Father John Gerard – the legendary escapee from the Tower of London. It was likely Roger Lee who introduced John Gerard to her, and Father Gerard soon provided spiritual and material support for her project.

But all was not harmony in Liège. The prince-bishop of nominally neutral Liège was Ferdinand of Wittelsbach, the younger brother of the powerful duke of Bavaria. An ardent, some might say fanatical supporter of the Catholic cause, it was widely suspected that this had as much to do with furthering the prospects of the House of Wittelsbach as with any deep religious conviction. Indeed, although Ferdinand was a bishop, he had never been ordained as a priest, because he wanted to keep open the option of producing offspring for the family line if his older brother were to die childless. A classic case of the abuses denounced by Protestants, Ferdinand was also archbishop of Cologne, bishop of Hildesheim, and prince-bishop of Münster (and, from 1618, Paderborn). With such a choice of palaces to reside in, Ferdinand was not, in fact, in Liège all that often – according to one calculation, he managed a grand total of six months and eighteen days in Liège during his twenty-three years as its prince-bishop. The Council of Trent required all bishops to be resident in their bishoprics – but Rome was clearly more willing to turn a blind eye in this matter than in the matter of enclosure for women.

Despite his long absences, Ferdinand had no compunctions about issuing decrees that impacted on the city. In 1614 he barred non-Catholics from citizenship of the city, at a stroke driving out both Protestant and Jewish families who, with their technical know-how, could have contributed to Liège as they so conspicuously did to Antwerp and Amsterdam. Louis de Geer, for example, would establish the Swedish iron industries that supplied munitions for the Protestant cause in the Thirty Years' War. It was a local example of the shift in economic prominence from (largely southern) Catholic to (largely northern) Protestant countries in this period.

In 1613 Ferdinand had angered the Liège city council by revoking the more democratic constitution that had been granted by his predecessor, Prince Bishop Ernest of Wittelsbach. In 1614 the city council chose to ignore Ferdinand's repeal and to conduct elections according to the old manner, so the representatives of the people (or at least its richer burghers and guilds) were pitted against the absentee prince-bishop in a tussle that anticipated Charles I's stand-off with the English parliament.

Nor was it all sweetness and light between the many religious communities in Liège. As in England, the Jesuits were at loggerheads with the local clergy and established orders who resented the Jesuits' influence on the prince-bishop. In particular, they argued over who should be in charge of training priests in Liège. When Mary Ward arrived in the city in 1616, the prince-bishop was trying to take this remit away from the traditional clergy and put the Jesuits in charge instead.

Mary Ward's allies and sponsors were, then, let's be candid, what we would today call the reactionary forces in town – the prince-bishop, and the Jesuits who were rearing the next generation of absolutist rulers. So should we regard Mary as an agent of absolutist rule? I find the question hard to answer. Her family background, her friends, her sponsors were all in the landed classes. On the other hand, she and her companions provided free education to girls of all classes, and helped to empower women, rich and poor. Her cause was ultimately not in the political field. She was dependent on the favours of the ruling elite wherever she went, but – unlike her sponsors – she and her sisters were in daily contact with ordinary people and had first-hand experience of their needs. Being of her time, she simply did not think in class terms.

Surprisingly, perhaps, there already existed in Liège an order of women with aims similar to Mary's – the Ursulines. Founded by Angela de Merici in 1535 with a mission to teach girls, both rich and poor, the Ursulines had originally lived unenclosed. This had not been controversial in the days before the Council of Trent, and the Ursulines gained papal approval in 1540. Now they were running the largest network of Catholic schools for girls in Europe, so they were, on the face of it, natural allies for Mary Ward. It seemed almost too good to be true.

It was. For after Angela de Merici died in 1540, the men of the Church began to limit the freedoms that she had fought for. Like the béguines, Ursulines lived and worked in independent houses with no centralising figure of chief superior and were therefore easy prey for experienced bishops to 'guide' into more 'proper' channels. When, for example, Bishop Charles Borromeo welcomed the Ursulines to Milan, he 'regularised' their status by organising them into congregations – depriving them of the status of nuns. In France, Church authorities persuaded the Paris Ursulines to accept enclosure in 1612, the Toulouse Ursulines in 1616. Of course, this limited the Ursulines' ability to teach and deprived them of the ability to decide things for themselves. Some French women, indeed, clung to their independence by emigrating to Canada. There, beyond the control of Rome, unenclosed French Ursulines taught the Hurons, Algonkians and Iroquois.

The Liège Ursulines, then, were not positive role models for Mary Ward. Her vision was of a society of women, free from enclosure, organised under a female superior answerable directly to the pope. Only this structure, Mary believed, would allow the Institute to work effectively. And events in Liège proved Mary right. For although the Ursulines arrived in town two years before she did, and had already secured approval for their school from the pope's nuncio (or ambassador), Antonio Albergati, Mary Ward managed to open her school before they did. The speed with which Mary could act was proof positive of the advantages of the self-governance which she was determined to secure for her Institute. Indeed, less than two years later, in February 1618, Mary was able to open a *second* house in Liège: a novitiate, or training college for new companions.

Was Mary maybe moving *too* fast? After all, with backers reluctant to fund her project till it was formally approved by the pope, she was short of money. The new house in Liège was only made possible with money which Sir Thomas Sackville raised by mortgaging Jesuit property bought in his name. When Thomas Sackville subsequently went bankrupt, this complicated transaction landed both Mary's Institute and the English Jesuits in deep trouble. But we should see Mary's move in the context of the exponential growth of the Jesuits, who were universally admired for the astonishing speed at which their schools spread from Munich to Macao, and from Brussels to Bolivia. It seems quite logical to me that, convinced that papal approval was almost within her grasp, Mary Ward wanted to do the same. Had Rome moved faster, we might now look back on the foundation of the novitiate in Liège as an act of genius.

Mary brought Anne Gage from London to be the new superior in Liège in 1618. The school was near the Church of St Martin; the novitiate stood on the Pierreuse, the road that climbs steeply from the prince-bishop's palace. I found it a disheartening climb because the cobblestones are shockingly uneven and the fine houses of the cathedral clergy sadly dilapidated. But persevere, and just as you begin to run out of breath, there on the left is the Ferme de la Vache which was once the house of the 'English Virgins'. The property included a meadow and an orchard, and a path still leads through an archway, through orchards and gardens to the former college of the English Jesuits, now the administration building of the Région Wallonne. The prince-bishop himself came to call on one of his rare visits to the city. He said Mass in the companions' church, and was good enough to compliment the sisters on the quality of their singing. But the sweetness of the singing masked the rumbles of trouble.

1618 was, of course, a fateful year for Europe. Far away in Prague, representatives of another Ferdinand – the ruler of Austria and Catholic claimant to the title of king Bohemia – were thrown out of the palace window, and what first looked like a local dispute in distant Bohemia triggered thirty years of war which spread like a cancer across central Europe, sucking in armies from countries as far apart as Sweden and Spain – a ghastly, ominous and threatening backdrop to the remainder of Mary's life.

Nominally a war between Catholics and Protestants for supremacy in Europe, it was in practice a struggle between the Habsburgs and their allies on one side, and, on the other, most of the rest of Europe, who feared and resented Habsburg power and dominance.[1] The pope, fearing Habsburg expansion in Italy, was only a lukewarm ally, Catholic France threw in its lot with Protestant Sweden and the Protestant 'prince of Transylvania', Bethlen Gabor sought the help of the Muslim Ottomans. Diplomatically, religiously, the Thirty Years' War was a messy affair[2] and in human terms it was a catastrophe from which the German-speaking peoples took decades, if not centuries to recover.

Few rulers emerged with much credit. One of the few who I feel deserves more credit than he generally gets is James I of England, who refused to enter the fray even though his daughter Elizabeth was married to Frederick V, the leading protagonist on the anti-Habsburg side. James thereby saved countless British Protestant and Catholic lives. In 1951 Pope Pius XII famously called his reign Catholic England's 'darkest and bloodiest hour' for the number of Catholic priests who were executed – but the death toll of English Catholics under James, shameful though it was, was nothing compared to Catholic and Protestant deaths in Central Europe, where, for thirty bloody years, armies reeled across lands like drunken giants, trampling the fields, ransacking towns and villages, raping or massacring the inhabitants. Estimates of (overwhelmingly civilian) deaths range from 5,000,000 to 8,000,000.

1618 was a difficult year for Mary, too. For a start, her efforts at securing papal recognition were getting nowhere despite good Bishop Blaes's best efforts. In February 1617 he had sent the prince-bishop of Liège a glowing reference:

> Most Serene Prince,
>
> English Virgins ... who abide here with us, have begged of me to commend to your Serenity their Mother and Sisters ... and this indeed I do most willingly ... because our Most Holy Lord, in consideration of their pious endeavours, has not long since commended them to me with most earnest words ... .

Bishop Blaes had also issued a public letter in which he had again insinuated that the pope himself was on side: 'The Most Holy Lord Pope, with the said Cardinals,' he wrote, 'have commanded us to help them with all the assistance we can ... .'

This was bending the truth as far as he dared, for the answer from Rome had of course not been from the pope, but from Cardinal Lancelotti acting for a committee. It was the last act of support from a man who – though sorely tested by the twists and turns of Mary Ward's career – had from the start recognised the magnificence of her vision, and had always stood by her. Bishop Blaes died in 1618. She would miss his unwavering support.

Mary was also facing a crisis closer to home, for dissent had flared up in her houses in Liège while she was away in England. It is, when I come to think of it, surprising that this had never happened before. For years Mary's companions had trusted her without question, even though her objectives were unclear, her aims apparently unachievable, and her convictions based on very personal messages from God. But supposing Mary were wrong? What if her projects were not based on God's will at all, but on her personal vanity? What if, as abbess Mary Gough had warned back in the Poor Clares convent, visions were a channel not for the word of God, but for the voice of the devil?

A number of sisters began to express such doubts in 1618, and they soon coalesced around the figure of Sister Praxedes. Mary, they said, had been led astray, and the sisters should jump ship and join regular female orders where their lives would be simpler, their status clearer, and their financial situation safer.

Sister Praxedes and her coterie were egged on by the English Jesuit fathers in Liège who felt that Father Gerard had got their college far too involved with Mary's Institute. Indeed, brave though he undoubtedly was, Father Gerard had a tendency to be carried away by his own enthusiasm. A Jesuit in Louvain had warned: 'I see a general fear … of the success of Father [Gerard's] government, and unless he hath a companion that may moderate him, his zeal will, I fear, carry him too far.'[3] Now Father Gerard had lent Mary Ward sums of money in a number of opaque transactions, and when it emerged that the English Jesuits themselves were in financial difficulties, many – quite understandably – blamed Mary Ward and her companions for it.

Mary arrived back in Liège, therefore, to find her community riven in two. It was a critical test of her leadership, and her reaction was typical of her. First she withdrew to seek guidance in prayer. Then she called a meeting of the Liège sisters and offered to resign as superior if this was what they desired.

But there was, as it happened, no need. Perhaps the revolt simply melted away once Mary was back on the scene. Perhaps, as Chambers tells the story, Sister Praxedes fell ill and – conveniently – died. A small number of sisters left the community in Liège, but most

remained loyal, and among those who stayed a process of healing could begin.

For Mary, the challenge to her leadership must have come as a shock. Yet, extraordinarily, we have no record of her leadership ever being challenged again. One reason must surely be that Mary led by example, sharing the sisters' daily routine of meditations, prayer, teaching and recreation. She claimed no special exemptions. Instead, she made herself a further list of resolutions, and tried to live by them:

> – A troubled dejected spirit will never love God perfectly, nor do much good to His honour.
> – Do good, and do it well.

Two of her resolutions put a striking emphasis on cheerfulness:

> – Show thyself at all times glad and joyful, for Almighty God loves a cheerful giver.
> – In our calling, a cheerful mind, a good understanding, and a great desire after virtue are necessary, but of all three a cheerful mind is the most so.

And Mary Ward certainly needed all the cheerfulness she could muster. Since the arrival of Cardinal Lancelotti's letter in April 1616, requiring her to 'produce daily more abundant fruits of their labours', she had increased the number of women in her Institute, maintained the English mission against all odds, continued to run the school in St Omer, opened a new school and a novitiate in Liège, secured public endorsement from Bishop Blaes and obtained the support of the powerful prince-bishop of Liège – not bad for two years' work. But still there was no word from Rome.

The safe and rational thing to do was to hunker down, hope for the best and not put her houses under any more financial strain. The visionary and inspired course of action was to expand further, so as to be in a better position to fully exploit the situation when papal approval arrived. So when the prince-bishop asked Mary Ward to set up a house in Cologne, guess which course she took?

1621: The long road to Rome

Walking, walking, walking.
Walking, searching, getting lost.

Mary Ward has no maps. The Belgian Gerard Mercator has published maps of the Netherlands, Germany and France and a world map so revolutionary that it is still in use today – but ordinary folk are not in possession of such treasures.

Most maps combine the factual with the fanciful: empty spaces are filled with imagined mountains and monsters. This reflects people's perception of space in the early seventeenth century. Those who consider distant places at all think of them as a series of discrete, self-contained units. They show no interest in the spaces in between, any more than for desert spaces between oases. Mary Poyntz's description of Mary's journey, for example, tells us that she was in Nancy, Milan and Loreto, but ignores the itinerary in between. As Axel Gotthard puts it, people in the seventeenth century travel in order to arrive.[4] There is little interest in travel as such.

It is only when (mainly English) aristocrats begin travelling through Europe that the educational and aesthetic value of travel will be appreciated. What will become the great vogue of the Grand Tour has, in fact, just begun with the earl of Arundel's journey to Italy, with his wife and children, in 1613. But it has yet to catch on.

So Mary finds her way by word of mouth, exchanging news and information with those who share the road with her – fellow pilgrims, itinerant merchants and disbanded soldiers.

11

Resources: 'More fruits of her labours' (1618–1621)

Why Cologne?

Well, Ferdinand, the prince-bishop of Liège, was also the prince-archbishop of Cologne, so he was able to smooth the way. And Cologne was a Catholic stronghold that was particularly dear to Catholics in the early seventeenth century, for, within living memory, the city had very nearly been 'lost' to the Protestants. If it had been, the consequences would have reached beyond the city itself.

We tread here with Mary Ward into the bewildering shifting quicksand of central European politics. Most of what is now Germany, and some territories beyond, was organised (if that is the right word) into myriad more or less self-governing states, loosely gathered under the emperor of what was misleadingly called the Holy Roman Empire. The (mainly) German-speaking states in the Holy Roman Empire delighted in confusing names and borders. The leading Protestant contender in the Thirty Years' War, for example, was Frederick V of the Palatinate. The Palatinate was, in fact, a disparate, to look at the map you might almost think a random collection of unconnected plots of land scattered on either side of the Rhine. However, these lands had special importance for they constituted one of only seven electorates within the whole of the Empire – that is to say, its ruler was one of the seven men (and yes, they were all men) who had the right to elect the emperor. Following the convulsions of the Reformation, fate had decreed that three of the seven electors were Protestant, and four Catholic.[1] The Catholic majority was slim indeed – and what should happen in 1582 but that one of the Catholic electors, Gebhard Truchsess von Waldburg, Prince-Archbishop of Cologne, should announce that he was converting to Calvinism, thus giving the Protestants a majority. For good measure, he then married his mistress with whom he had already been living for two years.

The Catholic leaders within the Empire were shocked and scandalised – no, not at the fact that one of their chief archbishops had had a mistress, but at the prospect of the Protestants commanding four of the seven votes for the emperor. The emperor had always been Catholic, indeed one of the chief motors behind Catholicism in Europe: it was, they raged, inconceivable that the next emperor might be Protestant. In fact, the electors did *not* always vote according to religion: in 1619, the Protestant elector of Saxony voted for the Catholic candidate – Ferdinand of Habsburg. But the Catholic faction was taking no chances. The pope excommunicated Gebhard and several thousand Spanish troops were hired, under the duke of Parma, to evict him from his diocese.

But Gebhard raised troops too, and for six years, in a ghastly prequel to the Thirty Years' War, the two armies laid waste to towns and villages, abbeys and castles, fields and orchards, reducing the population in and around Cologne to starvation. The Catholic forces finally triumphed, and Ernst of Wittelsbach was enthroned as archbishop in Gebhard's place. He brought in the Jesuits and other orders to re-establish Catholicism within the diocese. But as if to show that there were no hard feelings about Gebhard's mistress, Archbishop Ernst had one too. Despite all the strictures of the Council of Trent, he lived with her from 1605 till her death in 1608.

When Mary Ward arrived in Cologne, therefore, Catholicism dominated the city once more. One estimate is that priests, monks, nuns and other 'religious' accounted for fully 10 per cent of the population – a staggering proportion. They celebrated Mass, organised processions to the cathedral's shrine of the three Magi, and provided help for the poor, many of whom were refugees from the recent wars.

In view of this dominant position, two things appear strange. One was that the territory administered by Mary's sponsor, Archbishop Ferdinand, did not actually include the city – as a 'free city' within the Holy Roman Empire, Cologne itself was outside his secular jurisdiction, and the archbishop did not reside within it. When he was not sojourning in one of his other dioceses, Ferdinand lived in a palace in Bonn or Brühl, within the large diocese around Cologne. The second surprise is that the greatest monument to Catholicism in the city, the soaring Gothic cathedral, remained unfinished during the whole of this period. St Paul's in London, we have seen, was bereft of its spire, but the situation in Cologne was even more extreme: building had ceased in 1530 – and the crane atop the half-built southern tower had been there so long that it had become a tourist sight in its own right. It is an irony of history that the cathedral was only completed when Cologne was governed by Protestant Prussia.

Mary acquired a house in the Breite Strasse in June 1618, but the Institute did not actually move in until 1620 due to a desperate lack of resources – a shortage of both of money and of trained sisters. Sisters were needed in St Omer, in Liège and for the English mission, all at a time when dowry money was short and sponsors hard to come by. King James's agent in Brussels, Trumbull, had already been informed by his spies that Bishop Blaes and the magistrates of St Omer had paid some of the Institute's debts in St Omer – information which he gleefully passed on to London.

When the sisters finally moved in, they opened a school for girls. But wait a minute! How come the sisters are suddenly fluent in German? The sisters' aptitude for rapidly learning foreign languages is an unsung accomplishment, easily taken for granted as the Institute spread from Liège to Cologne and on to Rome and beyond. A clue as to how the sisters learned their German comes, as does so much information about Mary Ward, from the pen of one of her enemies. In 1622 Matthew Kellison told the Inquisition that 'she has started many communities in the diocese of Cologne, not only of English ladies but of those of that country.'[2] This is the first mention of non-English companions: a practical step for learning the local language, and a sign that the Institute membership was becoming more international.

In the Breite Strasse, the companions found themselves in the bustling centre of Cologne, rubbing shoulders with inns like the *Brauhaus zum Falken* in the Kreuzgasse and *em decke Tommes* in the Glockengasse, an enclosed congregation of Ursulines, one of Cologne's first printing presses and the city's first tobacco shop. Outside, the Thurn and Taxis post coach clattered on its way to connect with the post route to Brussels and Rome. You get a feel of what the city must have felt like in the small area of winding lanes that has survived south of the cathedral. The narrow, six-storey brick houses that look so quaint today were the modern residences of the 1620s: the older houses would have been made of wood.

There were as yet no bridges across the river. Ferries plied across the Rhine, serving the trade routes eastwards and the small Jewish communities forced to live over the river in Deutz and Mülheim. Banned from living in Cologne proper, the Jews entered the city by day to work as merchants, doctors and glaziers. As they were still banned from England, these were maybe the first Jews that Mary Ward and her sisters had ever seen. They were not hard to spot, for in 1215 Pope Innocent III had decreed that all Jews must wear a yellow badge.

The year 1620 finished on a high point for Catholics in Europe. The opening phases of the Thirty Years' War had been rumbling on far away in Bohemia, with two contestants, the Protestant Fredrick V of the Palatinate in one corner, and the Catholic Ferdinand of Austria in the other, sparring indecisively for the title of king of Bohemia. But early in November 1620 the two rival armies clashed at the Battle of the White Mountain, outside Prague, and the Catholic forces, spurred on by the Carmelite monk Domenico di Gesù e Maria, carried the day. The Protestants were routed, Frederick fled from Prague and Ferdinand acceded to the throne. It was maybe the most decisive victory of the entire war and the news will have been welcomed with jubilation in Cologne.

And Mary, too, had a victory to celebrate. Her work in Cologne had impressed the prince-archbishop of Trier, Lothar von Metternich, and he now asked her to open a school in Trier. The archbishop of Trier was the second of only three ecclesiastical electors in the Empire – Mary was moving in high circles indeed.

CB———EO

And so began 1621, a momentous year for Mary, though she did not yet know it.

How, I wonder, was she feeling, as she travelled the 100 miles from Cologne to Trier? Excited by this further opportunity to show the cardinals in Rome 'more fruits of her labours'? Or worried about how the new house in Trier was to be financed? Her resources were now spread very thinly indeed: Mary Alcock would later allege that Mary Ward was prone to start a new foundation when only two or three months' funding had been secured. On this occasion, it is likely that Mary's old friend and sponsor, Isabella, helped out: at any rate, she was soon in a position to open a house in the Pferdemarkt square, just down the road from the Porta Nigra, the massive Roman gate that had survived because it was later used as a church.

If the Porta Nigra bore witness to Trier's importance in the past, its continued importance was assured by the tomb of St Matthias:[3] the only tomb of an apostle north of the Alps, it attracted pilgrims from all over Northern Europe. The city's strategic position was symbolised by its stone bridge across the river Mosel, its political power by the palace under construction for the prince-archbishop. Educated by (of course!) the Jesuits, Archbishop Lothar was fluent in Latin, French, Italian, German and Flemish, and, like Bishop Blaes, he was passionate about raising the standard of education in his diocese and ensuring that priests were better trained.

Mary Ward therefore suited Lothar's plans perfectly: the Jesuits would educate the boys, Mary Ward would educate the girls. One boy that Mary may have seen among the pupils trooping off to church with his Jesuit teachers was Nicolas Antoine. In his case the Jesuit education backfired: Antoine became Protestant, then Jewish, and was burned at the stake in Geneva in 1632. Violence was never far below the surface of life in Mary Ward's day, and indeed Trier had its own particularly dark secrets.

For Mary Ward's sponsor, the self-disciplined, educated Lothar, had a second, grimmer side to him: Trier was the scene of the highest number of executions of so-called witches in Europe. The trials, torture and burnings had begun under Archbishop Johann von Schönenberg, with 300 people executed on charges of witchcraft by 1589. In one village every single woman bar two had been killed. And the killings continued after Lothar was appointed archbishop in May 1599: Trein Schussel was executed as a witch in June 1604, Elssen Dicköpfer in the following month. Biographies of Lothar sing the praises of his intelligence and culture, and Pope Paul V was moved to call him 'the pattern of a bishop.'

Harewell Hall Mary Ward spent many years of her childhood away from her parents and family, including here at Harewell Hall, deep in the Yorkshire Pennines.

The Painted Life Mary's family home in Mulwith, not far from Ripon, Yorkshire, was damaged in a bad fire. This is one of fifty paintings of scenes in Mary's life in a series called the Painted Life. The originals are in the Englische Fräulein school in Augsburg and copies are displayed in the Bar Convent Museum in York.

The Painted Life While sewing alongside her cousin Barbara Babthorpe, Mary Ward listened to Margaret Garrett, a maid in the Babthorpe household in Osgodby, and decided to become a nun. This scene is, again, from the Painted Life.

Above: **The Gunpowder Plot, 1605** Mary Ward was related to most of the Gunpowder Plotters, and her father became embroiled in the events following the discovery of the plotters.

Below: **London in the seventeenth century** London had a population of about 200,000 in the early 1600's. In 1605 Mary Ward stayed in the house of a well-to-do Catholic family in Baldwin's Gardens, a new, fashionable street that had been laid out north of Holborn, between the City of London and the City of Westminster.

Above: **Boats off Dover** Mary Ward felt forced to emigrate from England because of the religious persecution against Catholics. Government agents on the look out for emigrating Catholics, the vagaries of the weather and the threat of being attacked by pirates made the journey from Dover to Spanish-held Flanders a dangerous one.

Below: **A saint for walkers** As a lay sister in the Poor Clares convent in St Omer, Mary Ward had no contact with the choir sisters. She maybe prayed at the tomb of St Erkembode in the cathedral. Like Mary, Erkembode was a walker: as bishop, he walked all over his diocese to get to know his people and their problems. To this day, pilgrims leave shoes on his tomb.

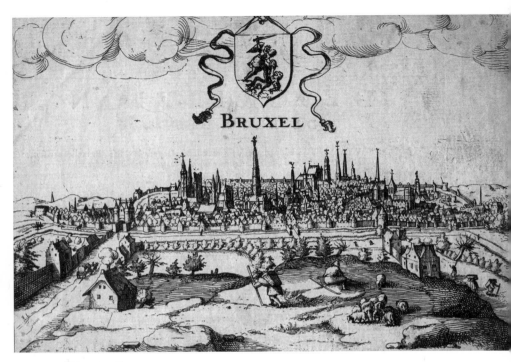

Above: **Brussels** Brussels was under Spanish rule when Mary Ward came to petition Archdukes Albert and Isabella in 1607.

Left: **Archdukes Albert and Isabella** Isabella was of equal rank to her husband, as both Albert and Isabella were Archdukes in their own right. As a strong, independently minded woman, Isabella was first a role model for Mary, and later a good friend and supporter.

Above: **The Coudenberg Palace** Undaunted by the pomp and ceremonial at their royal palace, Mary successfully petitioned Archdukes Albert and Isabella to allow her to found her own convent and on her own terms. This was an extraordinary achievement for Mary, who was only 22 years old.

Below: **Visions** Mary Ward experienced a series of visions which guided her towards her destiny. Following this second vision, Mary understood that she was not to become an enclosed Carmelite nun, but that 'some other thing' had been prepared for her. This is another of the paintings in the Painted Life series.

Companions Mary named the seven young women who joined her in her risky enterprise her companions. This picture in the Painted Life series makes clear that they were all from well-to-do families, but does not yet suggest the courage and tenacity that their life in Mary's Institute would demand of them.

Liège This is the Pierreuse – the hill in Liège on which Mary opened a novitiate, or training college for new companions. Liège was in one of the territories of Prince-Archbishop Ferdinand of Wittelsbach.

Cologne Mary opened a house in the Breite Strasse in the centre of Cologne in 1618, the year in which the Thirty Years' War began. Many houses in the city were still built of wood, and there were as yet no bridges over the Rhine.

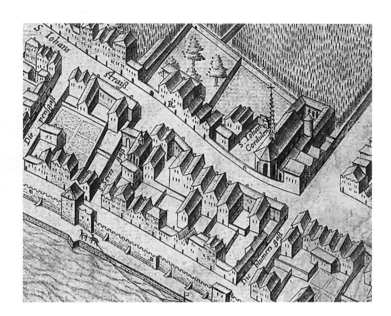

Unfinished cathedrals In an age in which thousands of people were slaughtered in the name of religion, it is striking that the same religious fervour was lacking as regards attention to buildings. Old St Paul's in London was bereft of its spire. Work on the cathedral in Cologne had been abandoned for so long that the crane (seen in this picture on the half-built south tower) had become a tourist attraction. Prague's St Vitus Cathedral was unfinished too.

The Battle of the White Mountain This Catholic victory in 1620 was one of the few decisive battles in the Thirty Years' War that devastated central Europe and was an ever-threatening backdrop to the life of Mary Ward.

Burnings Hundreds of women, and some men too, were burned across Europe as witches, some under Mary Ward's backer in Trier, Prince-Archbishop Lothar. After Mary Ward incurred the wrath of the Pope, her companions feared that Mary herself was in danger of meeting this fate.

Crossing the Alps Travellers in the seventeenth century did not cross the Alps for fun. The route was dangerous, with unprotected ledges, and even in winter travellers were equipped with no more than gloves and nail-studded boots.

Pope Urban VIII For most of her time in Rome, Mary was dealing with Pope Urban VIII, more famous for his dealings with Galileo. While Pope Urban always received Mary kindly, he was suspicious of her project and in the end banned it.

Right & opposite above: **The old Splügen Pass** Parts of the old Splügen Pass, which weaves its way through the mountains between Italy and Switzerland, were carved out of the bare rock, and there is a sheer drop to the left of the steps. You can walk it today as part of the dramatic Via Spluga trail.

In Munich The promise from Duke Maximilian I of Bavaria and his wife Elisabeth Renata that they would give Mary a house in Munich, and fund a school, gave new life and impetus to Mary's Institute.

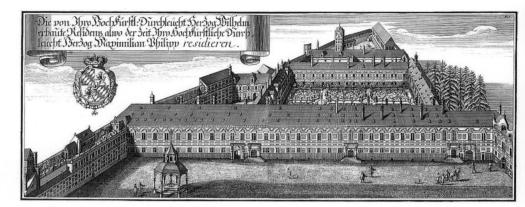

Above: **The ducal palace in Munich** This is where Mary Ward met Duke Maximilian and his wife Elisabeth Renata. The Duke gave Mary Ward the *Paradeiserhaus*, a property close to the palace. The 'house of paradise' became the nerve centre of Mary's Institute.

Below left: **Ferdinand II** As Emperor of the Holy Roman Empire, Ferdinand II ruled over most of central Europe and it is amazing that Mary Ward was able to meet and negotiate with him. While he was a supporter of her Institute, he ruthlessly suppressed the Protestants in his Austrian lands.

Below right: **Melchior Klesl, Archbishop of Vienna** Klesl and Ferdinand became bitter enemies, and Mary Ward and her Institute was damaged by the fall-out of their quarrel. Klesl's report on Mary's school in Vienna was so damning that it began the process that led to the suppression of her Institute.

Prague This print from between 1612 and 1630 shows the castle in Prague with the unfinished St Vitus cathedral. Despite all Mary's efforts, her school in Prague was the last one that Mary was able to open herself.

Rome This is a 17th century view of the Piazza Navona in Rome. Mary's stay in Rome from 1632 to 1637 must have been one of the most frustrating and difficult times in her life.

A la fin ſes Voleurs infames et perdus
Comme fruibs malheureux a cet arbre pendus

Monſtrent bien que le crime horrible et noire engeance
Eſt luy meſme inſtrument de honte et de vengeance

Et que, ceſt le Deſtin des hommes vicieux
Déſprouuer toſt ou tard d'la iuſtice des Cieux

Thirty years of war Jacques Callot depicted the horrors of the Thirty Year's War in his series of prints called The Great Miseries of War. In this print, men hang from the tree – 'like fruit', as the text below bitterly puts it.

The Lady Chapel This simple building, half hidden on a hill near Osmotherley in Yorkshire, became a place of pilgrimage for English Catholics after the Reformation. Mary Ward lived nearby after the first stirrings of what would become Civil War forced her to flee London.

Right: **Besieged in York** Mary Ward was in York during the siege of 1644. Most streets in York would then have looked much as the Shambles, once the street of the butchers, looks today.

Below: **The Battle of Marston Moor** It was really a battle for York, and the Royalists lost. Following the Royalist defeat, Mary Ward moved back to her house in Heworth, then a village just outside York. Mary died there in January 1645 and was buried in Osbaldwick.

Above: **Mary Ward school in Nürnberg, Germany** Following Mary's death her companions regrouped in Munich and campaigned for her Institute to be recognised by the pope. They also opened schools. As a result there are Mary Ward schools in some twenty different towns in the south of Germany and in St Pölten and Krems in Austria.

Below: **The Bar Convent** The Bar Convent in York is on the site of the first school in England opened by Mary Ward's companions, just outside Micklegate Bar, the main entrance into the city. The raised frontage of the larger building hides the dome of the chapel. The Bar Convent contains a fascinating museum about Mary Ward with interactive, state-of-the-art displays.

How, I ask myself, was it possible for such distinguished learning to go hand in hand with such barbarity?

One reason must be the culture of intolerance so actively promoted on both sides of the Catholic/Protestant divide in the seventeenth century. So utterly convinced were people that they, and only they, had divine truth on their side that they viewed anyone who deviated from their line as an enemy of God. It was therefore their holy duty to have that person expelled or destroyed. It is no coincidence that Archbishop Schönenberg expelled the Jews and the Protestants from his diocese before he picked on so-called witches. They were all, in his eyes, the enemies of God. People's utter conviction in their own rightfulness led to a blind spot regarding the suffering of anyone with different views.

And what of Mary Ward, I ask myself? Having journeyed this far with her, how can I not wish to exempt her from any association with the burning of innocent human beings as witches? How dearly I would love to quote her outcry against their trials and executions. But there is none. Loud are her laments about the persecution of Catholics in England, but this champion of women is silent about the persecution of women condemned as witches, Jews or Protestants. Of course, Mary Ward never explicitly condoned the killings. But I have to accept that she was part of the bigoted, self-righteous world – Catholic and Protestant – that created the atmosphere in which witch trials could take place. Empathy for victims 'on the other side' did not exist.

On the other hand, if it was intolerance that allowed the killing of so-called witches, it was the warped view of women that fanned the fires. We have already seen that women were widely regarded as weak and inherently sinful by the Catholic and the Protestant hierarchies. Even Erasmus of Rotterdam, a supporter of a more enlightened Catholicism, opposed the education of women because, he said, they had been created for men's sexual pleasure. 'Nature requires the man to be dominant,' he wrote in *The Abbot and the Learned Lady*, 'because the woman is always politically subordinate, and he is her natural superior.'

Martin Luther concurred. As he told one congregation: 'the nature of women [is] to be timid and to be afraid of everything. That is why they busy themselves so much about witchcraft and superstitions and run hither and thither, uttering a magic formula here and a magic formula there.' His words might have been taken from the perverse *Malleus Malificarum* written in 1486 by the Dominican Inquisitor Heinrich Kramer, which told its readers that women were: 'more credulous; therefore [the devil] rather attacks them … they have slippery tongues … and, since they are weak, they find an easy and secret manner of vindicating themselves by witchcraft.'

It is true that many churchmen condemned the *Malleus*, but it reflected widely-held views. It is wrong to judge the past by today's standards; but it is justifiable to judge people by their contemporaries – and here Mary Ward can certainly assert her place in the vanguard of those who developed a new vision of the potential of women, and who thereby contributed to a society in which the burning of so-called 'witches' is unthinkable.

It was difficult to oppose the madness of witch trials in the sixteenth and seventeenth centuries. When the Catholic priest Cornelius Loos condemned the witch trials in Trier, he was forced to recant and the killings went on. More than 500 women would be executed as witches in the Cologne diocese of our friend Prince-Bishop Ferdinand – 280 of them in the village of Amt Balve alone. I find it hard to get my mind around that horrific statistic. Only in 1633 would the Jesuit Friedrich Spee be able to bring this particular cycle of witch burnings to a close – by which time Mary would be in Rome, herself facing charges of heresy.

As if witch trials were not enough, Mary Ward's time in Trier also brought her close to the erratic comings and goings of militias that were typical of the Thirty Years' War. Events in one part of Europe could trigger fighting hundreds of miles away, and the defeat of Frederick outside Prague prompted Spanish forces to invade his Palatinate lands, that hotchpotch of territories on either side of the Rhine. When they seized the castle in Trarbach, the Spanish soldiers were only some 30 miles from Trier.

Where there were soldiers, there was rape, pillage and then plague – and what it meant to ordinary people is movingly described by the Lutheran pastor, Caspar Streccius. On 20 October 1620, he writes, Spanish soldiers bivouacking in a nearby forest broke into his rectory and stole eleven sheep, one calf, three pigs, beds, pots, one saddle, one of his wife's skirts, and socks, boots and shoes. In November they stole his linen and valuables which he had hidden in the church of Raversbeuren. In 1621 the Spanish soldiers stole the village's entire flock of sheep, and in June they brought disease. Protestant communities suffered most in this round of the war, but soldiers were not choosy. The Catholic villages' turn would come when Count Mansfeld brought what remained of Frederick's army from Bohemia.

Early in 1621, however, news of a different kind reached Trier: the city learned that Pope Paul V had died. This was sad news, of course – but for Mary it was also a blow to her hopes for official papal approval of her Institute. Paul V had been a supporter of new orders: would his successor – Gregory XV – be as supportive as Paul?

As luck, or God's hand, would have it, two men who could advise her happened to be passing through Trier at this very juncture. One was Antonio Albergati, the papal nuncio in Cologne, whose importance had leapt overnight, as he was related to the new Pope Gregory. Mary lost no time paying her respects to him at the abbey of St Maximin. The other was Father Domenico di Gesù e Maria, the man who had spurred the Catholic forces to their great victory at the Battle of the White Mountain. Such was his standing now, it was said, that no pope could refuse him anything – so Mary will have been bending Father Domenico's ear, too, when he stopped by in Trier. Father Domenico had visited the English Carmelite convent in Antwerp earlier in the year, so he will also have been able to bring Mary Ward news of her sister Frances.

Nuncio Albergati and Father Domenico persuaded Mary to draw up a new plan for her Institute. But plans and constitutions were not enough. Perhaps Mary had come to the conclusion that waiting for the cardinals was a dead-end game. Perhaps the financial predicament of her houses forced her hand. Possibly Nuncio Albergati whispered in her ear that the aged Gregory XV was not expected to live long. Or maybe Father Domenico, who was on his way to Rome, suggested that he might be able to help. We do not know who first made the suggestion, but during the summer of 1621 Mary Ward decided that enough was enough. If the cardinals would not actively support her, she would go over their heads and do the unthinkable: she would walk to Rome, and – yes, even though she was only a woman! – seek an audience with the pope himself.

Did she ever pause to question whether the pope would busy himself with the pipe-dream of a 35-year-old English woman who had already antagonised powerful sections of the Catholic Church? Or whether, even if he did grant her an audience, he would allow her Institute the right of non-enclosure, which no other female order had ever obtained? If she did, she certainly did not let such worries put her off.

1621 would be the year of Mary's epic journey to Rome.

12

Remedy: The first journey to Rome (1621)

It was, confusingly, the Spanish Road that led from the Netherlands to Italy. Not, of course, that it went by way of Madrid. But it is a reminder of Spain's super-power status in early seventeenth century Europe that most states along the well-trodden route between Spain and its most valuable territory, the Spanish Netherlands, were to a greater or lesser extent beholden to the Habsburg king of Spain. Southwards came tax revenues to fill the Spanish coffers, and Flemish choirboys to sing in the king of Spain's choir; northwards marched Spanish soldiers, more than 100,000 of them between 1567 and 1620. The soldiers sailed from Barcelona to Genoa, and then marched to Milan, which had been under Spanish control since 1525. From Milan the route led westward over the Alps of allied Savoy to the Habsburg territory of Franche-Comté, and then turned north through allied Lorraine and Habsburg-controlled Luxemburg to the Spanish Netherlands. The Spanish Road avoided the sea route infested with English and Turkish pirates, and studiously avoided any territories controlled by Spain's arch-rival France.

Indeed, the Spanish Road looped around France like a noose around a neck, so of course the French made repeated attempts to cut it. They almost succeeded in 1601, when the Treaty of Lyon left the Spaniards with one narrow valley and a single bridge over the Rhone, the pont de Grésin, for their precious road. This left it vulnerable to attack, so in the early seventeenth century Spain was trying to create new routes further east, away from France. The Brenner, the only Alpine pass that could be crossed by wheeled traffic, would have been ideal had its southern end not been under the control of another of Spain's rivals, Venice. So, as a sub-plot in the Thirty Years' War, Spain was fighting to gain control of any suitable Swiss valley that could connect Milan via an Alpine pass to Habsburg-controlled Breisgau in south-west Germany.

From the point of view of our story, the importance of the two routes – the original Road through Franche-Comté and the newer route through Switzerland – is that when Mary Ward set off on her epic journey to Rome in 1621, she almost certainly used one of them. But we do not know which. In her account of the journey, Mary Poyntz tells us that Mary stopped in Nancy to write to Isabella, in Milan to pray at the tomb of St Charles Borromeo, and in Loreto to pray at the Holy House. But as to the route in between, we are left to speculate.

Very well then, I'll speculate. What factors would have influenced Mary's choice of itinerary? The need to avoid armies on the rampage eliminated the obvious route: up the Rhine from Cologne to Basel. Throughout 1621, Tilly's Catholic soldiers were falling like locusts on Frederick's Palatinate lands on either side of the Rhine, while Mansfeld's Protestant army, which was supposedly defending this land against Tilly's, was ravaging it just as thoroughly. One estimate is that 50,000 soldiers were laying waste to the land and slaughtering the population.

There was fighting in eastern Switzerland too. In an effort to seize control of the strategically pivotal Valtellina (Veltlin) valley for its vital new north-south route,[1] Spain was fomenting Catholic resistance to rule from mainly-Protestant Graubünden. In retaliation, Graubünden allied itself with France against the Spaniards, and the scene was set for eighteen years of fighting. It was certainly an area best avoided.

That left Mary Ward with one of the more westerly passes, and here a different set of factors came into play. One was the weather: she would be crossing the Alps at the onset of winter when higher routes would be impassable. Then she would want to avoid areas affected by plague, and, as Henriette Peters points out, would prefer a route along which her letters from Isabella would dispense her from paying tolls.

Chambers, and most biographers after her, suggests that Mary travelled from Brussels to her house in Trier, then up the Moselle to Nancy in Lorraine, through Alsace to Basel, and over the St Gotthard Pass to Lake Maggiore, Como and Milan. Through Alsace? Mansfeld's army, tiring of pillaging the Palatinate lands, made raids into Alsace in 1621: in Riedseltz, for example, they set fire to thirty houses and massacred so many inhabitants that the population was not regained for a century.[2] If Mary used this route, there was danger not far away. Perhaps, then, as Henriette Peters suggests, Mary instead travelled from Brussels to Liège, then – skipping Trier – up the Meuse via Namur to Sedan,

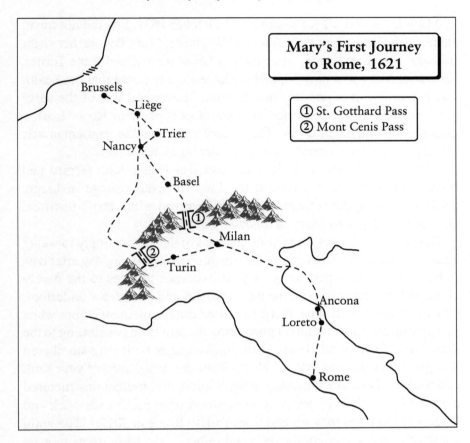

Verdun and Nancy, up the Saone and Rhone valleys to the easterly Mont Cenis pass over the Alps, coming down via Turin to Milan. This was the classic route of the original Spanish Road.

Before setting off for Rome, Mary called once more on Isabella in Brussels, to obtain letters of introduction for her journey. The court in Brussels was strangely changed since her first visit, for Archduke Albert had died in July and Isabella was in mourning. However, Isabella not only wrote letters of recommendation for her friend, but obtained a letter from the king of Spain, another from Ferdinand, the Habsburg emperor of the Holy Roman Empire, and even a pilgrim's garb for Mary, with the wide-brimmed pilgrim's hat still preserved in Altötting in Bavaria.

Mary finally set off for Rome on 21 October 1621. She did not travel alone. In the little party were Winefrid Wigmore, Mary Poyntz, her sister Barbara, Margaret Horde, who acted as her secretary, and Anne Turner, her nurse. Mary was now 36, and we have already noted that her health was not strong. It is possible that Susanna Rookwood was of the party too. The women were escorted by a priest (a nephew of Roger Lee), a man-servant and a gentleman. Only Mary knew that the gentleman was a cousin of hers. He would accompany her on all her travels.

The journey began with the bad news that Father John Gerard had been dismissed from his post at the English Jesuit college in Liège, partly for getting the college too closely involved with Mary's Institute. His removal deprived Mary of a key ally in Liège.

But what's bad news when your business of the day is simply to walk? There is something wonderfully therapeutic about walking day after day. Cares and concerns peel away as your existence reduces to the purely elemental: the sun, the rain, the nip in the air, and conditions underfoot. Of course, knees will ache, feet will blister, but the moment comes when you give up all vain attempts at preventing the rain from penetrating to the skin. Then, freed of all clutter, your mind engages with long-smothered thoughts and emotions that bubble up from the very depths of your soul, and walking becomes a musing, a meditation, and perfect unstructured prayer. Mary will have perfectly understood what my friends Nick and Angela noted when they walked from York to Rome in 2012:[3] 'The brain constantly wants to count the days and miles ... the body wants to have regularity: regular sleep, food and drink ... and the soul wants to dawdle and soak up sensations and feel the spirit of each place.'

Mary Poyntz has given us a record of the daily routine. The day started with prayers before breakfast. The party had two horses, one for the luggage, the other to carry anyone who was too tired or too weak to walk. Winefrid did the translating. There were rests at midday and again during the afternoon when Mary made time for more prayer. They sang a *Te Deum* on approaching their evening destination, thanking God that the perils of the day now lay behind them. Nick and Angela booked their overnight accommodation online; Mary Ward's equivalent of couch surfing were the religious houses which offered pilgrims an evening meal and a bed for the night – in the Catholic territories, of course. Once in her room, Mary set up an improvised altar. There was a reading from the Lives of the Saints before the evening meal, and during the meal Mary gave the company what we might call a spiritual pep talk to keep up their spirits. Mary apparently left the rooms tidy and showed her appreciation to maids and coachmen.

Oh, but what wouldn't I give to know more! We have become used to prying much deeper into our heroes' thoughts and feelings. I want to get under Mary's skin, I want to read about the mishaps, the squabbles, the obstacles that she faced and overcame. But it is the Romantics who would teach us the value of the subjective and incidental; seventeenth century biographers had their sights firmly fixed on the eternal. Mary Poyntz's account is, it must be said, disappointingly dry. We have to make do with such rare shafts of light as a description of Mary's sister, Barbara Ward, in a letter from Margaret Horde to the sisters in St Omer in 1623. 'If we were weary,' wrote Margaret of their journey to Rome, 'she was ready to animate us ... if melancholy she had ever some pretty jest, well-seasoned with virtue to recreate and make us merry.'

Cheerfulness, it seems, was a Ward family trait. Apart from such rare chance references, we are left to make deductions from the few facts we know. Mary, for example, wrote to Isabella from Nancy that they hoped to be in Rome for Christmas. The journey lasted two winter months, the route led through regions that none of them had ever seen before. And when did they arrive in Rome? On Christmas Eve! That speaks of tenacity, will-power and leadership on the part of Mary, and of loyalty, devotion and teamwork on the part of her followers.

The company's journey was mainly through fields and forests. Towns were few and far between, for a Venetian ambassador to Britain noted in 1613 that England was unique in Europe for having a sizeable town every few miles.[4] So the capital of the independent territory of Lorraine, Nancy, with a population of about 15,000, an impressive New Town, a magnificent collection of paintings, and a revolutionary water system that prevented waste water from mixing with drinking water, will have seemed large indeed. But did Mary perhaps sense a cold wind of change blowing from the east? Henry II of Lorraine had so far managed to remain neutral in the Thirty Years' War, but incursions were already being made into his territory. And in 1621 plague struck villages near Metz and the town of Mirecourt, not far off Mary's route south from Nancy.

However, our travellers emerged unscathed, and, if they proceeded south through Alsace as Chambers speculates, they will have made their way to Basel, a Protestant stronghold since 1529, when the prince-bishop had been forced to flee to his fortresses at Porrentruy and Delémont. Many areas in the Swiss Confederation, however, were Catholic – and visitors were struck by the mutual tolerance that usually reigned between the two communities: 'I look upon this country to be the safest spot of all Europe, neither envied nor envying … they live in great simplicity and tranquillity,' wrote John Evelyn in 1646, 'and although of the fourteen cantons, half be Roman Catholic, the rest Reformed, yet they mutually agree, and are confederate with Geneva.'[5]

Beyond Basel, Mary will have made her way up the Reuss valley, a north-south corridor from the Rhine to the Alps, where Catholic institutions such as Luzern's large Jesuit college will have been comfortingly familiar sights. Today the spectrum of cultural and religious tolerance has grown beyond anything Mary could have imagined, with Swiss Hindus authorised to use the Reuss for the scattering of human ashes.

Ahead, now, loomed the most formidable natural barrier on Mary's journey – the Alps. Not that crossing the Alps was anything new, of course: Roman legions, after all, had built passes like the Great St Bernard. But it was a hazardous undertaking, and people talked about having 'a good crossing' as we might talk about crossing the sea. Later generations would learn to gawp at the sublime beauty of the peaks and gorges; in the seventeenth century the mountains were seen as a wilderness or desert. The danger of succumbing to the cold, to the wolves or of falling off a precarious mountain track left no room for romantic wonder. 'The ways are very offensive to foote travellers,' wrote Thomas Coryate after crossing the Splügen pass, 'for they are pitched with very sharp and rough stones that will very much punish and greate a man's feete.'[6]

The mountains gave you pain. Beauty did not come into it.

The most direct route across the Alps – now the E1 long-distance footpath used by Nick and Angela – was the St Gotthard pass, made passable in about 1220 when a chain bridge was thrown across the precipitous Schöllenen Gorge. The chain bridge gave way to a wooden bridge, and in 1595 to a stone bridge that was such a wondrous feat of engineering that popular lore held that it must have been built with supernatural help. Interesting, then, that the help was deemed to be not heavenly, but diabolical, and the bridge was named the Devil's Bridge. Crossing it called for strong nerves. It was narrow, with low parapets to allow for donkeys' wide loads, and the track that led from it clung so tenuously to the sheer cliff face that it would be replaced in 1708 by the first tunnel in the Alps. It was a daunting route for travellers equipped with no more than gloves and nail-studded boots.

If Mary avoided Basel and took the route through Savoy, she will instead have used the Mont Cenis pass, where she will have sat on a chair strapped to runners and been hauled by professional carriers. This sounds more comfortable in theory than it was in practice, for the carrier in front had a strap around his chest, and the chair on the runners bounced sickeningly from rock to rock. A hefty payment was exacted for this service and travellers were lucky to come through alive, especially in winter, when monks from the St Nicolas hospice would look for bodies along the track that was marked by poles set at a spear's length from each other.

Whether from the Gotthard or the Mont Cenis, it will have been with joy and thanksgiving that Mary and her companions descended into Italy – which, in the seventeenth century, was of course a geographical and not a political term. Like Germany, Italy was divided into numerous rival states; but unlike in Germany, they were not grouped together under a single emperor, but ruled by different powers. Top right, Venice was a world power, and such a challenge to papal authority that the whole state had been excommunicated as recently as 1606. Top left, the duchy of Savoy straddled both sides of the Alps. Between them lay the duchy of Milan, which was in Spanish hands, as was the enormous kingdom of Naples which occupied the whole of the southern half of Italy. Its capital was the second largest city in Christendom after Paris, and both larger and wealthier than Rome. Squashed between Naples and the north were the duchies of Mantua, Parma, Tuscany and others, and of course the extensive Papal States.

Rivals though they were, the states were all Catholic, and, despite the grandeur that radiated from their libraries, art galleries and civic and religious buildings, they had all entered a state of gradual decline vis-à-vis the more dynamic states of Northern Europe. These two points were not unrelated. The triumph of the Catholic Church had driven out most Protestants, and as in Liège, they took their skills with them – clock-making to Switzerland, for example. The chilling hand of the Catholic Church was felt in both innovation and research. The works of Copernicus had just been put on the index of forbidden books, and Galileo, working in Florence, was treading as carefully as he could.

These controversies, however, seemed far away as Mary made her way through the Po valley's harvested vineyards to Milan, the first seriously large city that Mary had seen since leaving London. Its population rivalled Rome's, and its cardinal archbishop from 1560 to 1584, Charles Borromeo, had been one of the towering figures of the Counter-Reformation. In a super-human effort to raise the standard of literacy in the city, he had founded schools, colleges, seminaries, and one of Europe's first public libraries. He had taken a leading role at the Council of Trent, but when plague struck Milan in 1576, and the city governor fled, Borromeo had stayed at his post and personally ministered to the sick and dying. Such was his importance that the Catholic Church had canonised him (declared him a saint) in 1610, only twenty-six years after this death.

There was, however, also a darker side to Borromeo and his religious zeal. He had evicted Protestants, forced Jews to wear an identification badge, and overseen trials in which women accused of witchcraft were executed by being pushed head first into a fire. He had restored grilles to convents that had abandoned them and, as we have seen, 'regulated' the Ursulines into a lower-status congregation – measures that ran counter to what Mary was trying to achieve. Still, Mary took a precious day's break in her journey to pray at the great saint's tomb. She had heard of his good deeds from Jesuits back in her childhood, she admired his energy and courage, and maybe had an inkling that she might soon need these strengths herself.

It was then time to press on again. Winter had set in, and the roads were so boggy that the journey from Ferrara to Bologna, which took half a day in summer, took a whole day in winter.[7] This is maybe why Mary did not travel south, as we should expect, but eastwards down the Po, then by sea past Ancona to Loreto, for a final, shorter land journey to Rome. From Mary's point of view, this route had the added advantage that it would allow her to pray at one of the most famous shrines in the whole of Italy: the Holy House of Mary of Nazareth.

Most readers will probably do a double-take at the last sentence. What? Had Mary's house in Palestine been dismantled and transported by boat across the Mediterranean? No, the story is even stranger. Angels, it was said, wishing to prevent the house from falling into Muslim hands, had miraculously flown it to Italy. It is the sort of story that painfully exposes the almost insuperable gulf between the mind-set of people in the seventeenth century and what I like to call my more rational way of thinking. Rational? Maybe I should not be too smug. Among those who saw value in such stories were Galileo Galilei, who made a pilgrimage to the Holy House in Loreto in 1618, and René Descartes, who almost certainly did in 1620.

And so to Rome. The Apennines in midwinter will have been bleak, and progress difficult, but Mary was determined to arrive in time for Christmas. And image her joy when, some sixty-three days after setting out from Brussels, she at last set her eyes on the glorious dome of St Peter's, glinting in the distance. Larger and nobler than any dome she had ever seen before, it must have been like a vision of heaven itself. Mary and her party fell to their knees with prayers of thanksgiving, and who, frankly, had they travelled with her, would not have done the same?

Mary entered the Eternal City itself on Christmas Eve to find the streets bustling with preparations for the great feast. No less than 180,000 pilgrims flocked to Rome in the Holy Years 1600 and 1625 – an incredible number considering Rome's actual population of 100,000. Fewer pilgrims would have arrived in a 'normal' year like 1621, but there will still have been jostling for beds in the national hostels – the Germans at Santa Maria dell'Anima, the Flemish at Saint Julian, the Bretons at Saint Yves, the Lorrains at Saint Nicholas, etc. And the brightly-lit churches will have been full to overflowing.

It is never easy to arrive after a long journey on foot. Nick and Angela felt 'dazed' when they arrived in Rome, and 'puzzled by [their] shifting identities from "pilgrim" status ... to ordinary, slightly shabby-looking tourists,' and I can imagine Mary feeling much the same. Pilgrims today stop at the Church of San Lorenzo; Mary made her way to the tomb of St Ignatius in the Jesuit church (the *Gesù*), where, we can be sure, she prayed from the bottom of her soul. She had travelled all this way in blind faith that she would gain access to the pope and have the opportunity to explain her mission to him. But now that she had arrived, the improbability of it all must have pressed in on her. How was an audience to come about?

And then the miraculous happened.

For the extraordinary fact is that despite all the hubbub of Christmas festivities, Pope Gregory XV granted Mary Ward an audience on 26 December – within hours, as it were, of her arrival in Rome. What's more, the pope was the kindly figure she had imagined since childhood. He put her at her ease, listened intently to what she had to say and graciously accepted the plan of the Institute that Mary had brought with her. When he dismissed her, it was with words of encouragement that must have touched her to the quick. And indeed the pope then penned a letter to Isabella in Brussels,[8] assuring her that Mary's petition 'should be weighed with no little favour,' indeed that it 'should be immediately taken into consideration.'

Sweet words indeed. How can Mary fail to have been elated? It must have seemed as though all her hopes were about to be fulfilled. Little can she have realised that the journey had been the easy bit. Her stay in Rome would last five years. Five of the most difficult years in her life.

13

Results: New schools in Italy (1621–1624)

'The nuns in York fell out with the Church authorities, they were excommunicated, and their leader, a woman, set off on foot to put her case to the pope … .'

The year was 1192. The archbishop of York wished to grant the nunnery of St Clement's, in York, to Godstow Abbey in what is now Port Meadow in Oxford. When the nuns objected, he excommunicated them, barring them from Holy Communion and Christian burial – a drastic measure in an age when many people died young, and believed that the souls of the excommunicated went straight to hell. But Prioress Alice of St Clement's was not one to be brow-beaten by Church authorities. She believed in the justice and fairness of the pope himself, and, putting on her stoutest shoes, she apparently walked to Rome to petition the pontiff in person. There was a precedent, it seems, for the pope dealing with a hard-headed Yorkshire woman who traipsed half-way across Europe to put an awkward case directly to him.[1]

Back in 1192, Pope Celestine III decided in Prioress Alice's favour, and St Clement's priory retained its independence. Would history now repeat itself? Would Gregory XV recognise Mary Ward's Institute and grant it the freedom of action that Mary sought for it?

Mary was convinced that her Institute could enable women to play their part in the spiritual renewal of Catholicism in England and across the world. How could the pope fail to embrace such a vision? It was, Mary believed, Vatican bureaucrats who had blocked her so far. Now that she had put her case directly to the pope, she was sure that recognition must follow. Indeed, she expressed some surprise in a letter to Isabella on 8 January – less than two weeks after her arrival in Rome – that the go-ahead had not yet been given.

Oh, one could weep for the waves of innocent enthusiasm crashing against the rocks of experience, caution and prejudice. For Mary's assumptions were based on a series of false premises. Gregory's comforting words during the audience on the Feast of Stephen were diplomatic niceties, nothing more. The decision-making processes in Rome were far more complex than Mary had ever imagined, and far from being above the politicking, the pope was part of it. And in no way was he inclined to overturn doctrine in matters concerning women.

Italian views on women, Mary was to learn, were light years behind those in Northern Europe. English women of Mary's class, commented a German visitor to London, 'have much more liberty than perhaps in any other place',[2] and foreigners were surprised to find men and women mingling freely at the theatre. Mary's role models were tough, independently-minded women like Ursula Wright and Grace Babthorpe, who ran entire households while their menfolk hid from the authorities. When brought before the courts, these women gave their prosecutors as good as they got. Behind them hovered the shadow of Elizabeth I, whose policies the recusants might detest, but whose power and independence of spirit they could not deny.

In Flanders, too, Mary had the example of Isabella, who ruled in her own right, and of the béguines, who had run their own houses. Throughout the Netherlands it was quite usual for women to go about their business on their own. Men and women could eat together in taverns, and even share a drink after the meal.

Against this background, it is not surprising that Mary did not consider the issue of enclosure to be insuperable. In her view, Rome had overturned centuries of tradition when Pope Paul III had granted the Jesuits independence from the local bishops, and the right to organise themselves under a father general answerable directly to the pope. These concessions enabled the Jesuits to carry out their mission – a mission which was celebrated on 13 March 1622 in a solemn Mass in St Peter's in which Ignatius of Loyola was declared a saint of the Catholic Church. If the cardinals honoured her role model so publicly, how could they fail to welcome the creation of a similar organisation for women? Extending the concessions from men to women seemed to her to be less radical a departure from tradition than granting them in the first place.

A further positive sign, in Mary's view, was that within weeks of her arrival in Rome, Gregory XV approved a teaching order that was strikingly similar to her own: the Piarists. Their founder, the Spanish priest José de Calasanz, dedicated himself to mission work for the Catholic Church, and, like Mary, saw his calling in education. He opened his first school in Rome in 1597: like Mary's schools, it was free and open for rich and poor. Like Mary, Calasanz not only taught reading, writing and basic maths, but subjects such as Latin that were normally the preserve of the rich. And like Mary, Calasanz organised his teachers as a fully-fledged religious order, based on the three vows of poverty, chastity and obedience, and a fourth vow of devotion to teaching. So if Gregory XV approved the Piarists, why not Mary's Institute? For one crucial difference. Calasanz's Piarist school was for boys and his teachers were men: Mary's schools were for girls, and her teachers were women.

Now, if the view of women was conservative in Italy as a whole, this was nowhere more so than in Rome, where men outnumbered women by about two to one. Indeed, women were largely unseen. Nuns were enclosed in their convents, ladies stayed at home, or were escorted if they went out. Women seen in the streets were either from the lower classes or prostitutes – or at least regarded as such. To Roman eyes, therefore, the very sight of Mary and her companions publicly going about their business was shocking, and the thought of allowing a band of women exemption from enclosure anathema.

When did Mary begin to realise that obtaining recognition for her order would take far, far longer than she had ever imagined? That her life of commuting between Flanders and England would morph into a frustrating, sedentary existence in Rome, waiting for the wheels of the Vatican bureaucracy to turn another notch? We cannot know, for no word of criticism or bitterness ever passed her lips. Rather, she launched herself into a heroic campaign to lobby for her Institute, taking on the most powerful, most sophisticated institution in the Western world.

Oh yes, Rome was enormously powerful. On the macro level, power was shifting from the south of Europe to the north, but Rome itself was flexing its muscles again. Grand new buildings were transforming what had been a run-down ex-metropolis, sacked as recently as 1527, into a sophisticated European capital. Its grandest edifice of all, the new St Peter's, was the most magnificent church in Christendom.

The new buildings and monuments were the outward expression of the Vatican's new spirit of confidence. The Council of Trent had given Catholics a new manifesto and new zeal. Protestant minorities had been expelled from the Catholic heartlands of Italy, Spain, Austria and southern Germany, France had been recovered from the Huguenots, the wealthy cities of the southern Netherlands – Antwerp, Ghent and Brussels – had been held against the Dutch. In England, Rome was about to appoint its first Roman Catholic bishop since 1585. In the east, large areas of Hungary and Transylvania had been regained, while in Central Europe, the Battle of the White Mountain had provided the Catholic cause with a stunning victory. Tangible evidence of the victory arrived in Rome in 1623 in the form of 200 mules bearing 3,500 manuscripts and 13,000 prints looted from Frederick's palace in Heidelberg. They were a 'gift' to the pope from the leader of the victorious Catholic troops, Maximilian of Bavaria.

Rome was, of course, not only the seat of the Catholic Church, but also the capital city of the Papal States. The area had to be governed, roads built, taxes raised, the valuable alum mines exploited, wars waged. The territory was sandwiched between Spanish Naples, Spanish Milan and Spanish Sardinia, so Vatican diplomacy had to reconcile backing Spain in the Thirty Years' War with resisting Spain as a rival within Italy itself. But the Vatican establishment, with centuries of experience to draw on, took such convoluted diplomatic gymnastics in its stride. The cardinals that Mary now had to wrestle with were as well versed in European power politics as they were in Church law and the decrees of the Council of Trent.

Mary did what she could. She wrote letters to potential supporters, she chivvied sponsors like Isabella, she petitioned such Vatican heavyweights as Ambassador Vives, Isabella's representative in Rome, she submitted and re-submitted mission statements to clarify the aims of her Institute – but it was a Kafkaesque game of Blind (Wo)man's Buff. Mary was a woman operating in a world of men, an English exile negotiating in Latin and Italian, an outsider grappling with a labyrinthine system peppered with bewildering titles and names.

Nothing was straightforward. Who, for example, would actually decide the fate of her Institute? Gregory XV pitched her case over to a congregation (the word for a Vatican 'department') of bishops and regulars – but some among the thirty cardinals on this worthy body had more clout than others, so Mary had to find out who the big hitters were. Moreover, some cardinals were members of more than one congregation, so Mary could never be sure in which forum her case was being discussed. Ottavio Bandini, for example, was a member both of the congregation of bishops and regulars and the sacred congregation for the propagation of the faith (*Sacra Congregatio de Propaganda Fide*): were both congregations now discussing her case? And if so, which one had the greater say?

Pope Gregory had set up Propaganda Fide as recently as 6 January 1622, to oversee Catholic policy in non-Catholic countries like England.[3] It worked hand in hand with the Vatican's oldest congregation – the congregation of the Roman Inquisition, which was responsible for enforcing dogma, and, if necessary, punishing those it deemed heretical. Within living memory, the Inquisition had had Domenico Scandella burned at the stake in Venice (1599) and Giordano Bruno in Rome (1600). These were dangerous times to come under the scrutiny of such powerful yet nebulous committees.

Such a tangle of congregations did not lend itself to Mary's negotiating strategies. In Brussels, Liège, Cologne and Trier Mary had gone straight to the top, but in Rome power was more diffuse. Powerful cardinals jostled for power and influence, knowing that the elderly pope would not live long, and that a successor must be elected soon. Mary lobbied hard, but different cardinals had their own agendas. They might be for or against the Jesuits, for example, or they might support France against Spain, or vice versa. If Mary bent the ear of one cardinal, she almost certainly made an enemy of another.

It was difficult even to be sure who really supported her. Ambassador Vives, for example, received Mary politely and arranged meetings with important players. As Isabella's representative in Rome, he could do no less – but we know from his correspondence that he was sceptical about Mary's cause.

Father Mutius Vitelleschi, the father general of the Jesuits, listened attentively to Mary and was gracious towards her. But he did not tell her that he had been receiving negative comments about her from English Jesuits for at least two years, nor did he share with her the nature of the complaints. This meant Mary could neither know that his actions were motivated by a perceived need to protect the society from her, nor could she defend herself against the allegations made against her. Vitelleschi did order the Jesuits to help her in Naples and Perugia, but he also advised Pope Gregory against approving the Institute, and he later banned Jesuits in Liège, Cologne and Trier from co-operating with her Institute.

As to Cardinal Ottavio Bandini, he tutted sympathetically when Mary put her case to him – but did not let on that he was working hand in glove with John Bennett, the English clergy's agent in Rome, who was passing on smears and slanders against her.

Were Vives, Vitelleschi or Bandini guilty of duplicity? Or were they merely seasoned diplomats and tacticians, not averse to using Mary as a pawn in their own elaborate games? Or is the difference academic?

Mary and her companions were offered accommodation by a congregation of women in Rome, but even so Mary's funds soon ran low. She had not anticipated being in Rome so long, and she was soon so short of money that she could hardly afford the paper on which to write letters to her houses in Flanders. She had exhausted all avenues for putting forward the case for her Institute, and still no decision was forthcoming. Who could have blamed her if she had given up? Who could have blamed her companions if they had lost faith in their leader?

But Mary was not done yet. She made her points by example and results. And she now hit on a plan both eminently practical and breathtakingly audacious. The cardinals, she reasoned, were withholding their approval because they had not seen her Institute in action. Her schools in Northern Europe were too far away. Very well then, she would show them what she could do. She would do what they least expected: she would open a school in Rome. The school would make her case more powerfully than any documents, however perfect her Latin.

As was her way, Mary moved fast and her school in Rome opened in mid-1622. Although she was short of funds, Mary resisted the temptation to charge fees: the school was free and welcomed girls from poor families. And the need was great: food shortages in Rome were so acute that by 1625 a priest recorded that poor people were dying in the streets. Small wonder the number of Mary's pupils quickly rose to 120. The girls had classes in reading, writing, maths and needlework – but not in religion, for Mary was careful to make sure she could not be accused of 'preaching'.

The cardinals noted the school, even had it inspected, but never gave it formal approval. But it was such a success that Mary summoned reinforcements from Flanders, and eight companions duly made the same epic journey that Mary had made before them, facing all the same obstacles and dangers.[4] Mary's companions trusted her implicitly, and gave her the strength to pursue her cause. The biggest blow that Mary suffered in Rome was the death of her sister Barbara in January 1623, the result of an illness. Loyal, cheerful Barbara, who walked with her sister over the Alps to Rome, was only 31 when she died.

The reinforcements from Flanders allowed Mary to make a second bold move: in 1623 she travelled south to explore the possibility of opening a school in Naples. Naples! Here was Mary Ward, some 1,400 miles south of Yorkshire where her travels had begun.

Yet Naples was not as foreign as we might think. Like Flanders, the territory was ruled by Spain: its protocols, customs and bureaucracy would have been comfortingly familiar after the bewildering politics of Rome. And Naples was a more prosperous city than Rome, with some of its grandest buildings, such as the Certosa di San Martino, the enormous Carthusian monastery, taking shape before Mary's eyes. Claude Lorrain and other leading artists were at work in the city which was equally famous for its music and lavish drama performances featuring, interestingly, male and female performers.

In Naples, Mary was able to go straight to the top again – to the Spanish governor, Don Antonio de Toledo, Duke of Alva, to Cardinal Giovanni Pamphili, the nuncio in Naples, and to Archbishop Decio Carafa. That explains why the school could get off the ground so quickly. It opened in 1623, and was a free school again, open to girls from poor families. There were plenty of them here too, despite the city's flamboyant trappings, the product of the crushingly high taxes that paid for Spain's wars in Germany and Switzerland. The sisters in Mary's school will have seen the pinched faces of their pupils when a bad harvest in 1624 led to high food prices and hunger for the poorest families.

Susanna Rookwood was the school's first superior in Naples, having presumably learned Italian during her few months in Rome. However, Susanna fell ill and died in May 1624 – the second of Mary's original band of companions to die in just over a year. Mary Ratcliffe took over as superior early in 1625, assisted by Winefrid Wigmore, Joanna Browne, Chrysogona Wakeman, Lucy Shelley, Margaret Genison and Jane de la Cost. This was the team that had to cope with a disaster that – literally – shook the school in 1626: the devastating earthquake of 30 July. Naples was used to occasional shakes, but this disaster claimed the lives of thousands of people, some say as many as 10,000. It is a scale of calamity that I find hard to comprehend, and the sisters will have had to comfort and counsel pupils suffering from its physical and psychological consequences.

Mary Ward herself had already left Naples, however, for the Catholic Church had been hit by a metaphoric earthquake of its own: the death of Pope Gregory in July 1623, after only twenty-nine months in office. The death of a pope always meant all change in Rome, and Mary Ward travelled to Rome at once, to secure an audience with Gregory's successor, Maffeo Barberini, elected in August 1623 under the name of Pope Urban VIII.

Urban was a strong character from an immensely powerful family. Not afraid to put his own stamp on things and quite willing to ignore the Council of Trent's ban on 'enrich[ing] relations or domestics from the revenues of the Church' he appointed a brother and two nephews to the rank of cardinal. Ominously, he kept Mary waiting for a full year before he granted her an audience.

Not that Mary spent this time twiddling her thumbs – for a rich widow by the name of Ottavia Caimi had noted Mary's work in Rome and Naples, and had invited Mary to set up a similar school in her home city of Perugia.[5] A new school would stretch the Institute's human and financial resources to the very limit, but Mary could not turn down a call for help. In January 1624 Mary set off with Mary Clayton, Joyce Vaux, Elizabeth Cotton and Margaret Horde on the 100 mile journey to Perugia – 100 miles on foot, with Mary increasingly fighting the pain caused by her gall and kidney stones.

And it was while Mary was in Perugia that Prince-Bishop Ferdinand in far-away Liège made a bold move on her behalf. Like the bishops in Naples and Perugia, he valued Mary's schools, but with a longer experience of the schools in Liège and Cologne he could see the damaging effect of the withholding of papal recognition. He knew very well that sponsors would support the Institute more willingly if it were seen to be officially approved, so in an effort to give it some official standing, and to nudge the new pope in the right direction, he declared in March 1624 that from now on the 'English Ladies' were to be considered 'religious' in his diocese – in other words, to be acknowledged as nuns, until such time as the pope himself gave general approval. It was not, of course, in Ferdinand's remit to make such a declaration, but the savvy prince-bishop had covered his back as far as Rome was concerned. He had made sure that his declaration was backed by the pope's nuncio in Liège.

And here I shall pause, to allow Mary to enjoy her moment on the cusp of a wave.

She now had schools operating in seven cities from the English Channel to Mediterranean: St Omer, Liège, Cologne, Trier, Rome, Naples and Perugia. More sisters were working in secret in England. New sisters were being trained in her novitiate in Liège. And now a prominent prince-bishop and elector of the Holy Roman Empire had publicly recognised her companions as unenclosed nuns. All this Mary had achieved without official recognition.

But with finances at crisis point, the crunch moment had arrived. If the new pope were now to recognise the Institute as prince-bishop Ferdinand had done, everything was in place for a dramatic transformation of the education of girls across Europe and beyond. On the other hand, if he continued to prevaricate, Mary's Institute was in danger of imploding.

Expansion or collapse?

All would now depend on Urban VIII.

14

Rebuff: Debacle in Rome (1624–1626)

We have seen Mary Ward riding a wave. But the problem with waves is that they come crashing down in myriad fragments of froth and foam. For Mary, the crash came in a series of setbacks starting in the summer of 1624. So far she had wrestled with the Church's inertia; from now on she increasingly faced its hostility.

All might yet have been saved at Mary's first audience with Pope Urban VIII in October 1624. A clear signal from Urban, even a nod of tacit support could have caused funds to flow. But it was not to be. The pope spoke kindly, as popes do, and Mary put a brave face on it, as petitioners do, but there was no denying that after two and half years of lobbying in Rome, the Vatican had not budged an inch.

Quite the opposite. In April 1625 four cardinals appointed by Pope Urban to look into the case of Mary Ward ordered Mary's three schools in Italy to be closed. The move struck Mary like a thunderbolt; she felt, she wrote, 'as if I had been condemned to death.' The school in Rome did not re-open in the autumn of 1625. The school in Perugia foundered. Only in Naples did the authorities manage to ignore the order for a few more years.

Nevertheless, Mary was now forced to admit to herself that the chances of convincing the pope and the cardinals of her cause were zero – and by the end of 1626 we find Mary Ward leaving Rome, defeated, empty-handed. Such was her hurry to put Rome behind her that she did not even wait two weeks to see the dedication of the new St Peter's Cathedral.

What had caused this debacle?

One factor was quite simply that Mary Ward had run out of money.

Established orders derived much of their income from land donated to them over the years. Marske Priory in Yorkshire, for example, had before the Dissolution drawn over 80 per cent of its income from rents and the sale of crops, wool and meat, while the nuns of St Mary's Thicket Priory, south of York, had received 'grain, vegetables, apples, milk from sheep and cows, and fish ... Meat from their estates ... timber from their woods and wool from their sheep.'[1] This is how convents traditionally survived.

Mary's Institute, in contrast, had no such sources of food or income. New houses in this situation were always desperately short of money. The abbess of Mary Ward's Poor Clares in Gravelines, for instance, noting that her convent did 'not have any Landes, Rentes, or Annuityes,' appealed to sponsors for a 'little Butter, Cheese, oyle, Hony, oatmeale, corne, or salt, fish, wax or tallow candles, flax, or wool.'[2] A little cheese or oatmeal: the list of necessities is humble indeed.

In the absence of any income from land, Mary depended on donations and dowry money, but while richer convents expected dowry payments of between £200 and £400, Mary's Institute, lacking papal approbation, attracted much lower amounts. And now that she was bogged down in Rome, Mary was unable to tap any English dowry payments at all.

The results were dire. In Rome, Mary was dependent on hand-outs from Isabella. The house in Trier was desperately poor. Mary's two houses in Liège were hit by debts arising from the complicated legal entanglements of their chief sponsor, Sir Thomas Sackville, with Father Gerard. In St Omer one Symphorien Machin declared before the town council that the 'English Ladies' owed him 560 guilders; butcher Maxime Juet claimed they owed him £345. The sisters contested these figures, but the bailiffs carried off their beds, mattresses, tables, chairs and cooking pots. The sisters were now eating and sleeping on the floor.

It is a moving picture: young English gentlewomen, brought up in wealthy homes, reduced to making do on the bare floor. It took a seventy-two-hour power failure one December for me to appreciate how long, cold and tedious winter evenings are without heat and light, and to scupper any romantic notions of reading by candle light. The sacrifice made by the sisters in the stone-cold houses in St Omer, Cologne and Trier was quite as heroic as that made by those who undertook the more dramatic journeys. For some, indeed, it was too much, and they returned to their families or joined another order. But most put up with the hardship – an unseen, unsung demonstration of their loyalty to Mary and their belief in the vital importance of her mission.

A second reason for the debacle in Italy was that Rome simply could not stomach Mary's shopping list of demands. Irresistible force had met immovable object. Mary's insistence on non-enclosure clashed with the decrees of the Council of Trent. Her vision of a female superior who would organise and develop the Institute was irreconcilable with Rome's view of women. And her wish to place her Institute under the immediate jurisdiction of the pope, free from obedience to the local bishops, smacked of insubordination.

Never mind that Mary's demands were valid for the task in hand: a mission to England could not be achieved by women if they were enclosed. Never mind that in raising the issue of the jurisdiction of bishops, Mary was addressing a real issue, one that Dom Basil Whelan describes as the 'bugbear of the convents.'[3] The unedifying tussle over jurisdiction that we saw at Mary's Poor Clares convent in Gravelines was no exception – the English Carmelite convent in Antwerp had the same problem. But Mary's points were never seriously considered by the cardinals. They cited Catholic tradition, and declared the issues non-negotiable.

The cardinals rested their case for total enclosure for nuns on the edicts of the Council of Trent. It was, they felt, a cogent argument – and it would strike me as tenable if the edicts from Trent had been applied with equal zeal to both sexes. But this was blatantly not the case. The 23rd session of the Council of Trent banned the 'accumulation of benefices' and stipulated that bishops must reside in their diocese – but Rome turned a blind eye to our friend Ferdinand, the absentee bishop of Liège, Cologne, Münster, Hildesheim and Paderborn, resident in Bonn. Appointed bishops, said Trent, must become ordained priests within three months – but unordained Prince-Bishop Ferdinand happily flouted this rule too. Trent insisted on the celibacy of the clergy, but the Church tolerated Prince-Bishop Ernest's liaison with his mistress. Bishops must be at least 14 (!) years old, said Trent – but Gregory XV himself had just appointed a bishop all of 9 (!) years old.[4] Trent was so often quoted against women, and so regularly ignored by men, that I can't help seeing it as the convenient fig-leaf for a far more deep-seated antagonism towards women – an antagonism derived from the Church's traditional identification of women with sin, nurtured by men in authority who had little experience of women.

And in any case the Catholic tradition of enclosure for women was less rock-solid than is often assumed. The very fact that the issue was raised in synod after synod is evidence that it was largely ignored. Pope Boniface VIII insisted on female enclosure in his bull (= edict) *Periculoso* in 1299, but as Eileen Power put it, 'for the next three centuries, Councils and Bishops struggled manfully [the adverb is well chosen!] to put into force the Bull Periculoso but without success.'[5]

Professor Power gives the example of Bishop Dalderby, who handed the nuns of Markyate Priory a statute imposing enclosure on them. 'Certain of the nuns,' a Register of 1300 records, 'hurled the said statute at his back and over his head, and as well the Prioress as the convent appeared to consent to those who threw it ... declaring unanimously that they were not content in any way to observe such a statute.'

Or take John of Ayton, a fourteenth-century church lawyer who supported the principle of enclosure. Even he was dismissive of the notion that bishops could cause the decree of Boniface to be observed. 'Cause to be observed!,' he exclaims. 'But surely there is scarcely any mortal man who could do this ... For the nuns answer roundly to these statutes ... saying "In truth the men who made these laws sat well at their ease, while they laid such burdens upon us by these hard and intolerable restrictions!" Wherefore we see in fact that these statutes are a dead letter... .'[6]

As late as 1681 – over a hundred years *after* Trent – Jean-Baptiste Thiers noted in his treatise on female enclosure that 'no point of ecclesiastical discipline was in his day more completely neglected and ignored.'[7]

If, then, there was a tradition of men imposing enclosure on women, it is also true to say that there was a long tradition of women resisting 'the intolerable restrictions' imposed by men who 'sat well at their ease.' Mary Ward was not as unique in this respect as the cardinals were trying to suggest.

ෆ————ඏ

A third reason why Mary Ward failed to secure recognition for her Institute was the cumulative effect of the negative campaign mounted by her opponents. As Mary ruefully put it in a letter to Winefrid, 'Our adversaries have been very busy, and have troubled themselves not a little to trouble us.'

The English Catholic clergy, as we have seen, saw Mary's Institute as an easy target through which to undermine the Jesuits, and when they sent William Harrison to lobby the pope for an English Catholic bishop, he took the campaign against Mary Ward to Rome. 'Lately,' he told the Vatican, 'there has sprung forth out of our nation a certain society of women ... which professes to be devoted to the conversion of England, no otherwise than as priests themselves.'

To accuse women of conducting themselves 'as priests' was, of course, a red rag to a bull.

The Jesuitresses, as Harrison called them,

> have a habit of frequently going about cities and provinces of the kingdom ... anyone will easily see how dangerous it is, and occasionary of many scandals, that women should go about houses in this fashion, wander hither and thither ... now publicly, now privately, now many together, now alone, among men, seculars, and not seldom of bad morals.[8]

The language – 'wandering, running hither and thither, bad morals, meeting men, scandal' – was of course chosen to convince the establishment in Rome that enclosure was more than justified.

The accusations were always of a general nature, with no particulars given. Bandini's friend John Bennett, accused the Jesuitesses of moral laxity – citing no specific examples. Matthew Kellison, the president of the English seminary at Douai, alleged that English Catholics were 'scandalized' by the 'boldness' of the 'women' whose lives, he said, were 'none too religious', and cited 'faults in conduct, which were sufficiently unworthy even of lay people.'[9] Kellison had his own anti-Jesuit agenda – and omitted to admit that he had never actually had any contact with the Institute. And in 1625 John Bennett's successor, the aptly named Thomas Rant, alleged that the 'Jesuitesses', 'run about all over England and associate with men ... In doing so, they are a threat to the women of England and a scandal to catholics.'[10] 'Mr Rant,' Mary Ward wrote ruefully to Winefrid, 'makes himself hoarse with speaking against the English gentlewomen.' Rant was one of the first to advise the total suppression of the Institute.

We know of the allegations made against Mary from documents in the Vatican archives. But Mary was never shown them, so she had no way of defending herself. The cardinals decided for themselves whether the slurs were valid or not – and they were woefully ill-informed about the conditions in Northern Europe. Anybody with any knowledge of the Institute's work in England or Flanders would have seen through the calumnies that were thrown at it, but the cardinals had none. They never asked the hundreds of pupils, parents, teachers and clergy who could have vouched for her. They listened instead to the voices of those who had an axe to grind against her.

Seeing which way the wind was blowing, Vives urged Mary to merge her Institute with the Ursulines while she still could. But Mary declined. As she wrote in 1622, her project came from God, and brooked no earthly discussion. 'By divine appointment we are to take upon us the same holy Institute and order of life already approved by divers popes of happy memory... .'

This was frank and direct, not to say blunt and uncompromising. The only compromise Mary was willing to make was for the exemption from enclosure to apply only to companions working in England, Flanders, and Germany – but this offer was rejected by the Vatican.

On 10 November 1626, therefore, Mary Ward left the Holy City and headed northwards once more. How, I wonder, was she feeling? It would be dangerous to surmise that she was despondent. Mary had extraordinary spiritual reserves, and a deep faith that everything would work out as God willed. As she wrote to Winefrid of 3 February and 6 April 1625: 'The Cardinals ... are bent to do what hurt they can. Here hath been seen ... hot businesses betwixt the good Cardinals and us.' But, 'The gain will be ours every way in the end.'

What matter that she was penniless? That two of her schools had been forced to close? That her foundations in Northern Europe were holding on by the skin of their teeth? These were earthly dimensions. Much more important to Mary was that her relationship with God was intact. 'It only remains that I be faithful on my part,' she had written – and she had not let Him down.

My perspective, however, is not hers. Some 400 years later, I have the advantage of distance, the power to judge and the right to rage. Yes, my judgements will be clouded by the values of my own age and circumstances, and yes, it is hard to assess the damage caused by actions *not* taken, the benefits that Mary's Institute *might* have brought had she *not* been blocked. That said, it is clear to me that Gregory XV and Urban VIII and their advisors in Rome in the years 1621–1626 stopped dead in its tracks the best opportunity in generations to develop female education in Europe and further afield, and thereby set back the cause of female education by hundreds of years.

Thousands, tens of thousands of girls were denied a decent education as a result, with a cost to humanity that is incalculable.

15

Reprieve: The House of Paradise (1626)

To travel hopefully is a joy. Your heart sings, your eye delights in every flower, every friendly face that passes by. But to travel despondently is bleak indeed. Step after step is taken in silence, the world is unseen, unacknowledged. Your focus is inwards, your brain rehearses not so much the words that you said, as those that you maybe should have said, but never did. As Mary plodded towards the snow-covered Alps in November 1626, I imagine her asking herself the same litany of questions a hundred times over. Could she have acted differently? What should she have done? What shouldn't she have done? How might she have won over the cardinals to her point of view? And, above all, what should she do now? Never had Mary had more need of her resolutions to steady her mind; never had she had more need of her faith.

The sisters in her houses in Liège, Trier, Cologne and St Omer desperately needed her support. Mary knew that only too well from her correspondence with companions who had not seen her for five years or more. Yet astonishingly, instead of heading straight back to Flanders, she struck north-eastwards towards Munich. And that detour shows us that Mary had not given up the fight. Far from it.

For Mary had a plan. She had failed to obtain the pope's support in Rome. Very well. She would instead endeavour to enlist the support of one of the most powerful secular Catholic leaders in Europe, Duke Maximilian of Bavaria.[1] It was an extraordinarily daring bid at a time when reason and caution screamed for her to hasten back to Flanders and shore up her houses there. But this act of faith was to save her Institute from oblivion.

In Milan Mary prayed again at the tomb Charles Borromeo, maybe for safe passage back over the Alps. This time she was following the route of the Lindauer Bote, a postal service that had operated between Milan and Lindau since 1322. It crossed the Alps over the old Splügen pass, making use of a narrow ledge carved out of the cliffside of the precipitous Cardinello gorge.[2] When I walked this way in Mary's footsteps in summer 2017, sudden swirling fog thwarted my first attempt through the gorge, and the vertiginous drop on one side made me feel giddy when I finally made it. That was in mid-August. Mary Ward came this way in November, when days were short, temperatures freezing, and paths icy and treacherous. Even the modern road over the Splügen pass often closes between November and May.

Nor was the worst behind them when the travellers made their way down on the Swiss side, for ahead was another formidably deep and narrow canyon where travellers often slipped and fell to their deaths. Not for nothing had the Romans called it the Via Mala (the Bad Road). It looks impressive today; it was positively scary before the narrow stone bridges built in the eighteenth century enabled travellers to avoid the most dangerous sections.

The Via Mala led to Graubünden's capital city, Chur, where Protestant citizens were keeping their Catholic prince-bishop holed up in the precincts of his ancient cathedral. Mary and her companions will have hurried through as unobtrusively as possible, and I pick up a distant echo of their relief at putting Chur safely behind them in the text accompanying Picture 43 of the *Painted Life*: 'On Christmas Eve 1626, Mary arrived in Feldkirch in Tyrol.'

Readers of the time would have understood that emphasis on Tyrol: this was Austrian territory, the travellers were back on Catholic soil. On Christmas Day Mary attended Mass in the church of the Capuchin monastery. Her thoughts, we are told, flew back to England, where English Catholics were praying for the new king, Charles I, hoping he might be good to Catholics. Here in this distant Tyrolean town, Mary added her prayer to theirs.

How then to proceed from Feldkirch to Munich? The question is a no-brainer today: the 140-mile journey northwards is just two and a half hours along the motorway. Interesting, then, that Mary Ward struck east over the 1,793 metre Arlberg pass to Hall in Tyrol, where time could

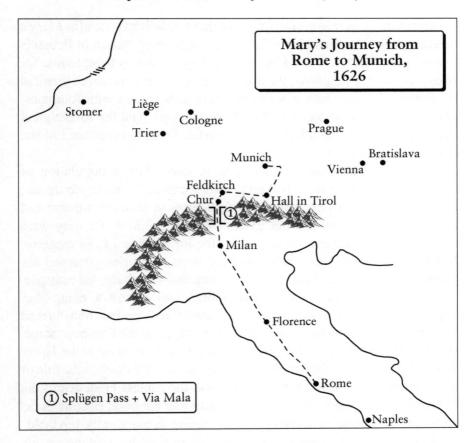

Mary's Journey from
Rome to Munich,
1626

Stomer

Liège

Cologne

Trier

Prague

Munich

Bratislava

Vienna

Feldkirch

Chur

Hall in Tirol

Milan

Florence

Rome

Naples

① Splügen Pass + Via Mala

be made by boating down the river Inn to Wasserburg, just 40 miles east of Munich. Hall teemed with boatmen who thrived on the lucrative salt trade, and were not averse to carrying passengers, anything from regiments of soldiers to Vienna's first elephant. Mary's little party presented no problem, then, even though it had grown by one: a young Austrian, Anna Maria Grünwald, had decided to leave home and join Mary on her uncertain journey.

From Wasserburg to Munich Mary travelled through a landscape punctuated with Romanesque and Gothic church towers, for though Bavaria's first *Zwiebelturm* already adorned the convent church of Maria Stern in Augsburg, the fashion for onion-shaped domes had not yet taken off.

They entered Munich through the mighty three-towered *Isartor* on 7 January 1627, and then put up at the Gasthof Ylmberger in the wide street called Tal.

And so the stage was set for a meeting that was fully as crucial as Mary's meeting with Albert and Isabella in the Coudenberg Palace in Brussels twenty years before. Indeed the setting was almost as sumptuous, for Munich's elegant Residenz, the ducal palace, boasted entrances guarded by massive bronze lions, a series of courtyards graced with fountains, and the largest Renaissance hall north of the Alps. And the sovereign at the centre of it all was a European superstar: Duke Maximilian I of the House of Wittelsbach.

Maximilian had had a tricky hand to play. With a population of 20,000, his capital Munich was an upstart compared with Augsburg and Nürnberg, southern Germany's age-old centres of industry, finance and art. Maximilian's writ did not extend over these cities, for they were *reichsfrei* – free imperial cities, under the jurisdiction of the emperor. Nor did Maximilian have sway over the large territories governed the Church – by the prince-bishops of Augsburg and Würzburg, for example.

For all these qualifications, Maximilian was indeed a rising star. Highly-educated, hard-working and self-disciplined, he had transformed Bavaria from a sleepy backwater into a key player on the European stage. He had made his army so indispensable to the Catholic cause in the Thirty Years' War that in 1623 Emperor Ferdinand granted Maximilian the title of *Kurfürst* (elector) when it was stripped from the hapless Frederick of the Palatinate. There were, as we have seen, only four temporal electors in the whole of the Empire, so Bavaria was now taking its place at the top table.

What's more, Maximilian achieved all this without plunging his duchy into debt, thanks to a rigorous economy drive, and a canny exploitation of Bavaria's most popular tipple. The Bavarian state had a monopoly on *Weissbier* (wheat beer), and Maximilian vastly expanded its production.[3] The more Bavaria's beer-drinkers slaked their thirst, the louder the clang of coins pouring into Maximilian's state coffers – and the fuller his coffers, the less Maximilian depended on his *Landtag*, or state parliament. Maximilian called only two sessions of the *Landtag* during his reign, earning the title of 'the first true absolutist ruler in the Holy Roman Empire.'[4]

Such was the man whose favour Mary Ward had to win. She had the advantage that he was the brother of Prince-Bishop Ferdinand, her enthusiastic supporter in Liège. Maximilian's interest in education and support for the Jesuits bode well, too. Educated at the Jesuit University of Ingolstadt, Maximilian saw the State and the Catholic Church as two mutually-supportive pillars of society. He had helped the Jesuits to build St Michael's, the largest Renaissance church in Europe, and a Jesuit college which ranks as one of the most beautiful. But the stakes were high. Spurned by the pope, on the verge of financial collapse, Mary's Institute desperately needed Maximilian's backing if it was to survive.

In the event, Maximilian and his wife Elisabeth Renata made Mary two offers, and it says much for Mary's skills in diplomacy that she was able to accept the first while politely but firmly rejecting the second.

The first offer was startlingly magnanimous. Impressed with Mary's vision, Maximilian and Elisabeth Renata offered to provide a suitable house and to pay the teachers' salaries if Mary founded a free school for girls in Munich. A new house! A new school! It would, of course, torpedo any chance of her returning to Flanders or England in the near future, but it would transform the outlook for her Institute after the impasse in Rome. There would be a secure source of income, while a school in the capital of one of Europe's most prominent Catholic rulers would display to all and sundry what her Institute could deliver for the education for girls. It would surely finally persuade Rome of the value of her venture. It might even be a springboard for expansion in this new part of Europe. No wonder Mary graciously accepted this first offer.

The second offer was for Mary to merge her Institute with a group of Ursuline sisters from Porrentruy whom the Catholic prince-bishop of Basel – he who had been hounded out of his city – wished to send to Munich, a safe haven now that the Thirty Years' War was engulfing much of Europe. The Ursulines were to set up a school for girls in Munich so a merger would both boost the number of pupils that could be taught, and relieve the prince-bishop of Basel of his headache.

However, while the foundress of the Ursulines of Porrentruy, Anne de Xainctonge, had like Mary Ward promoted non-enclosure, her followers had been unable to maintain their independence. They had accepted enclosure, and their destinies now depended on the say-so of the bishop. This was precisely what Mary had fought against in Rome, so she politely declined the second offer. And the Ursulines were never mentioned again.

Maximilian and Elisabeth were as good as their word, however, and they found Mary premises arranged around a yard and a garden, close to the Residenz itself. This was the inspirationally-named Paradeiserhaus. The house of paradise! What a divine gift of a name! Never mind that the house was not actually named after the celestial spheres, but after Christoph von Paradeiser, who had bought the property in 1611 and donated it to Maximilian for pious use. The house became the centre of the Institute's existence, and its heavenly name inspired the Institute during the long years in which the *Englische Fräulein*, as Mary and her companions soon became known in Munich, were denied recognition in Rome.

It is well that the name had such positive vibes, for the house stood on a site that had a grim past. The former Judengasse (Jew Street), now the Gruftstraße, had led to the Jewish baths, and the house next door occupied the site of the old synagogue in which sixty-seven Jewish men, women and children were burned to death in 1285. When Munich's Jews were expelled in 1442, the synagogue was made into the very chapel to which the sisters in the Paradeiserhaus now had access. They will have prayed next to the statue of the Virgin Mary placed here to cleanse the building from its Jewish past.

And anti-Semitism was still rampant in Mary's day. The law banning Jews from Bavaria had been renewed as recently as 1616 – by Mary's new backer, Maximilian. And the paint was still fresh on a painting depicting the old lie of Jewish men paying a Jewish woman to steal a Communion wafer – the most heinous of crimes, since Catholics believe the wafer to be the body of Christ himself. The ghastly painting, the work of Peter Candid and featuring Maximilian as the saviour from these dastardly Jews,[5] has now for good reason disappeared from view.[6] In Mary's day, however, it was on public display in Munich's large Marienkirche. Paradise and hell were never far from each other in the age of Mary Ward.

The Munich school opened its doors on 21 April 1627, with Winefrid Bedingfield as headmistress. It had a large free section for day pupils who learned reading writing, arithmetic, needlework and catechism, and a smaller fee-paying section for fourteen boarders, who had French,

Italian and Latin added to their curriculum. Mary also set up a novitiate to train six new candidates, who included a local woman, Anna Röhrlin. Mary Poyntz was appointed superior of the entire house: she was only 23 years old, but time would confirm this was another of Mary's inspired appointments.

At last, Mary had a house that was established on a firm financial footing. Maximilian paid the salaries of ten teachers, several of whom were brought from the Institute's houses in Liège, Cologne and Naples: at 200 gulden annually, this was the rate of pay of Jesuit teachers in their school for boys – one of the earliest examples, surely, of equal pay for women!

Mary's school was very much the duke's personal project. No bishop was consulted. Maximilian took personal responsibility, and a question crosses my mind: why should such a devout Catholic as Maximilian so publicly promote the Institute which had been rebuffed in Rome? Perhaps it suited Maximilian to demonstrate to Rome that he was his own man. Contrary to Protestant propaganda, Catholic rulers did not like to kow-tow to the pope, and Maximilian's sponsorship of the 'English Misses' was maybe a relatively harmless way of reminding the pope that he depended on Maximilian's army for victory in the Thirty Years' War.

With Maximilian's time taken up with affairs of state and war, Mary and her companions were free from interference by duke or bishop. And Mary wasted no time to use this freedom to make her next move.

She had arrived in Munich in January 1627, opened her school in April, and on 20 June she was on the road once more – not westwards, as she had once planned, but eastwards – to open a school in Vienna. And she was travelling in hope once again.

16

Resurgence: Vienna, Bratislava, Prague (1627–1628)

So far the story of Mary Ward has led us in a linear narrative from Mulwith to Munich, but our tale now becomes a more complex twin-track story. On the one hand we shall continue to follow Mary who, like a butterfly in the sultry heat before a thunderstorm, flits ever more frantically between Munich, Vienna, Bratislava and Prague. But we must also keep an eye on Rome, where a web was being spun to catch the butterfly and pin it down once and for all.

All began promisingly, with Mary arriving in Vienna in July 1627 with letters of introduction to the emperor Ferdinand II. This was extraordinary: the Yorkshire lass from the banks of the River Ure was meeting, indeed negotiating with, the ruler of Austria, Bohemia and Hungary, emperor of the Holy Roman Empire, and, since his victory at the Battle of the White Mountain, king of Bohemia.[1] The victory had been won with the help of Maximilian of Bavaria, with whom Ferdinand had much in common. They shared the same Jesuit upbringing, both believed in the transforming power of education, and both put a house at Mary Ward's disposal. But while the Paradeiserhaus in Munich had been given to Maximilian for religious use, the house in Vienna had been confiscated from a Protestant. This detail is revealing of Ferdinand's treatment of non-Catholics in his Austrian lands.

Ferdinand was convinced that Protestants were his enemies, wherever they might be. So while his predecessors had turned a benign eye on the growing number of Protestants in their Austrian lands, Ferdinand closed their schools and churches and had some 10,000 Protestant books burned in Graz. He even forbade Catholic doctors to treat Protestant patients.

This was, of course, the mirror image of the situation in England, where a toxic mix of fear, rage and prejudice caused Catholics to be seen as potential traitors. We saw earlier in our story the misery and cruelty this led to: the harassment of households, the suppression of schools, the financial penalties and prison sentences, the persecution and execution of priests, and the resulting mass emigration. All these measures were now meted out against Austrian Protestants, the vast majority of whom had, like English Catholics, had always considered themselves loyal subjects of their monarch.

And Protestants were not the only minority to be persecuted in Austria. By coincidence, the Institute's house in Vienna, like the Paradeiserhaus in Munich, stood in what had once been the Jewish quarter, and the Judenplatz just around the corner had once housed the synagogue, the Jewish baths, the Jewish hospital and the Jewish school. In a terrible pogrom in 1421, 200 Jews were set on fire outside the city, and those who sheltered in the synagogue were starved into committing collective suicide. An innocent-looking carving of the baptism of Christ in the Jordan on the house at 2 Judenplatz celebrates this 'cleansing' of the district from the Jews. For anyone who might miss the visual allusion the Latin inscription reads:

> The waters of the Jordan cleansed the bodies of filth and evil.
> Thus the flame of hatred arose in 1421, it raged through the city
> and purged it of the horrible crimes of the Hebrew dogs.

Mary Ward, who was fluent in Latin, will have often have passed the plaque – and it still stands today, a bizarre companion to Rachel Whiteread's Holocaust Memorial on the same square.

Vienna's houses had no numbers in Mary's day, but were known by their names, *zum braunen Hirsch* (the Brown Stag), for example, or *zur kleinen Weintraube* (the Little Grape). Among the more unusual were *Küss den Pfennig* (Kiss the Penny), *Schab den Rüssel* (Scratch your

Snout) and *Wo der Wolf den Gänsen predigt* (Where the Wolf preaches to the Geese). Mary opened her school in the house called *Stoss am Himmel* (Knock at the Door of Heaven). A heavenly name again! It was a grand five-storey house that once housed eighteen families; now house number 3 in the short street called Stoss im Himmel, I recognised it at once by the typically-Jesuit IHS monogram over its grand central doorway. It is a listed building, and when I googled it I found one of the flats on the second floor advertised as a self-catering apartment.

Vienna was surrounded by city walls – the walls that would protect the city from Turkish attack as late as 1683. Packed tightly together within them, Vienna's houses were vulnerable to fire, and indeed in the year Mary Ward arrived a fire destroyed some 140 buildings, including the archbishop's palace, which remained a burnt-out shell throughout her stay. Walking in Vienna's profusion of baroque and classical buildings, it is hard to re-capture the older, late-medieval Vienna of Mary Ward. But I did find one place where this is possible, only a few steps away from Stoss am Himmel. The columns, the stone carvings, the medieval paintings of the Gothic church of Maria am Gestade still exude the quiet, introverted piety that characterised the world in which she moved, and sitting there, I felt for a rare moment tangibly close to Mary Ward, in a place where she will likely often have come to pray.

Mary's school in Stoss am Himmel opened in the autumn of 1627, with the girls learning reading, writing, sewing, religion and drama. Mary believed that drama encouraged the girls' self-confidence, and I like to think that she imbued the very walls with the spirit of female self-assertion, for the Wiener Frauen-Erwerb-Verein, the first organisation in Austria to campaign for equal pay and conditions for women was inaugurated here in 1866. This was almost 240 years later – a measure of how far Mary Ward was ahead of her time.

The new school stretched the Institute's resources to the limit, but despite a shortage of teachers, within a year of opening Mary's school was teaching 465 girls who would otherwise have had no education. From Mary's perspective, momentum appeared to be building up once more behind her Institute, and it was in this confident spirit that she set off from Vienna in January 1628 to found a school in Bratislava.

The committee of cardinals – 21 March 1628

Unknown to Mary, trouble was brewing. And it sprang from a personal feud between Emperor Ferdinand and the archbishop of Vienna, Cardinal Melchior Klesl.

Klesl had once been a close ally of Ferdinand's, but when Ferdinand backed the Jesuits' bid to seize control of the university, he and Klesl fell out so badly that the archbishop had been obliged to seek sanctuary in Rome. When Klesl finally arrived back in Vienna in October 1627, therefore, he was determined to get his own back on Ferdinand – and he soon found that an easy way of doing so was to pick on the emperor's protégée, Mary Ward. The pretext? Easy: Mary had opened a school without first obtaining permission from the Church. She had not obtained the Church's permission in Munich either, of course, and there it not been a problem. But that was there, and this was here – so on 19 November 1627, Klesl carried out a visitation (inspection) of Mary's school.

No school looks forward to an inspection – but this was no ordinary inspection. The 'visitors' ignored the teaching and any good that Mary was doing for her pupils. All that mattered, as Klesl wrote to Cardinal Bandini on 5 February 1628, was that Mary had opened a school without the archbishop's permission and had invested authority in a female superior.

Klesl's damning report was read out at the eighty-ninth session of *Propaganda Fide* in Rome on 21 March. Inferring that Mary had refused to place herself under the archbishop's authority, the incensed cardinals set up a sub-committee to investigate whether Mary's Institute should be suppressed.

The sub-committee sat down to work just as Mary, unaware of its existence, was opening a new school in Bratislava.

Why Bratislava?[2] Like Munich and Vienna, Bratislava was a European capital. Not, however, of Slovakia. It was the capital of the rump kingdom of Hungary, the part which the Ottomans had *not* occupied after their victory over Austria at the Battle of Mohacs.

The Muslim victory had limited Catholic power in this region, and as a result the Reformation had been allowed to take place here peacefully.

Religious divides, such as they existed, were less clear cut than elsewhere. And a patchwork of different denominations lived side by side in a way that was virtually unknown in Europe outside of Hungary and the Polish-Lithuanian Commonwealth.

A rich plurality reigned. There were men and women who attended Protestant services all their lives, but who chose the Catholic burial that their parents had had before them. Others, associating Lutheranism with German-speaking culture, became Calvinist to prove their Hungarian cultural credentials. For their part, there were Catholic priests who led lives and celebrated Masses that were distinctly Protestant in character. Sixty-two of the 119 priests who attended a Catholic synod in 1561 were married, and forty-four gave their parishioners both bread and wine at Holy Communion, in the Hussite tradition, discouraged by Rome.

As recently as 1606 Ferdinand had been forced by the Peace of Vienna to allow a freedom of worship in Hungary that he denied his people in Austria. The treaty's attempt to meet the needs of both sides is neatly summed up by David Daniel: 'The Peace of Vienna (1606) … accorded to the Protestant nobles, cities and towns … the right to practise their faith freely, without discrimination or hindrance, save that nothing in the treaty should be interpreted as detrimental to the Roman Catholic Church.'[3]

The very concept that freedom of worship for Protestants might *not* be detrimental to the Roman Catholic Church would have been beyond the comprehension of most in Western Europe.

It was the Catholic archbishop in Bratislava, Péter Pázmány, who invited Mary Ward to Bratislava to found the city's first school for girls. Here then, unlike in Vienna, the local archbishop was on board. Either he did not know about Rome's campaign against Mary, or, more likely, he dismissed it as irrelevant. Like Bishop Blaes in St Omer, Archbishop Pázmány was passionate about promoting both education and Catholicism in his diocese, and he welcomed Mary's Institute. He had firewood ready for her when she arrived, and enabled Mary to open her school on 14 March 1628, extraordinarily soon after her arrival.

This was Mary's first school in a city in which Protestants wielded power. Half the senators in Bratislava's Old Town Hall were Protestant, and they kept the Jesuits out of Bratislava until 1627, much later than in Vienna. They authorised Mary's school, because they recognised the benefits for the city's girls, but limited the number of teachers to four. It would remain a tiny outpost, then, requiring sensitive leadership, and Mary appointed Barbara Babthorpe as headmistress, assisted by two German sisters and one Italian. Barbara's letters tell us that conditions were not easy. Rain came in through the roof, girls from poorer families skipped school to work in the vineyards, and some girls from richer families only turned up when they felt like it. Still, within a month of opening, the school pulled off an impressive publicity stunt by fielding more than sixty pupils in a procession through the streets of Bratislava.

Archbishop Pázmány was delighted, and in July 1629 he sent Rome a glowing report that could not have been more different than the report sent by Klesl a year and a half before.

The committee of cardinals – 13 April 1628

The sub-committee set up to investigate Mary's Institute met on 13 April 1628 and studied a paper put together by the secretary of *Propaganda Fide*, Francesco Ingoli. It was a re-hash of Klesl's negative comments and the old generalised slanders gathered by Harrison, Rant, Kellison et al. Most allegations were just plain wrong, and many were spiced with nasty sexual innuendo: the Institute's members were 'garrulous' and had a 'bad reputation', their 'depraved chaplain' had 'ruined their reputation', and in England they had been called 'whores'. In other words, the women were first branded whores and then criticised for being so called.

Ingoli's document should, of course, have been rejected out of hand, but it played to the cardinals' worst prejudices. The sub-committee decided to recommend that Mary's Institute should be suppressed once and for all. The recommendation was rubber-stamped by *Propaganda Fide* at its ninety-fourth session, on 7 July 1628. The Jesuitess houses, it was decreed, should be closed for good.

It was, surely, one of the most catastrophic decisions taken in the history of the Catholic Church. 'In its condemnation of Mary

Ward,' writes Walter Nigg, 'the Catholic Church failed to live up to its name – to its universal (i.e. catholic) mission across the world.'[4]

It would have been bad enough if *Propaganda Fide* had studied Mary's plan, discussed it with her and then rejected it. But the sad fact is that the cardinals never really got to grips with the plan at all, never really grasped its importance.

And yet the cardinals could easily have invited Mary to discuss her project with them, for they knew exactly where she was. At their meeting of 13 April, a letter from Nuncio Carafa informed them that Mary had arrived in Prague.

So far in this chapter we have seen Mary setting up new schools while Rome was deciding to suppress them. Clearly, this could not go on – and the crunch came in Prague.

Mary had been invited to Prague in April 1628 to set up the city's first school for girls. The city, once a Hussite, then a Protestant stronghold, was now firmly in Catholic hands. Calvinists had been expelled in 1621, the Lutherans in 1622. Only the Jews were still allowed to remain in their Josefov ghetto.

Mary will have walked past the old Town Hall with its astronomical clock, and under the Powder Tower with its wizard-like hat to the Charles (then called the Stone) Bridge, where her eyes will have lifted to the palatial Hradschin Castle. She will not, however, have had our magnificent view of Prague's cathedral, for it still lacked its nave and west towers. Ferdinand's religious fervour was of the sort that preferred to suppress Protestants than to complete cathedrals.

The truncated cathedral was perhaps symbolic of the religious wrangling in the city. Here too, the emperor championed the Jesuits, while the Church authorities resented their influence. Here too they quarrelled about the Jesuits' role at the university. And here too the archbishop insisted that Mary's Institute must be put under his jurisdiction. The battle lines were drawn, then, as in Vienna – except that in Prague Ferdinand was not on his home turf. Archbishop Harrach wielded real power.

And there was a further complicating factor. In Prague, Mary Ward faced not one nuncio, but two. Considering Nuncio Carlo Carafa too meek, Rome had charged Giovanni Pallotto with giving its mission backbone. Pallotto was the sort of man who, when he was governor of Rome, had had a woman whipped for flouting his ban on wearing carnival masks.[5] Conscientious, not to say ruthless in carrying out a mission, he was to play a crucial role in our story.

Pallotto arrived in Prague when relations between Ferdinand and the pope were particularly strained because they had taken opposite sides in a war in distant Mantua. The pope feared that this local quarrel might give Ferdinand a pretext for quitting the Catholic cause in the broader, more important theatre of the Thirty Years' War, so Pallotto's brief was to identify any thorny issues between the emperor and the Church, and neutralise them. And Pallotto soon decided that the thorniest issue was Mary Ward. He therefore devised a three-pronged strategy to remove her from Prague. We know this from a source which puts the best possible light on his actions – Pallotto's own letters.

First, Pallotto undermined Mary's support in Prague by reminding her backers of her problems with Rome, and hinting that it might be dangerous to back a school before the pope had given her Institute his blessing.

Secondly, Pallotto opened a charm offensive towards Mary herself. He sang the praises of her work, and whispered in her ear that this was the ideal moment for a second journey to Rome, because the pope, he claimed, was tending in her favour. Of course, he knew this was not true. On the contrary, he knew from his connections in Rome that *Propaganda Fide* had already decided to suppress her order.

And thirdly, Pallotto painted Mary in the worst possible light in his reports to Rome. We can see how he spun his reports by comparing two letters sent to Rome on 7 June 1628, one from Nuncio Carafa, one from Nuncio Pallotto. Carafa's letter is measured, factual. Mary's school, he writes, has many good points about it, but the issue of non-enclosure remains unsolved. Pallotto's tone is incriminating: Mary and her companions, he writes, pestered Harrach for a church in Prague (harassment?), dismissed an oratory in their house as too small (greed?), and did not want Carafa to consult Rome about the new school (something to hide?). Was she, mused Pallotto, trying to evade the judgement of Rome (disobedience?)?

Pallotto chose his words to confirm the cardinals' worst fears – and they fell for his ploy hook, line and sinker. In his answer, Francesco Barberini laments the 'ever-mounting shamelessness of the Superior of the Jesuitesses.' One slander had spawned another.[6]

And Pallotto's strategy was crowned with success. Mary's backers withdrew their offer of a house in Prague, and Mary decided to undertake a second journey to Rome.

A second journey to Rome! It would have been a daunting prospect for a healthy young person, it was positively dangerous for somebody of Mary's age and health. The problems with her gall and kidney stones had flared up again. The traditional treatment for the pain was to drink gin or eat robins or sparrows. In practice, you either put up with the pain or submitted yourself to the unimaginable agony of crude surgery with no painkillers, disinfectants or anaesthetics. Samuel Pepys famously underwent such an operation to have his stones removed in 1658. He was lucky to emerge alive. With a survival rate of only one in ten, most doctors were not prepared to risk their reputation on the procedure, and left it to less qualified barber-surgeons.

But Mary was prepared to do *anything* to establish her Institute – even if it took the last ounce of strength out of her. From her perspective, a Vatican insider was recommending a way out of the hopeless situation she had faced in Rome in 1624–26. If it was a straw, she was willing to clutch at it.

First Mary steeled herself for the journey by taking the waters in Eger,[7] then she discussed her travel plans with Pallotto in Vienna. From Vienna she travelled to Munich to arrange matters in the Paradeiserhaus, and then she returned to Vienna to finalise arrangements with Pallotto. By now she was in such excruciating pain that she could hardly sit, stand or lie in her bed – and all the time, Pallotto knew that Mary was on a hiding to nothing. Even Mary's biographer Sister Margaret Littlehales is stung into a rare outburst: 'What sort of a man,' she writes, 'could send a very sick woman on a fool's errand across Europe simply because he wanted her out of the way?'

And who could find it in their heart not to agree? For to be candid, the chances were pretty high that once she set out, Mary would never arrive.

Mary Ward finally set off on her second journey to Rome at the end of November 1628. Watching her go, Pallotto will have smiled. His choreography had worked to perfection.

That's more than can be said for Ferdinand's choreography for Prague. Protestant forces seized the city in 1631, the Catholics wrested it back in 1632. Swedish forces returned in 1639, and in 1648 they looted the palaces and cathedral, and took Archbishop Harrach as a hostage. But though the Swedes occupied the Hradschin Castle, they never managed to fight their way across the river. Catholic forces held out here thanks to the money and the fighting men provided by an unlikely source – the Jewish community from the Josefov ghetto who had not forgotten that Ferdinand had spared them in 1620.

17

Reality check: The second journey to Rome (1628–1630)

Mary's first journey to Rome is the memorable one, with all the pluck and daring of an irresistible feel-good story. Her second journey to Rome, lacking the infectious optimism of the first, is less celebrated. But it was no lesser feat. The walking distance from Vienna via Munich to Rome is only 100 miles or so shorter than from Brussels. Mary was eight years older, in worse health, and travel is more arduous when your steps are not buoyed with exuberance.

Of course, Mary was carried by her unshatterable faith in God: she was unwaveringly convinced that He would, in time, see her project through to fruition. She also had Pallotto's assurance that the time was ripe to put forward her case in Rome once again. Nonetheless, realism born of experience must have led to wonder whether papal approval for her Institute would really be forthcoming. So about the only common factors between the two journeys was that, from Munich, she had the same companions – Winefrid Wigmore, Anne Turner, Robert Wright and Henry Lee (plus, on this occasion, Elizabeth Cotton) – and that the journey over the Alps again took place in winter.

The first leg of the journey was to Munich. And for all that the pain from her stones was now so acute that she had to be rocked to sleep, I can imagine Mary's relief at being back home among her companions, and away from the politicking in Prague and Vienna.

Outside the Paradeiserhaus, however, the atmosphere was less friendly than before. Vitelleschi had instructed Mary's Jesuit supporters to have less contact with the *Englischen Fräulein,* and Maximilian had been targeted in the mud-slinging campaign against Mary. Henry Silisdon, the Rector of the English Jesuit Novitiate in Liège, alleged in a letter to Maximilian that Mary's companions in Flanders lived in wanton and wasteful luxury (!). Letters from Rome alleged that Mary's Institute had been involved in illegal activities. But Maximilian saw at first-hand the benefits of the sisters' school in Munich, and he wrote in defence of Mary to Cardinal Francesco Barberini in Rome.

Christmas 1628 was celebrated in Munich, then Mary set off for Rome on 2 January 1629. In my mind's eye I picture the scene as in a seventeenth-century Dutch winter landscape painting, with a small group of travellers picking their way past wooden houses along snow-covered tracks. The days were short, the daily distances limited, and for the first stretch of the journey Mary lay on a litter provided by Maximilian's wife Elisabeth Renata. She ate little more than a watery porridge. *Schleimsuppe*, the Germans call it – 'slime soup', and the description is apt. The little party will have spent nights along the way in convents and in the castles of local aristocrats, one of whom provided Mary with a carriage for the snow-covered Brenner Pass.

From the Brenner, Mary's route will have taken her down to Lake Garda and on to Mantua. She was not alone. In the winter of 1628–29 tens of thousands of troops were amassing in the region, with the Habsburgs aiming to take control of Mantua, and France and the Papal States trying to prevent them. It was in order to soothe Ferdinand's anger over this inter-Catholic struggle that Pallotto had been sent to Prague. Nobody knew when exactly the siege of Mantua would begin, but when it did, it would involve a larger concentration of forces than any Catholic versus Protestant battle in the Thirty Years' War.[1]

In the event, Mary slipped through Mantua in late January 1629, just in time to avoid the fighting, although she would have had to deal with the food shortages caused by the presence of so many soldiers in northern Italy in 1628 and 1629. Mary prayed once more at the shrine of the Holy House in Loreto, and she finally reached Rome on 10 February.

Drained and exhausted as she will have been on arrival, Mary sat down at once to compile a document for Pope Urban VIII. First she re-capped the reasons for founding her Institute, then she defended herself, as best she could, against the allegations which she guessed might have been made against her. Astutely, she questioned the basis on which they had been made. Why, she asked, did those in Munich allege scandal in the Netherlands, those in the Netherlands allege scandal in England, and those in Rome allege scandal in Naples? Because it was no more than hearsay! It was the sheer repetition of the unfounded allegations, Mary complained, that appeared give them credibility. Once more Mary declared her total obedience to the pope and again she promised to obey any order he gave. She knew she had enemies in some cardinals at the Vatican, but still believed that the pope himself was supportive, or at least non-committal.

This impression was strengthened when Urban granted Mary an audience in May 1629. Mary was again received with customary kindliness, for as Christina Kenworthy-Browne delicately puts it, 'under the diplomatic conventions of the time, the pope and many of the Cardinals received ... Mary Ward with an elaborate courtesy which belied their real attitude to the English women.'[2] The pope failed to mention that he had been at the crucial meeting of *Propaganda Fide* that had decided to close Mary's Institute.

Was Mary naïve to believe the pope? I try to put myself in her shoes. No doubt she was receiving anguished letters from her companions in St Omer, Naples and Vienna, warning her of a campaign to close what the Vatican saw as Jesuitess institutions. The sisters were bewildered, frightened, unable to make sense of what was happening. Not knowing who was behind the campaign, of course Mary will have appealed to the pope for help – and how, under these circumstances, could she have failed to interpret his gentle words as grounds for hope?

Mary was further encouraged when the pope gave her leave to argue her case before a committee of four cardinals. He did not tell her that *Propaganda Fide* was about to hand her case over to the Inquisition. Nor that the four cardinals that Mary would address were members of the Inquisition.

The committee of cardinals – 1629 / 1630

When *Propaganda Fide* ordered the nuncios in Flanders, Naples and Vienna to close all houses of Jesuitesses, they well and truly set the cat amongst the pigeons. The cardinals do not seem to have realised that Catholic Northern Europe was riddled with groups of women living together in small communities and doing charitable work. Some were survivors of the béguine movement, some were involved in teaching, others helped the sick and the poor. Some were supported by local bishops, some by the Jesuits, others operated independently. And the bishops across the Spanish Netherlands were now tearing their hair out trying to work out which of these myriad communities were the ones that *Propaganda Fide* had in its sights.

The bishops were confused, and their reports sound frantic, almost farcical. The bishop of Antwerp reports communities of devout women who are doing good works outside their convent under the guidance of local Jesuits. Are they Jesuitesses and should they be shut down? And what about the five or six women who teach poor children in Tournai to read and write? Or the women who live together and do good works in Bruges? Nuncio Lagonissa, an Italian newly arrived in Brussels, was out of his depth. He tried to close down a community of English sisters in Brussels, only for Archduchess Isabella to leap to their defence, pointing out that they had been approved by the archbishop of Mechelen. It was enough to make Lagonissa's head spin, and by October 1628 he was urging Ingoli not to press ahead too quickly with the ban on the Jesuitesses because he had come to the conclusion that they were doing good work. The cardinals had lifted the lid on a can of worms that they had never imagined in their worst nightmares.

What was anything but laughable, however, was the effect of the cardinals' blunder-buss measures on the lives of the most vulnerable people in society – the children who, at a stroke, lost their one chance of schooling, or the widows, the orphans, the old and the destitute who, out of the blue, were deprived of their only support. None of them had anything to do with Mary Ward.

The cardinals' measures were also disastrous for the women who had performed these good works. Having carved themselves a meaningful existence in a world in which the cards were stacked against them, their world was now turned upside down. They were never told why their communities were shut down, nor were they ever given an opportunity to defend themselves. Many had no homes to return to. Mary had warned Urban in her document that, if her schools were shut, the young female teachers would be made homeless. But compassion for women was not the cardinals' strong suit.

The bishops who knew the situation on the ground were appalled. Archbishop van der Burch in Cambrai and others fought a dogged rearguard action to protect the female communities in their dioceses from this incomprehensible and senseless destruction, but their appeals to Rome on behalf of the women fell on deaf ears. The cardinals who lapped up any critical unsupported allegations ignored any positive reports of women's good works, however many explicit examples were given.

And bit by bit the cardinals' campaign against the alleged Jesuitesses produced 'results'. Mary's school in Naples finally closed August 1629 – a month after Archbishop Pázmány wrote his glowing report from Bratislava.

In September Archbishop van der Burch wrote a final letter to Rome, pleading that the communities of women in his diocese were doing fantastic work as teachers and social workers. To no avail. In October *Propaganda Fide* widened the scope of the suppression to include Cologne, Trier and Liège, and in November 1629 van der Burch finally threw in the towel and the last two houses in his diocese – one in Tournai, one in Arras – were finally forced to close.

The cardinals' orders had, of course, targeted Mary Ward, but of all the houses mentioned above, not a single one had anything to do with her. What then of Mary's house in St Omer? Given that the sisters there had not seen Mary since at least 1621, I think it is actually extraordinary that the house and school had survived at all. For ten lonely, poverty-stricken years, the sisters maintained both their work in the community and their loyalty to Mary's cause. We do not know whether they heard rumours that Lagonissa was closing Jesuitess houses in Flanders, or whether closure caught them unawares. Their local bishop, Bishop Pierre Paulet of St Omer, maybe tried to thwart Lagonissa's orders as long as he dared, but the inexorable pressure from Rome took its toll, and the sisters were ejected from their house in November 1629. Perhaps the bishop still hoped for a reprieve from Rome for he did not formally close the house till September 1630.

The cardinals could then congratulate themselves on their 'victory'.

The closures of her communities in Naples and St Omer must have hit Mary like a kick in the stomach. It was not a matter of pride: what hurt was the feeling that Mary had let down the women who had voluntarily placed themselves in her care. The houses in Munich, Vienna and Bratislava appeared, thank God, to be safe. But those in Liège, Cologne and Trier were vulnerable. What could Mary now do to protect her companions there?

It is typical Mary Ward that she did not resort to blame or attack. First she prayed for divine guidance, then she wrote a letter to all her remaining houses in Northern Europe, assuring her companions that she was doing everything in her powers to keep the Institute afloat. And, convinced as she was that it was a coterie of cardinals that were attacking her houses, but not the pope himself, she urged her companions to resist any attempts that might be made to close their houses down while she fought their corner in Rome. The letter was dated 6 April 1630.

Having done what she could to shore up her communities, and realising that – despite Pallotto's assurances – that there was nothing at all to be achieved in Rome, she upped sticks and returned to Munich at the end of April 1630.

18

Wreckage: Rooted out, destroyed and abolished (1630–1631)

Events now drew to a climax.

Mary, persecuted by her 'severe fits of the stone', travelled back to Munich via Venice. Fewer friends were now willing to give her a welcome along the way, and she and her little band of travellers were virtually penniless. Mary made do with just one pair of shoes – and even these were not the right size for her.

Nor was Munich any longer a haven of peace and security. The war was going badly for Maximilian and his allies, for a botched siege of Stralsund had brought the Swedes into the fray. A string of bad harvests had caused trade to dwindle and disease was raging unchecked. The stench of death and a mood of fear and despair were abroad,[1] and, as people looked for scapegoats, they were soon accompanied by something much uglier still – renewed outbreaks of witch trials and burnings.

The numbers are horrific: 73 killings in 1590 in the diocese of Freising, 450 in the prince-bishopric of Ellwangen before 1618, 1,000 in Bamberg between 1612 and 1632, and hundreds more in the diocese of Würzburg. The fires were alight from Protestant Coburg in the north to the Duchy of Bavaria itself, with forty-three killings between 1629 and 1631, thirty-nine of them in the one small town of Wemding.[2]

And the number of accusations of witchcraft (as opposed to actual burnings) was at an all-time high in Bavaria in the years 1629 and 1630. There was a real danger that if Rome were to label her a heretic, Mary Ward might find herself accused of witchcraft. For class, reputation and status were no guarantee of protection. In Eichstätt three former Bürgermeister (mayors) and four town councillors were executed as witches, and in Würzburg members of the nobility were among the victims.

To make matters worse, several of Mary's Jesuit backers were active in the witch-burning lobby.[3] If they now turned on her, she would stand no more chance of proving her innocence than Katharina Henot, the respected postmistress in Cologne, whose high social standing and patrician background did not prevent her being strangled, then burned as a witch, on the mere say-so of a nun, in May 1627.

It was against this dangerous background that Mary received bleak news from her houses in Northern Europe. St Omer, we know, had been closed, but now she learned that her houses in Liège, Cologne and Trier were under threat as well. And still Mary did not know who exactly was behind the campaign against her. All she knew was that some powerful faction in Rome had ratcheted up its campaign, from lobbying against her Institute to carrying out an all-out attack on it. So she did two things. Still believing that the pope was not involved, she again appealed to Urban VIII for help. And lacking hard information, she did what the cardinals signally failed to do – she sent a Visitor, or inspector, to see what was happening on the ground. For this most challenging of missions Mary chose her most trusted and fearless companion, Winefrid Wigmore. She set off in June 1630, across a Europe wracked by twelve years of war, starvation, destitution and rampant localised violence. Valiant Winefrid triumphed over all of these. The one adversity she would not be able to overcome would be the power of the Roman Inquisition.

And then all Mary could do was to wait in Munich for events to unfold. By night she will have prayed for strength and guidance; by day it will have done her soul good to touch base again and involve herself in the teaching of the girls in the Paradeiserhaus. If Mary's destiny was to consort with princes and cardinals, her heart was always in the smaller things of life. 'This is verity, to do what we have to do well,' Mary had written to the sisters in St Omer. 'Many think it nothing to do ordinary things. But for us it is. To do ordinary things well, to keep our constitutions, and all other things that be ordinary in every office or employment, whatsoever it be, to do it well, this is for us, and this by God's grace will maintain fervour.'

And extraordinarily, even as the Institute was facing meltdown, young women were still coming forward to train as novices. A fierce loyalty to Mary's Institute ran through some families: three novices were related to Winefrid Wigmore and four were nieces of Barbara Babthorpe. The storm clouds might be about to burst, but there were still young women out there who wanted to be part of the venture – no matter what Rome might throw at it.

The committee of cardinals – 15 June 1630 / 13 January 1631

Having 'successfully' closed all Jesuitess houses in Flanders, Francesco Ingoli, secretary of *Propaganda Fide*, now turned to those in Liège, Cologne and Trier, and urged the local nuncio to take action there. The man in question was Pierluigi Carafa, who had taken over from Nuncio Albergati. You may have noticed that this is the third Carafa in our story – nepotism was alive and well.[4]

And Carafa swung into action. First he worked on Prince-Bishop Ferdinand of Liège to close Mary's schools in Liège and Cologne. Ferdinand delayed a little, but Mary's school in Liège closed in April 1630, and the Institute's house in Cologne in May.

Carafa then tackled Philipp von Sötern, the prince-bishop of Trier.[5] It was lucky timing for the nuncio, because Philipp, having allied himself with the French in the Thirty Years' War, now had Habsburg forces closing in on his territory and only the pope had the diplomatic clout to get him out of his hole. Mary's Institute was a cheap card to play to earn the pope's good will, so at 7 am on 16 July 1630, Philipp informed the eight sisters in Trier that their house was closed. Trier had always been the very poorest of Mary's houses, but the sisters still had fight in them. As the pope had not yet approved their order, they protested, their vow to live together must be a civil, not a Church, contract, and the Church therefore had no authority to annul it. It was a gutsy riposte, but of course Philipp closed their house all the same.

And that was the sorry state of affairs when Mary's emissary, Winefrid Wigmore, arrived on the scene in August 1630. Exhausted from her long journey from Munich and expecting to inspect four houses, she found that three of them had now been closed. Only the house on the Pierreuse in Liège remained open – just. Threatened as it was with closure, and saddled with debt, Winefrid found its community in great confusion. So, vested with the authority that Mary had delegated to her, she decided that a strong hand was called for.

First, Winefrid challenged any sisters who questioned Mary's leadership and wished to leave the house to do so. Then, when

Nuncio Carafa arrived to close down the house, Winefrid refused to let him in. She would obey the pope, she said, and nobody else.

Faced with a barred door, the nuncio lost his temper and let slip that Mary Ward was 'no gentlewoman'. Goaded by this slur on Mary's standing, Winefrid hit back that Mary's position came from birth, whereas the nuncio's title had been purchased.[6]

Carafa's allegation was factually wrong, for Mary Ward was a gentlewoman. And Winefrid's retort had substance, because nepotism was condemned by the Council of Trent. But biographies of Mary Ward have tended to focus on the emotions rather than the facts, and most have shown understanding for the man while condemning the woman. Both Winefrid and Carafa were angry. Biographers have used Carafa's anger to excuse his insulting remark, while condemning Winefrid's anger as evidence of her 'rash' and 'impetuous' nature. As one writer puts it, she 'blundered from one mistake to another, and made a bad situation much worse.'[7]

Of course, with the benefit of hindsight, we know that Winefrid's resistance was not only futile, but played into the hands of those who saw Mary and her followers as rebels against the Church. But Mary had chosen a fighter as her official representative, and I can't find it in me to criticize a fighter for choosing to fight. Was Winefrid wise to resist a papal nuncio? Probably not. But I admire her guts.

For all that, Winefrid's stand was of course in vain. With the weight of the Roman Inquisition behind him, Carafa soon brought the sisters in the Pierreuse to heel. He seized control of their house and subjected them to cross-examination, the minutes of which make sorry reading. It was not a trial. Nobody represented the inexperienced sisters. Each was questioned on her own, and in every whispered answer to every question put, oh so cleverly by the churchmen trained in rhetoric and Church law, we hear the quivering voice of a desperately frightened young woman, loyally attempting to remain true to Mary, but scared stiff of saying anything that might land herself in yet deeper trouble.

What makes the interrogations worse is that they were quite unnecessary because evidence that was far more incriminating than any of the women's confessions had already fallen into Carafa's hands. This 'smoking gun' was a copy of the letter that Mary had sent to each of her houses in Northern Europe on 6 April 1630. In it, Mary had urged her companions to resist attempts to close their houses: 'Whatever is imposed on us by anyone on the basis of this order is to be rejected by Ours everywhere,' Mary had written.

This letter to the house on Mont Saint Martin arrived in Liège a few days *after* the house was closed, so Carafa was there to receive it. Mary had of course written in total ignorance of who was trying to close her houses, but, read out of context, her letter offered *prima facie* evidence of resistance against the authority of the Catholic Church.

The letter was bad enough, but what Carafa did with it now was positively Machievellian. Rather than sending it to Rome, he had only its most incriminating passages translated into Latin, and it was these selected passages that he sent to Ingoli, without mentioning that the letter had been truncated.[8]

The edited excerpts gave Ingoli the evidence that the cardinals had been waiting for. Here was 'proof' that Mary had urged disobedience to the orders of the Inquisition, and now the cardinals went for the jugular. They demanded not only the closure of Mary's schools, but the annihilation of her Institute.

The truncated version of Mary's letter reached the Inquisition on 15 June 1630.

On 22 November *Propaganda Fide* handed the case of Mary Ward to the Roman Inquisition.

On 5 December the Inquisition ordered the imprisonment of Mary Ward in Munich and Winefrid Wigmore in Liège.

On 13 January 1631 Pope Urban VIII decreed that the Jesuitesses should be suppressed completely.

Mary probably learned of Urban's decree from the sisters of the Institute in Rome. It was, of course, the most shattering bombshell imaginable. All her certainties were now clashing irreconcilably with each other. The pope, God's representative on Earth, was suppressing the Institute that God himself had directed her to set up. It was beyond her understanding.

But if Mary could not fathom the reasons, she knew her duty. It was now clear that the pope himself wanted to close her Institute, and Mary had always promised the pope her unconditional obedience. She therefore wrote to the sisters in all her houses and ordered them to submit to the order of suppression. Her letter, dated 2 February, states unequivocally: 'In the event that His Holiness, through Nuncios or other religious officials in the places where you live, forbids you to continue your regular practices … obey at once.'

Nearly 400 years later, in an age when for most of us loyalty is something to be deserved rather than expected, Mary's reaction is surprising, maybe even disappointing. How could she sacrifice her schools and obey a pope who was now bent on destroying everything that she had attempted to build? How could she remain loyal to the Church that so thoroughly rejected her aims and ideals? Could she not see the contradiction?

The answer is that she *did* see the contradiction. Of course she did – and it caused her untold anguish and suffering. But Mary had an unshakeable faith in God, and a firm belief that the Catholic Church, whatever its weaknesses and faults, was God's church on earth. Pain, suffering and defeat were the gateway to ultimate triumph. Why this should be so was not for her to understand. What Mary believed was that if she held true to what she firmly believed, then God would in His time reconcile the irreconcilable. Her task was not to set the timescale; it was to remain true to her convictions. So Mary continued with her teaching and waited in the Paradeiserhaus for the inevitable knock on the door.

It came at 4 pm on 7 February 1631, and the arrest proceeded as arrests do. The dirty work was done by a hapless, not unsympathetic minion, Dean Golla from Munich's Frauenkirche. He arrested Mary Ward in the name of the Inquisition as a heretic, schismatic and rebel against the Holy See. Friends and supporters were scared away. Cardinal Francesco Barberini had warned Duke Maximilian against any interference. Asked whether the arrest signified that the Institute had been suppressed, Golla could honestly reply that he did not know.

The prisoner's papers were seized. She was allowed to pray one Lord's Prayer and one Hail Mary but no more. The prisoner was allowed to say goodbye to Mary Poyntz and Elizabeth Cotton, but not to the other sisters in the house. She was then bundled into an awaiting carriage and taken to be held in solitary confinement. Lack of communication and information was part of the terror, but inadvertent death was to be avoided, so in view of the prisoner's poor state of health, Anne Turner was authorised to accompany her as a nurse. Once incarcerated, the prisoner was allowed no visitors, and all correspondence was censored.

Most jurisdictions, even totalitarian ones, give prisoners the benefit of a trial, sham or otherwise. But the Inquisition did not deal in trials. Mary was never shown any evidence.[9] She was never given the chance to speak in her own defence. Nor was she told what her sentence was: Mary and her nurse had absolutely no idea whether they would remain imprisoned for a few hours, a few days, a few weeks or a few years. They were held in a guarded cell in the Anger convent of the Poor Clares, and the sisters of the convent were forbidden to make any contact with them on pain of excommunication. The order for the arrest was signed by Antonio Barberini, the pope's brother, so it is highly unlikely that Urban VIII was not in the picture.

It was only after Mary was locked away that the full text of Urban's bull, or decree, suppressing the Institute was made public. Entitled *Pastoralis Romani Pontificis*, it was published in Rome on 31 May 1631, then sent to the nuncios in Naples, Cologne, Vienna and Brussels for translation. Even allowing for the florid style of such documents, it ranks, in Littlehales' words, as 'the harshest Bull ever to emanate from Rome.'[10]

The work of the women that the bull calls Jesuitesses is 'most unsuited to their weak sex and character, to female modesty and particularly to maidenly reserve.' The women are 'heretic[s], schismatic[s] and rebel[s] to [the] Holy Church'; they 'arrogantly and obstinately disobey' the pope's warnings, leaving him no option but to suppress them.

Suppress them? Not strong enough.
Completely suppress them.
Totally and completely suppress them.
Totally and completely suppress and extinguish them.
Totally and completely suppress and extinguish them and condemn them.
Totally and completely suppress and extinguish them and condemn them to perpetual abolition and remove them entirely from the Holy Church of God.

And even that was not enough. The Jesuitesses:

> must be torn up by the roots
> are null and void
> are of no authority or importance
> We destroy and annul them.

The document ends in a tautological tirade:

> We command all Christian faithful to consider them and
> think of them as ...
> ... suppressed,
> ... extinct,
> ... rooted out,
> ... destroyed,
> and
> ... abolished.

And that, you may be forgiven for thinking, was that.

19

Reflections: In prison (1631)

The heavy bars are rammed shut and bolted, and Mary Ward and Anne Turner find themselves alone in their darkened cell. They are isolated and bewildered. Only a partially blocked window set high up in a wall lets in a little light.

Time hangs heavy. Thoughts go round in circles. And my guess is that Mary Ward is haunted by a question that has long hovered over her story. Could she possibly have avoided the confrontation with the Vatican? Might another woman have acted differently? In other words, is she to blame for what has happened to her?

Well, there is time in abundance now, for Mary has no idea how long she will be imprisoned. So let's ask the awkward question, and seek answers to it.

In an ideal world, of course, we would carry out a comparative experiment. We would find a young woman, living in the same age and bent on the same mission as Mary Ward, and we would then compare her successes and failures with those of Mary.

The extraordinary thing is that, in the real world, there was not one other such woman. There were several.

Anne de Xainctonge, born in Burgundy some twenty years before Mary Ward, had a strong Catholic faith, high-ranking parents and an excellent home education. Her order of teaching nuns were to be exempt from enclosure. They ran a free school for girls, funded by dowry money. Daughter communities followed, including the sisters in Porrentruy who were nearly foisted on Mary Ward in Munich. Anne died in 1621, the year of Mary Ward's first journey to Rome, and was declared 'venerable' (the second step towards being recognised as a saint) in 1900. 'We have talents and capabilities as women,' wrote Anne, 'and it is not forbidden us to use them to draw those of our own sex to religious life and to teach them what they are able … .' The words might easily have been from Mary Ward.

And there was Regina Protmann, who ran schools for girls in far away Braniewo in north-east Poland. She too had wealthy, high-ranking Catholic parents and a good education. Influenced by the Jesuits, in 1571 she founded a female order one of whose aims was to teach girls. Her nuns were to be exempt from enclosure. Regina died in 1613, and was beatified by Pope John Paul II in 1999.

'Do not flee from the world,' wrote Regina Protmann, 'but instead confront, engage and embrace it, constantly. Service to the needy and sick humanity shall have precedent over any formal regulation.' Again, the words could have been Mary Ward's.

Or Alix le Clerc. Born in 1576 in Lorraine of wealthy, aristocratic Catholic parents, and directed in a vision to assemble a band of companions, Alix opened her first school for girls when Mary Ward was just 13. She set up an order of women to teach the girls, and opened nine more schools by the time Mary Ward walked through Lorraine in 1621. Alix le Clerc was beatified by Pope Pius XII in 1947.

And there's Louise de Marillac. Six years younger than Mary Ward, she founded an order of unenclosed nuns to work in hospitals and run schools for orphaned children. Louise died in 1660. Declared a saint in 1934, she is the Catholic Church's patron saint of social workers.

There's Jeanne de Lestonnac in Bordeaux, who set up a female order to teach girls in free day schools for poorer girls and fee-paying boarding schools for richer ones. There's Jeanne-Françoise de Chantal, who established a community of women operating outside enclosure in Annecy in 1610: she was declared a saint of the Catholic Church in 1767. And Marie de l'Incarnation, who, in 1639, left France for Quebec where, free from enclosure, she taught both French and Indian girls. And we have already met Luisa de Carvajal who left her native Spain to open a school for girls in London.

These women have much in common. They are from well-off Catholic families, benefit from leisure time and have a good home education. Several are weak in health. Most live on the fringes of Catholic territories. They all see that educated women can make a contribution to shoring up Catholicism by teaching girls. And they all recognise that non-enclosure is essential to their task.

How, then, do these women avoid the wrath of Rome?

One reason is absurdly simple: they never go there. The women are savvy about Rome in a way that Mary is not. Brought up in Catholic territories, they are versed in the realities of Catholic administration, and realistic about the chances of negotiating with the pope. When Angela Merici, the founder of the Ursulines and therefore the grandmama of them all, is asked by Pope Clement VII to stay and work in Rome, her response is to hurry home to Brescia where she knows she will be able to operate more freely. The women in France, Lorraine, Italy and Germany recognise, in Henry Coleridge's words, that it is one thing for Rome to 'encourage a manner of life' at an arm's length, 'but quite another to give formal approbation to the abstract framework which gives this manner of life its form.'[1]

Alone among these women, Mary Ward is brought up in a country with no Catholic bishops or nuncios, where Masses are makeshift and secret. It is a context which encourages an idealised, unrealistic view of Rome.

As an Englishwoman, too, Mary has a different experience of the role of women. Tudor women are visible in society, and have more say over their lives than do women in many other countries. As a child, Mary sees Catholic priests entrusting their lives to women such as Ursula Wright and Grace Babthorpe – scenarios that are inconceivable in Catholic France and Italy.

There is also, crucially, a key difference in Mary's vision. Anne, Regina, Alix and the others work locally, and Louise de Marillac limits herself to France. Rome can therefore praise them, secure in the knowledge that the local bishops will keep them under control. Mary's vision, however, is global. The first plan for her Institute envisages a chief superior responsible for different provinces, each with their provincial superiors above the superiors of the actual houses – this is the hierarchy of a large-scale organisation. And Mary's third plan of 1621 expresses a willingness to serve 'those who live in the region called the Indies, or among any heretics whatever.' The global scale of the project is a potential threat to Rome.

What's more, a large-scale, centralised organisation requires the powerful figurehead of a chief superior – and Rome was never going to contemplate entrusting so much power to a woman. Most of the other foundresses never envisage such a post: this removed a stumbling-block with Rome, but left their orders vulnerable to manipulation by local bishops. We have seen how the bishop of Basel disposed of Anne de Xainctonge's sisters without their say-so. Mary Ward saw the post of a powerful chief superior as a bulwark against such a loss of independence.

Interestingly, Jeanne de Lestonnac *does* originally call for a female chief superior, but Pope Paul V drops any mention of the role when he approves Jeanne's plan.

How does Jeanne react to the terms dictated by Paul V? She accepts them as the best deal she can cut. And this is the crux of the matter. Anne de Xainctonge, Jeanne de Lestonnac, Jeanne de Chantal and the others duck and dive, yield and compromise in order to keep their projects afloat. Anne de Xainctonge is happy to call her sisters Ursulines if this will buy her peace from Rome: 'a name neither increases nor diminishes the perfection of a state of life', [2] she says airily. The women are deliberately vague about whether their sisters are fully-fledged nuns (subject to enclosure) or congregations (exempt from enclosure). They are as keen to blur the exact delineations as Rome is keen to uphold them. They resort, as Sioban Nelson puts it, to 'subtle circumvention of canon law'[3] and fudge definitions if this leaves them free to carry on with their work.

In contrast, Mary Ward refuses to fudge and compromise. No, her Institute will not be a congregation – her sisters must have the status of nuns. No, they will not be enclosed. No, they will not become Ursulines. And no, they will not be under the authority of the local bishop. Was this admirable honesty and principle? Or stubborn inflexibility and inability to compromise? Some commentators have thought the latter: 'In her responses to her antagonists,' writes Laurence Lux-Sterritt, 'Mary Ward sometimes lacked tact, defending her vocation with a virulent assertiveness which, in turn, lent weight to clerical complaints about her failings in the timidity and the modesty befitting a religious woman.'[4]

But Mary had good reasons for not making concessions. 'Take the same of the Society,' her vision had said: her God-given mission was an all-or-nothing venture. Any compromise suggested by the cardinals, she realised, would prevent her Institute from launching her transformational programme of education for women. She was playing for the very highest stakes. And the blame for the fact that her world-changing vision never came to be must surely attach to those who blocked the project, rather than to Mary Ward for holding out for it.

At the end of the day, Mary Ward and the other women won their battles in their own way. Anne, Jeanne, Alix, Regina and the others triumphed by stealing little local victories that allowed them, at a local level, and for a short period at least, to circumvent the limitations imposed by Rome. Mary Ward triumphed by sticking to her principles through thick and thin, a strategy that doomed her project to setback after setback during her lifetime, but that put down an unequivocal marker in the global quest for female emancipation.

And a second set of comparisons, in this case with the Piarists, convinces me all the more that a large-scale, female-led organisation on the Jesuit model never stood a chance of being approved, whoever its leader was. The Piarists, the male teaching order founded by Joseph Calasanz and recognised by Pope Gregory in January 1622, ran a number of (boys') schools in Italy, including one that opened in Naples soon after Mary's own school there. However, Calasanz made catastrophic appointments as headmaster and inspectors of the school, and rumours of 'roguery' and 'the worst sin' were soon flying around it. These terms, as Karen Liebreich describes, were code for the sexual abuse of the boys in the Piarists' care.[5] And documents in the Vatican show that the rumours were based on fact.

The procedure to follow was clear. Pope Pius V's Constitutions of August 1568 stated that offenders were to be 'severely punished and immediately delivered to the secular power to be punished as the current law dictated.' But Calasanz ignored this guidance, and instead removed the chief offenders from the scene by promoting them. This of course gave them the opportunity to abuse boys in more schools. Calasanz's chief concern was not the well-being of the boys, but the reputation of his order. 'See that this business does not become public but is covered up,' he wrote to the school in Naples. 'Your Reverence's sole aim is to cover up this great shame in order that it does not come to the notice of our superiors, otherwise our organisation, which has enjoyed a good reputation until now, would lose greatly.'

Calasanz only confessed the terrible truth in 1643 when the chief offender, Stefano Cherubini, removed him from the leadership of the Piarist Order. Amidst claim and counter-claim, the order was closed down by Pope Innocent X in 1646 under the pretext that there had been internal dissent.

So we have two orders closed down in the mid-1600s: Mary's Institute for flouting the Catholic Church's rules on enclosure for women, and the Piarist Order for the sexual abuse of children. We can predict which will get the harsher treatment. Two women were imprisoned; no Piarist ever was. The women were declared 'heretics', exposing them to the danger of being burned as witches; no Piarist ever was. The women were accused of defying Church doctrine; the Piarists were not. Mary Ward would not be rehabilitated until 1909, almost 380 years after Pope Urban's bull; the ban on the Piarists lasted a mere ten years, with the order reconstituted in 1656.

To be clear: the point at issue is not whether we, today, judge the Piarists' crime to be more heinous than Mary Ward's. My argument is that when the Vatican punished two orders which had erred *by its own rules at the time*, it acted more harshly, out of all proportion more harshly towards the women than towards the men. And that the Vatican came down so heavily on the women convinces me that Urban VIII would have clamped down on such a female-led project whoever its leader happened to be. In the face of such blatant, implacable misogyny, no woman could realistically have obtained authorisation from Rome for a project on such a scale. Mary's character, then, was not to blame: her only crime was to be ahead of her time in terms of the global project she was proposing.

Calasanz is honoured today as the Catholic Church's patron saint of popular schools; the campaign to recognise Mary Ward as a saint has dragged on since the 1930s. Pope Urban VIII's bull *Pastoralis Romani* of 1631 has a long reach indeed.

20

Release: In the hands of the Inquisition (1631)

It's time to return to Mary in her darkened prison in the Angerkloster. As a prisoner of the Inquisition, she was cut off from human life. She did not know where she was. There were guards outside her door. She was not allowed to attend Mass or make a confession. However, prison regimes at the time expected the prisoner's 'family' to provide food and drink and see to the laundry, so baskets of provisions and clothing passed to and fro between the sisters in the Paradeiserhaus and the cell in the Angerkloster. Some of the food was wrapped in a very precious commodity – paper. Now, I have already mentioned that Mary often had so little money that she could not afford the paper on which to write letters. Odd, then, is it not, that such a commodity should be used to wrap food?

It is fortunate that the gaolers – less used to poverty than Mary Ward? – did not register the discrepancy, and did not investigate the paper more closely, for Mary and the sisters in the Paradeiserhaus were using a ruse perfected by Catholic prisoners in English gaols: they were smuggling secret messages. They wrote on the paper with lemon juice: the words, invisible to the naked eye, turned black when heated over a flame. In their coded letters, Mary and the sisters in the Paradeiserhaus called the lemon juice 'liquor': 'I have little or no liquor left,' wrote Mary, to alert her companions when her reserves were running low.

Extraordinarily, twenty-three lemon juice letters have survived, and they show us that Mary remained up-beat during her imprisonment: 'Never be given to sorrow, therefore be merry and not sad,' she urges her sisters from what she cheekily calls her palace. And when she reads that the sisters are keeping up a twenty-four-hour vigil to pray on her behalf, she tells them to be sensible and go to sleep at night – with a cheerful song. Nor did she abandon her vision: If God give health, she wrote in lemon juice, we shall find another way to serve him than by becoming Ursulines.

Not surprisingly, Mary's health gave way in jail, so seriously in fact that Dean Golla feared that she might die on his watch – without having been given the Last Sacraments, for these were denied to prisoners of the Inquisition. Torn between a rock and a hard place, Dean Golla offered Mary a macabre compromise: he would offer her the last rites if she first signed a paper confessing the error of her ways.

This presented Mary with an impossible choice. To face death having refused the Last Sacraments was the worst scenario that a committed Catholic could possibly contemplate; on the other hand, to recant would be to give up all she had all she had ever fought for. This indeed was Mary's Galileo-moment.

Mary held firm and refused to sign Golla's document. 'I will cast myself on the mercies of God,' she is said to have replied, 'and rather die without the sacraments.'

That was pluck.

For good measure, Mary wrote a document of her own in which she stated categorically that she had never thought or said: 'the least that might be contrary to the Catholic Church,' but on the contrary had 'employed her life and labours in the service of the Holy Church.' She begged the pope for forgiveness if she had in any way displeased him, and asked to be released from prison and allowed to travel to Rome to prove her innocence.

Luckily for Dean Golla, luckily for us all, Mary recovered.

The committee of cardinals – 1 May / 10 May 1631

The pope and cardinals of the Inquisition read Mary's letter on 1 May. They showed no sense of urgency. It took them a week to agree to release Mary from jail, and they made no mention at all of Winefrid, who was still in prison in Liège.

Released is the right word – not freed. For as Galileo was to discover, once a prisoner of the Inquisition, always a prisoner of the Inquisition. The Inquisition never let you go. From now on, Mary would no longer be in charge of her person, no longer be allowed to direct her life as she chose. The Inquisition would dictate her every move. It not only ordered Mary to travel to Rome, for example, but stipulated the terms under which she would travel, the bail that would have to be paid, and by what date she was to arrive in Rome.

The instruction to release Mary was sent to Golla on 10 May 1631.

Back in Munich, however, Dean Golla had taken matters into his own hands, and had released Mary from the Angerkloster on 14 April.

Partly this was because the thirty-three sisters in the Paradeiserhaus had signed a joint letter renouncing any claim to be a religious community and accepting lay status instead, thereby demonstrating unconditional obedience to the pope. And a second reason, as Golla wrote to Rome on 17 April, was that an English cleric in Munich by the name of Henry Ansloe, a friend of Father John Gerard's, had come forward and offered to stand bail for Mary Ward to the tune of 1,000 thalers. Only too eager to have Mary off his hands before her health gave way once more, for the purposes of the bail document Golla appointed 24 June as the date by which Mary should arrive in Rome.

Poor Dean Golla! He had grossly under-estimated the bureaucracy of the Inquisition. Golla wanted Mary to leave, Rome wanted Mary to travel, and Mary wanted to travel to Rome to clear her name – but, absurdly, she could not leave without permission, and the Inquisition bickered about the terms of travel. First the cardinals insisted that Mary be accompanied by a commissary who would make sure she did not abscond. Good Lord, did the cardinals really think that Mary would do a bunk? Where did they think that she could abscond to? Golla, however, was unable to find anyone willing to be a commissary, as he reported on 5 June. This condition was then dropped, but now the Inquisition insisted that Mary's bail be open-ended, and not terminate on Mary's arrival in Rome. That caused the good Henry Ansloe to withdraw his offer – so Dean Golla was back to square one. Mary was still in his charge, forbidden to leave.

Weeks passed in deadlock, and it was September before a Dr Alphonso Ferri, whom Mary had helped in Rome when he was ill, agreed to stand bail of 500 scudi. Finally on 5 October Mary Ward was given permission to leave Munich. Five months had been wasted on totally unnecessary quibbling. From the start, Mary had assured Golla 'on the word of an honourable woman' that she would travel to Rome as the Inquisition commanded her. Could her word not have sufficed? The journey would now have to take place in winter, as the Inquisition stipulated that Mary must arrive in Rome for Christmas.

But every cloud has a silver lining. Thanks to the delay, Mary Ward was still in Munich when one day Barbara Babthorpe appeared at the Paradeiserhaus. In Prague, Barbara had heard rumours of Mary's arrest, so she had walked from Bratislava to Vienna, and then on to Munich to see what had happened for herself. Her presence will have done the companions good.

And God knows the women needed all the moral support they could get, for on 18 August 1631 Dean Golla assembled the sisters of the Paradeiserhaus and finally read them Pope Urban's bull, which he had received from Nuncio Carafa a week before. As we know, it not only banned them from living together as a community, but branded them heretics. Heretics faced the threat of death by burning – the fate of Giordano Bruno on Rome's Campo dei Fiori in 1600. Was that to be Mary's fate when she arrived in Rome?

The bull had to all intents and purposes completed the destruction of Mary's Institute. All her houses in Northern Europe had been closed, although a few sisters still lived together in Liège under the leadership of Mary Wivell. The school in Naples was closed; the school in Bratislava received payments from the Hungarian court treasury till the end of 1632. The school in Vienna survived by cutting its ties with Mary Ward. That left six sisters under Elizabeth Keyes in Rome, and the eleven sisters whom Mary was now leaving in the Paradeiserhaus in Munich. The scale of the wreckage might have reduced a lesser leader to despair.

But not Mary Ward, for before leaving Munich she did a wonderful and extraordinary thing: she appointed Mary Poyntz, the youngest of her original companions, as superior of … well, of what exactly? The house was no longer a religious house, it was no longer a school, and according to the terms read out by Golla it was no longer even a community. With Maximilian keeping his head below the parapet, its funding was unclear, and with the Swedes sweeping southward through Germany, its survival was uncertain. None of this mattered. Whatever the prelates, lawyers and military men had in store for her, and whatever status the men in Rome declared was permissible or not permissible, Mary was making a clear statement of faith that her Institute would survive.

The appointment of Mary Poyntz was classic Mary Ward. On the one hand she totally, humbly and sincerely obeyed each and every instruction of the Inquisition; on the other hand, she still displayed a streak of resilience and independence that, intentionally or not, irritated the cardinals of the Inquisition to the quick. Imprisonment had failed to break Ursula Wright, and it failed to intimidate her grand-daughter.

Mary finally left Munich on 24 October 1631.

So much for Golla's plan for her to arrive in Rome by 24 June.

21

Resurrection: Besieged in Munich (1632–1635)

The sisters of the Paradeiserhaus wave goodbye to Mary Ward, Anne Turner and Elizabeth Cotton late in October 1631, then return into their cold, echoingly-empty corridors. Parting is hardest on those who stay behind, and life for the sisters in Munich did not look much like paradise now. In the streets they faced the suspicion of a population that knew them to be, as Immolata Wetter puts it, 'under the shadow of the Inquisition.' Indoors, there was so little food that Anna Röhrlin went out begging. With her Bavarian accent, people were less likely to recognise that she was one of those 'heretical' *Englische Fraülein*.

Maximilian had paid for Mary's journey to Rome, and privately gave the sisters a further 1,200 florins in December 1631. But he had yet to make a public show of support, and before he could do so, the whole situation was turned upside down: Munich, the Wittelsbachs' cocky capital, suddenly found itself threatened with invasion. The Swedes, under King Gustav Adolf, had swept south and taken Würzburg and Augsburg. By May 1632 they were poised to take Munich itself – and the date was ominous. Almost exactly one year before, Catholic forces had taken the city of Magdeburg and massacred some 20,000 of its citizens. Would the Swedes avenge Magdeburg when they took Munich?

Maximilian, for one, was not prepared to risk it. Throwing his reputation of invincibility to the winds, he and his wife packed their bags and fled to Austria. Munich's richer citizens and many religious communities followed suit: entire convents sought refuge in South Tyrol. Not, however, Mary Poyntz and her companions. They remained at their post and were in Munich when the Swedish soldiers seized the city. It was a courageous stand, prompted at least partly by the fear that if they ever abandoned the Paradeiserhaus they might never get it back again.

The Swedes entered Munich on 17 May 1632. The sisters will have been surprised to learn that the new governor of the city was a Catholic and a Scot, and relieved to hear that there would – officially – be no plundering. Instead, Gustav Adolf levied a fine of 100,000 thalers in cash, 40,000 thalers in jewellery and, famously, 361 buckets of Maibock beer and 22,000 litres of Hofbräuhaus brown beer. Ever since the proud boast of Munich's brewers has been that 'beer saved the city of Munich from total destruction in the Thirty Years' War.'[1]

There were soldiers everywhere – in the streets and billeted in monasteries and private houses. If widespread looting was avoided, there was plenty of petty theft of clothing and other possessions,[2] although the soldiers would not have found much to steal in the Paradeiserhaus. And beyond the city walls, the situation was dire. Here, the Swedes foraged, ravaged and pillaged at will, and the fields were littered with the bodies of men and beasts. An etching of 1632 shows a whole series of villages around Munich set on fire. In Moosach the only stone building left standing was the Church of St Martin, which had been used to stable horses. Only nine of Olching's sixty-seven farmsteads were still being worked in 1648.[3] Food supplies failed in Munich itself, and people resorted to eating cats, dogs and mice. Unfortunately we have no record of how the sisters made do.

Nor had Munich seen the worst yet. When the Swedes left, the 4,000 'friendly' Spanish soldiers who arrived to 'secure' the city for the Catholics brought bubonic plague, a horrible sickness that led to a horrifying, undignified death. Swellings (buboes) in the neck, the armpits and the groin grew till you were wracked with cramps and high fever, from which delirium, coma and death were, all too often, the only release. The cause of the disease was unknown. In the Paradeiserhaus, Katherina Köchlin recognised the signs of plague on her body. She stole out of the house to protect her companions, and became just one more sorry statistic of death. By February 1635 some three-quarters of the population had perished.

The Swedish occupation of Munich was certainly a frightening baptism of fire for Mary Poyntz's leadership, but the sisters' steadfastness and resolve impressed Maximilian, and they reaped their reward when he made them a gift of 340 florins. This was a significant sum of money, and it proved to be a game-changer in the life of Mary's Institute, because it guaranteed the survival of the house in Munich, and allowed

Mary – by now in Rome – and the sisters in the Paradeiserhaus to carry out a plan that was stupendous in its audacity. For the clever women had spotted that for all the hyperbole in the papal bull of 1631, for all its talk of 'eradication, destruction, extinction and suppression', it had not in fact specifically banned the women from teaching. Very well, then. Now they knew that Maximilian had not given up on them, they would try and secure his permission to re-open their school. It would be a clear sign that they, their project and their mission had not been crushed.

Of course, the bull had changed the terms under which they could operate. From now on they would have to keep their heads below the parapet, and compromise. Like Anne de Xainctonge, Louise de Marillac, and the others, they would have to accept the best deal they could get, in anticipation of better. They would have to put on hold their dream of a global network of schools on the Jesuit model, their desire for recognition of the status of unenclosed nuns. They would no longer insist on being recognised as an order of nuns rather than as congregation of religious women. They would blur this neat delineation – symbolically, four of the seven sisters in the Paradeiserhaus wore religious dress, three wore secular clothes. But postponement did not mean abandonment. The vision of Mary Ward, the mission to take 'the same of the Society', remained. Not for a moment did the sisters abandon their faith in Mary Ward and her vision, no matter what Rome might say.

Mary Ward called Mary Poyntz to Rome in 1633, so it was Winefrid Bedingfield, the new superior at the Paradeiserhaus, who approached Maximilian late in 1635 with the daring proposal to re-open the school.

On 8 December 1635 the duke gave his approval. The show was back on the road.

22

Reconciliation?: Five years in Rome (1632–1637)

We left Mary in October 1631, setting out on her third journey to Rome, and her most arduous. Her health had worsened and the pace was set by the Inquisition, who stipulated that she had to be in Rome by Christmas – a stiff goal to meet. There was also the worry about what fate awaited her in Rome.

However, Mary made remarkably good speed, and when she checked in with the local inquisitor in the walled city of Bologna late in November 1631, she was in high hopes of meeting her deadline for arriving in Rome. Then the bubonic plague threw a spanner in the works.

The disease was the consequence of the battles for Mantua,[1] and it swept across the Po valley at an alarming speed, killing almost half Milan's population and 280,000 people in Italy as a whole. Bologna was itself a plague hot-spot, with 15,000 recorded deaths by the end of 1630, so neighbouring states sealed their borders in an attempt to hold the disease at bay.[2]

Health Officers in Florence required travellers to obtain a special health pass, and urged villagers to ring church bells if they found strangers crossing the border without one. In the Papal States, the health authorities required all goods to be quarantined and fumigated before they were allowed in (measures which prevented Galileo from sending his *Dialogue concerning the Two Chief Systems of the World* to Rome as he had been ordered to). Moreover, no person was allowed to enter the territory on pain of death – so Mary's path was blocked. On 26 November she wrote to the pope's brother requesting a health pass for entry into the Papal States. And then all she could do was wait.

And meanwhile the clock was ticking on her deadline of arrival in Rome by Christmas.

Elizabeth Keyes, the superior of the Institute sisters in Rome, had realised the moment she heard of Mary's departure date that the date set for Mary's arrival was unrealistic. So she had immediately written to the Inquisition on Mary's behalf, requesting a postponement of the Christmas deadline. This was in October.

---

29 Oct 1631 Sitting of the Inquisition (Pope absent)

The cardinals read the letter from Elizabeth Keyes and agree to postpone the deadline for Mary Ward's arrival from Christmas 1631 to 31 March 1632.

    The cardinals inform Dr Alphonso Ferri of their decision, and the bail terms agreed with him are changed to tally with the new deadline.[3]

Yes, the cardinals contacted Dr Ferri. And they could easily have contacted Mary, because she checked in with the local inquisitor in every town she passed through. But they chose not to do so. They preferred to keep their prisoner on edge – so Mary still thought she had to reach Rome by Christmas.

---

15 Dec 1631 Sitting of the Inquisition

The pope and cardinals read Mary's letter of 26 November requesting a health pass.

Again they showed no great hurry. Only on 18 December did the pope order a pass to be sent to Mary Ward.

    Back in Bologna, of course, Mary was becoming frantic. She was desperate not to break the terms of her bail, but as December wore on, it became clear that there was no way she could make Rome by Christmas. On seventeenth December, therefore, with some trepidation, Mary wrote to warn the cardinals that she would be delayed, quite unaware that the cardinals had already postponed the deadline some seven weeks earlier.

When Mary finally did reach Rome, she informed the Inquisition that she was at their disposal.

---

4 March 1632 **Sitting of the Inquisition**

The pope and cardinals read Mary's letter informing them of her arrival. The pope orders that she is to be received kindly, but must not be allowed to leave Rome without permission.[4]

Mary had come to Rome to clear her name, and clearly expected that there would now be a trial in which she could defend herself against the accusations that had been made against her. It will have taken a few weeks for her to realise that this was not how the Inquisition worked. No trial was planned, and no trial was ever held.

Instead, Mary was kept in the dark. Weeks, months went by with seemingly nothing going on, then out of the blue it would be announced that a decision had been taken. Sometimes it was good news, sometimes bad. On 26 May 1632, for example, the Inquisition suddenly acquitted Mary of heresy. No reasons were given. On 22 December 1633, however, the Inquisition rejected Mary's request for former members of her Institute to be allowed to live together: 'His Holiness,' note the minutes of the meeting, 'refused to grant them anything.'[5] Mary had no information about when decisions would be made, or why one request was granted and another refused.

The role of Pope Urban is particularly ambiguous. He granted Mary an audience during the first half of 1632, and received her with the usual kind words. Indeed, according to Elizabeth Cotton's description, the meeting was quite emotional: Mary, she says, flung herself at the pope's feet declaring 'I am no heretic,' and the pope raised her with the words 'We believe it, we believe it.' Some biographers have taken this as proof of a reconciliation after the papal bull of 1631, with Mary now rehabilitated.[6] Pope Urban, they point out, paid for Mary's food and accommodation, and requested that the younger sisters of the Institute be brought from Munich to Rome. Mary's work, the Catholic Encyclopedia concludes, suitably 'reconstituted with certain modifications of detail,' was now 'fostered by Urban.'[7] A happy end, then, after all.

But there are details that niggle. For example, Mary was extremely anxious about Winefrid, who, to the best of her knowledge, was still incarcerated in Liège. In her audience with Urban she begged for Winefrid's release, and some accounts maintain that the pope assured Mary that he would do as she wished. If this is true, Urban was being economical with the truth.

For the Inquisition – as the pope very well knew – had ordered Winefrid's release several months *before* Mary's audience with Pope Urban. Nuncio Carafa had arrested her in February 1631, interrogated her in September, and the Inquisition had ordered her release in November 1631. So the pope could easily have reassured Mary that the order had already been given for her friend's release, but he preferred to pull the wool over her eyes.

Worse, the Inquisition (of whom, let's remind ourselves, the pope was a member) had been intercepting the Institute's mail since at least January 1631:

---

22 January 1631 Sitting of the Inquisition

The pope and cardinals order the inquisitor in Perugia to find Joyce Vaux, lately superior of the house in Perugia, to initiate a search for her if she can not be found, and to intercept any letters to her from abroad.[8]

6 March 1631 Sitting of the Inquisition

The pope and cardinals order the inquisitor in Naples to find out what he can about the Jesuitess Anna and to intercept her letters.

10 April 1631 Sitting of the Inquisition

The Inquisition learns that the Jesuitesses' mail comes in via the Jesuits in Naples, and again orders the inquisitor in Naples to make every effort to intercept it.[9]

Taken along with the pope's order that Mary must not leave the city without permission, this does not sound like a man acting in the spirit of reconciliation. And as for the monthly food allowance – Good Lord! The pope was keeping the sisters prisoner in Rome. He could hardly do any less, short of letting them starve.

Mary and her companions, for their part, were always obedient and respectful towards the pope, and never said a word against him. But in private they communicated in code, fearful that their letters would be read by Church agents and taken in evidence against them. Mary went by various names such as Felice, Phyllis, Margery or simply the 'old woman'. Mary Poyntz was Ned, Elizabeth Cotton was James, and the sisters no doubt derived some wry pleasure by referring to Duke Maximilian and his wife as 'the miller and his mate'. But humour aside, this was hardly the behaviour of a community that feels fostered.

Mary's existence in Rome must in fact have been unspeakably frustrating. She had founded her Institute in order to teach girls across Europe and further afield – and here she was cooped up in Rome, with the months passing by, prevented from carrying out her task. But still she did not give up her dream. The sheer survival of her houses in Rome and in Munich was no mean feat, and the arrival in Rome of Winefrid Wigmore and Catherine Smith in December 1632, lifted her spirits. She was not beaten. In fact Mary the Irrepressible was planning her next moves.

In Munich, as we have seen, Mary re-launched her school with Maximilian's backing. In Rome, she had a trickier hand to play. Her first attempt to carve out some independence for herself was to move out of their rented house and into a house of her own. She raised money from her acquaintances in Rome – including the pope's sister-in-law, Donna Costanza – but of course funds were hard to come by. 'Marg hath not got her patents to set up shop, but labours and hopes,' she wrote to Mary Poyntz, meaning 'Margery [code for Mary Ward] has not yet received permission for her new house.' 'Jesus grant Ned some competent quantity of yellow silk,' translated as 'Jesus grant that Mary Poyntz raise the necessary funds.' As 1633 drew on, however, Mary felt confident enough to summon Mary Poyntz from Munich, and the sisters moved into their own house opposite the basilica of Santa Maria Maggiore before Christmas 1633.

Mary's next move was to request permission to travel. This did not begin promisingly.

---

23 February 1634 **Sitting of the Inquisition**

The pope and cardinals read a letter from Mary Ward. Due to her deteriorating health, Dr Alphonso Ferri recommends she spend time near the sea. A medical certificate is enclosed. It states that Mary Ward is suffering from an inflammation of the liver and kidneys caused by the stones. It is causing pain, fever, coughing and spitting of blood, and indigestion.

As a result, Mary Ward requests permission to be allowed to travel to England.[10]

England! Was this a bid for freedom? The cardinals were clearly suspicious, for they obtained a second medical opinion from a doctor of their choice. And the pope resorted to carrot and stick: he offered to increase his financial support for Mary and her companions if Mary agreed not to travel to England, but he also had the Inquisition repeat the travel ban.

---

9 March 1634 **Sitting of the Inquisition**

The session reminds Mary Ward that she is banned from leaving Rome without permission.

16 March 1634 **Sitting of the Inquisition**

The session again reminds Mary that she must not leave Rome without permission.

So Mary amended her request. Might she, instead, be allowed to take the waters at San Casciano, some 180 miles north of Rome? Her letter led to a flurry of meetings and measures that soon bordered on the farcical.

---

20 April 1634 **Sitting of the Inquisition**

The pope and cardinals agree to allow Mary Ward to take the waters at San Casciano. But she is at all times to be kept under the supervision of an inquisitor.

---

20 July 1634 **Sitting of the Inquisition**

The cardinals, informed that Mary has set off for San Casciano, order the inquisitors in Florence and Siena to keep watch on her. She is to be arrested at once if she takes a road other than to San Casciano.

9 August 1634 **Sitting of the Inquisition**

A grand session of passing the buck. The inquisitor in Florence writes that San Casciano is not in his district, but in the district of Siena. The inquisitor in Siena writes that Mary Ward is in Monte Santa Maria, which is in the district of Perugia.

6 September 1634 **Sitting of the Inquisition**

The inquisitor in Perugia denies that Mary Ward has ever been in Monte Santa Maria. But he has a helpful suggestion to make: perhaps the inquisitor in Siena should have her watched?

Somewhat bemused, the cardinals order *all* the inquisitors to watch Mary Ward.

7 October 1634 **Sitting of the Inquisition**

Going for brownie points, the inquisitor in Perugia can report that, even though this is outside his district, Mary is in San Casciano, preparing to return to Rome. He will try to ascertain which route she intends to follow.

9 October 1634 **Sitting of the Inquisition**

Not to be outdone, the inquisitor in Siena can report a scoop: he has obtained a report on Mary Ward directly from the wife of a nobleman who is staying in San Casciano. He can communicate the crucially important information that Mary has been wearing a black dress with silk trimmings, wide sleeves and a broad collar in French fashion, along with a close-fitting cap sewn with silk, a black hat … [11]

One can only hope that at some point in this session, the pope, the pope's brother, the pope's nephew, or indeed any other one of their eminences expressed the opinion that the Catholic Church might better be served if its most powerful princes spent less time listening to such trivia. The sorry saga was finally brought to an end when the Inquisition learned in November that Mary had returned to Rome – as she had always said she would.

It is of course utterly ludicrous that the cardinals should have been devoting so much of their time to frustrating the work of at most sixty impoverished women, scattered across Europe, and loyal Catholics to boot. Mary and her Institute were the subject of at least *fifteen* sessions of the Inquisition between 1632 and 1634 alone. And the Inquisition's obsession with Mary Ward – the word is surely justified – was truly extraordinary given that this was the height of the Thirty Years' War, and that the very same men were at the very same time dealing with the matter for which the Roman Inquisition is virtually synonymous: the case of Galileo.

Galileo came 'under the shadow of the Inquisition' when his *Dialogue Concerning Two Chief World Systems* finally reached Rome in 1632. Pope Urban VIII, hitherto a Galileo supporter, took umbrage at the work, and the inquisitor in Florence – the man who would later be asked to keep watch on Mary Ward in San Casciano – was ordered to summon Galileo to Rome. Galileo was 68 years old and suffering. But this was of as little concern to the Inquisition as Mary's gall and kidney stones. Like Mary, Galileo was required to make the journey in winter.

The fates of Galileo and Mary Ward were therefore both in the hands of the Inquisition in 1633. Like Mary, Galileo was never given a real trial, never had the opportunity to defend himself in a court of law. His guilt, like Mary's, had been determined in advance. And like Mary Ward, all Galileo could do was submit to the Inquisition's decisions.

Galileo, as we know, recanted. But he was not set free. By gracious permission of the Inquisition, he was allowed to live under house arrest in the home of Ascanio Piccolomini, the archbishop of Siena. And in 1634, taking time off from studying reports of the silk worn on Mary Ward's dress and cap, the cardinals drew up the terms under which

Galileo would return to his villa in Arcetri, outside Florence. They decided that Galileo was to be kept under house arrest, banned from going into Florence itself. They even determined how many guests the ageing scientist was allowed to receive. It was an ill omen of the kind of life that lay in store for Mary Ward.

And yet, somehow, Mary managed to avoid a similar fate. For in 1637, against all the odds, the Inquisition suddenly gave Mary permission to leave Italy.

Why the Inquisition should perform such a U-turn remains shrouded in mystery. Did Mary engineer this change of policy? Did it have to do with another crisis in Mary's health? Or had the pope and the cardinals decided to be shot of her? Maybe they felt it was unlikely that she would survive the journey. Or maybe they had finally recognised that she was no threat to them? We do not know the terms that were negotiated. All we know is that in August 1637 the Inquisition officially gave permission for Mary to travel to Spa, near Liège, to take the waters for her health.

But more had gone on than met the eye. For when, on 10 September 1637, Mary finally broke free after five and half years in Rome, she had more than just the Inquisition's permission to travel. Along the journey she produced a letter from the pope's nephew recommending her to Henrietta Maria, wife of King Charles I of England. And at some point it became understood that the ultimate destination was not Spa, but England.

Mary Ward was going home.

23

Return: The longest journey (1637–1639)

So Mary was finally on the road again. Once more she was breathing in the air rich with the scent of wild herbs and grasses, body and soul braced for the challenges of the daily stint...

Forget it. Mary was a seriously sick woman. Walking was out of the question. Henry Lee and Robert Wright carried her on a litter. Winefrid Wigmore, Mary Poyntz and Anne Turner walked alongside, trying to keep her as comfortable as possible. Mary was often in a high fever, close to delirium, tormented by spasms of searing pain from her gall and kidney stones.

In this manner the cortege stumbled 150 miles to Siena, where Mary was helped by Archbishop Ascanio Piccolomini, the man who had offered sanctuary to Galileo. Galileo himself, now almost completely blind, was by now home in Arcetri, waiting for the Inquisition to decide whether to allow him to enter Florence for medical attention. Mary's onward route to Florence passed close by Galileo's house, but Mary and Galileo were never to meet – so this, in more ways than one, was as close as they were ever to be.

From Florence Mary's little party travelled on via Bologna to Milan. She then struck westwards, and on 2 November 1637 a coach provided by a local governor brought her to Turin, the capital of the independent duchy of Piedmont. It was a city in crisis, for Victor Amadeus I, the ruler of Piedmont who had carried off the unlikely double-act of allying himself with France without actually declaring war on Spain, had just died. Everyone now expected the skirmishing between France and Spain in Piedmont to escalate into all-out war, and indeed Mary slipped out just before French troops poured in over the Alps. As in Prague, as in Mantua, Mary had narrowly missed the siege of a major city. It was a lucky streak that could not last forever.

Mary's route up the Susa valley took her past the abbey of San Michele, so notorious for its absentee abbots that it had been shut down by Pope Gregory XV in 1622 – a reminder that the closing of abbeys was not a Protestant monopoly. Further on stood the abbey of Novalesa, where Benedictine monks put up travellers who braved the busiest mountain pass between Italy and France – the daunting 2,083-metre Mont Cenis pass. These might be pilgrims, merchants or indeed papal nuncios, like Cardinal Guido Bentivoglio who crossed the Alps four times. 'These four times are fully enough,' he wrote, 'I am quite sick of the Alps, and so tired with travelling that I must have done with it.'[1] Mary will have sympathised. She was older, in much worse health, and was now attempting her *sixth* crossing.

The Alpine passes had become busier during the Thirty Years' War, and some families that monopolised the transport of goods had become seriously rich.[2] On the Mont Cenis, however, it was villagers who charged set rates for their services as guides. They hired out sledges in winter, mules in summer and even primitive sunglasses to protect your eyes from the glare of the snow. When Mary and her companions set out from Novalesa in mid-November, the hazardous zigzag track was marked out with poles but hidden in deep snow. As they fumbled their way forward, they were hit by a violent snowstorm, and four travellers who had attached themselves to Mary's party fell to their deaths. Mary and her companions could only hope that their bodies would one day be found and laid in the Chapelle des Transis.

At the top of the pass was La Ramasse, where travellers were transferred onto stretchers made of bundles of wood. A guide then dragged the stretcher down the French side of the pass, with the traveller jolting from rock to rock behind, which will have been agony for Mary.

Nor was the going much easier from the bottom of the pass. The track climbed onto another steep-sided massif; then, at Les Echelles, it dropped through a hole in the rock into the back of an enormous cave. Travellers groped their way between the stalactites in the semi-darkness to the mouth of the cave, where ladders fixed to the rock face provided a dizzying descent to the road some 30 metres below. Les Echelles (The Ladders) certainly deserved its name.

☙————❧

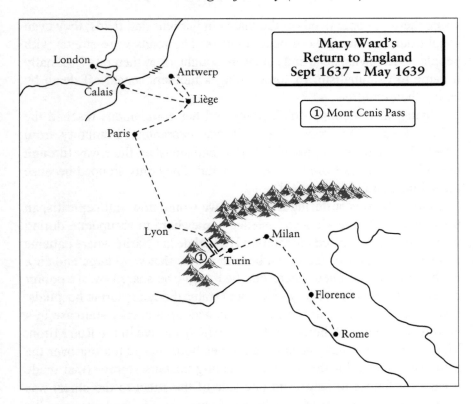

At last, however, Mary and her companions had the mountains behind them, and could head west to Lyon.

Why this uncharacteristically westward route for Mary, far from the Habsburg lands that were more familiar to her? The answer is simple: war. The Mont Cenis pass allowed Mary to avoid Germany, where for nineteen long years lumbering, blundering, plundering armies had been transforming entire territories into ghastly landscapes of unworked fields and abandoned villages. It also avoided Lorraine, whose catastrophic devastation since Mary had passed through Nancy sixteen years earlier is depicted in grisly detail in etchings called *The Great Miseries of War*, by the Lorrain engraver Jacques Callot. The plates show villages being pillaged, travellers being robbed, beggars starving by the roadside, people being shot, burnt, hung or broken on the wheel – and in Plate 11 so many people hang from a single tree that, as the commentary drily puts it, they hang there 'like fruit'.

Keeping to a westerly route, Mary could also circumvent the equally ravaged state of Franche Comté. 'Posterity will not believe it,' a survivor wrote there. 'People lived off the plants in gardens and fields; they even sought out the carcasses of dead animals. The roads were strewn with people ... In towns, dogs and cats were sought after, then rats ... Finally it came to cannibalism. In some villages mothers staved off death by eating their children ... .'[3]

Finally, in December 1637, Mary and her companions reached the safety of Paris. Not that even Paris was guaranteed immunity from attack. The year before, Spanish troops had smashed their way through to Corbie, 90 miles from the French capital. They only stopped because the soldiers had not been paid.

Mary, who was suffering from what we would now call nephritis, an inflammation of the kidneys,[4] needed somewhere to recuperate during the winter. Paris boasted the modern Hôpital de la Charité where patients enjoyed the luxury of their own beds in rooms that were large and airy, or the older Hôtel-Dieu where one bed might be shared by six poorer patients. But people of Mary's class and status did not resort to hospitals. Instead, a physician will have made his way up a creaky staircase in a narrow, wooden-built house of the sort which survive in the Rue Miron. Mary's room may have been on an upper floor that jutted out over the medieval street – for the ban on projecting upstairs storeys (that made it easy for flames to leap from one side of the street to the other) was widely ignored. And if Mary's landlord was one who had rendered his half-timbering with flame-delaying plaster, her house will have looked like the one at 51, Rue de Montmorency, now the oldest surviving house in Paris.

For Paris was not the city of broad boulevards and seven-storey residences that we know today. For all its boast of being the largest city in Christendom,[5] most of its 300,000 inhabitants still lived within its ancient city walls. The crowding was atrocious, with houses lining the bridges over the Seine[6] and had Notre-Dame caught fire in 1637 as it did in 2019, the flames would have engulfed the wooden houses crammed into the narrow strip of land between the cathedral and the river which is now a small park.

However, Paris was building newer, airier palaces, like Marie de Medici's Palais de Luxembourg, with larger windows and broad, symmetrical façades,[7] as Mary may have noticed when she took her health-improving walks in the spring of 1638. Or maybe not – for extraordinarily, in the light of all the opposition she had faced in Rome, this indomitable woman was exploring Paris to see whether she might be able to open a school. A school! Nothing came of the idea on this occasion – but Mary's efforts were not in vain. Thirteen years later her companions would be back in Paris, harvesting the seeds that Mary had sown.

By the second half of May 1638 Mary was well enough to resume her journey to Spa. She headed north-east from Paris, and took a boat down the Meuse.[8] At one point, a fierce-looking group of soldiers got on board, but the women arrived unmolested in … well, where exactly did they arrive? Not in Spa, as agreed with the Inquisition. Instead, Mary put up in Liège – yes indeed, to see about opening a school, maybe on the same model as that sponsored by Prince-Bishop Ferdinand's brother in Munich. Littlehales, indeed, speculates that Liège, not Spa, had 'perhaps been the real object of this horrendous journey from the beginning.'

The problem was that, as usual, Ferdinand wasn't at home – or to be more precise, he was in one of his several other homes. And, to make matters worse, following the assassination of the council leader Sebastien la Ruelle in 1637, the prince-bishop's stand-off with the town council of Liège had flared up into all-out civil war. French troops had invaded and seized the insignificant town of Brée. Spanish and Croat forces then re-took Brée and laid siege to the even-less-significant village of Bilzen. This was classic Thirty Years' War carnage: armies rampaging in the countryside, slaughtering people, destroying farms, villages and crops, spreading mayhem, disease and famine, achieving nothing.

It was certainly not a propitious moment for Mary Ward to petition Ferdinand, and although Mary remained several months in the area, it is not clear whether she, or maybe Winefrid Wigmore or Mary Poyntz, obtained an audience with the prince-bishop. Guilday speculates that Mary opened a school for a while,[9] but this is not certain. What we do know is that when Mary left Liège in December 1638, she headed west, not south. England was clearly her goal.

There was, however, one last poignant visit to be made before Mary boarded the ferry home: she travelled to Antwerp in order to meet up with her half-sister Frances, with whom – when they were both young things, so many years ago! – Mary had begun her adventures in St Omer, Brussels and Gravelines. Amazingly, when you come to think of it, Mary had since then travelled as far east as Vienna and Bratislava. Even more amazingly, Frances had been further east still – to Krakow in Poland!

Having professed as a Carmelite in Mons in 1611, Frances was one of five sisters who answered a call to found a Carmelite convent in Krakow. For their own safety, the sisters travelled to Poland dressed as men: with this Ward sister too, then, we are a million miles away from the Vatican's rules on clothing and enclosure. By 1613 Frances was not only sub-prioress of the new convent but mistress of novices too. Intriguingly, we know that the Jesuits tried to take control of Krakow university in 1617, and that the Carmelites opposed them. Was Frances involved in this power struggle – the same that Mary found herself embroiled with in Vienna and Prague? All we know for sure is that Frances was sub-prioress for six years.

Returning to Mons in 1619, Frances became one of the first three nuns in the new English Carmelite convent in Antwerp. Ironically, it was championed by Henry Silisdon, a ringleader of the smear campaign against Mary Ward, and indeed, as Littlehales describes him, 'the most bitter adversary of the English Ladies among all the Jesuits.'[10] The Carmelites established themselves in Hopland, a street just around the corner from where Pieter Paul Rubens had his studio, and this is where the two Ward half-sisters met for the first time in twenty-eight years.

But there were no embraces. Even *met* is stretching the meaning of the word – for, as a nun in enclosure, Frances sat hidden behind the sort of grille that Mary had fought so hard to resist for her own companions. Still, for all that, it must have been a heartfelt and intimate exchange.[11]

Mary had by now been on the road for over eighteen months since leaving Rome. Surely, surely she would now board a boat and cross the Channel?

Well, not quite yet. She must have received word in Antwerp that a school might, after all, be possible in Liège, so in the spring of 1639, Mary travelled 85 miles in the wrong direction in one last heroic bid to get her Institute back on its feet. You have to admire the sheer courage of a sick woman prepared to sacrifice her all for her life's work. Her hopes, however, were dashed yet again, the opportunity for girls in Liège to receive an education receded, as it had in cities from Bratislava to St Omer.

Now, at last, Mary headed via Tournai and St Omer for the coast. This was dangerous country, where the border between France and the Spanish Netherlands moved this way and that as the two territories fought for a few miles of land with the same tenacity and futility as the First World War armies two centuries later. Spain grabbed Cateau-Cambresis; the French snatched it back. The French raided Gravelines, the home of Mary's Poor Clares convent. They laid siege to St Omer in 1638; by the time Mary arrived in May 1639, Spanish troops had forced them to withdraw. After months of siege, St Omer was a shadow of its former self.

Mary, however, made it safely to Calais, and the end of a twenty-month odyssey in which, in her longest journey of all, she had criss-crossed Europe and dodged armies all the way from Rome to the English Channel. She had miraculously avoided becoming embroiled in any fighting, but for months she had travelled through regions ravaged by brutality, destruction and famine. So Mary will have heaved a huge sigh of relief as she boarded a ship for England – a haven of peace, as she thought, in a Europe that was tearing itself apart.

What Mary did not know was that just as she was setting foot in Kent, 2,000 men were marching on the Scottish town of Turriff, where Presbyterians who considered the Anglican Church too 'papistical' were reported to have assembled. It was the first action in a conflagration that, with gathering intensity, was about to sweep across the British Isles and form the back-drop to the last few years of Mary's life.

24

Revolution: Besieged in York
(1639–1644)

It is 1639, and we are fast approaching the end of Mary's life. We know, with the benefit of hindsight, that her Institute survived and blossomed – so can this remarkable woman yet snatch victory from the jaws of defeat?

In many ways, 1639 appears an auspicious year for Mary to return to England. The country has changed beyond recognition. In her childhood the queen of England persecuted Catholic priests; now the queen of England is Catholic. Her marriage contract to Charles I guarantees her the right to practise her religion. Monks minister to her in the queen's chapel, and her organist is the Catholic convert Richard Dering, recently returned from exile in Brussels. The queen's court includes its own papal nuncio. Elizabeth I was excommunicated by Pope Pius V as a heretic; Queen Henrietta Maria sports Pope Urban VIII as one of her godfathers. The symbolism could hardly be starker.

Nor is this Catholic renaissance restricted to the queen's inner circle. The king's painters are the Catholics Anthony van Dyck and Peter Paul Rubens, and his new Whitehall Palace is to be designed in Italianate style. William Laud, the Anglican archbishop of Canterbury, is replacing the wooden Communion tables favoured by Protestants with stone altars preferred by Catholics. 'The whole land,' complains the non-Conformist Nehemiah Wallington, is 'overrun with idolatry and popery.'[1] The time seems ripe, then, for the return of England's most famous female Catholic.

But that is only part of the picture. A maelstrom of contradictory currents are washing away the broad consensus achieved under Elizabeth. Alongside the Catholic revival there is a rising clamour from people demanding the right to interact with God on their own terms. The country's most popular book after the Bible is John Foxe's *Book of Martyrs*, and the hideous martyrdoms it describes are not those of

Catholic priests persecuted under Elizabeth and James, but those of Protestants executed during the reign of Catholic Queen Mary.

New religious communities burst into existence like fireworks in the night sky. Baptists, Anabaptists, Grindletonians, Unitarians and others tug the Church of England away from its archbishop, spawning a whole new terminology. Low church priests oppose Laud's reforms, and dissenting vicars dispense with their surplice and the Book of Common Prayer when they conduct their services. Three non-conformists have their ears cut off for criticising Archbishop Laud, and radicals are flogged for circulating unorthodox views on religion, but the tables are turned when Laud is impeached in 1640. England, and maybe the world, has never seen such an explosion of religious individualism. Coinciding with a rise in population,[2] unemployment and the cost of living, religious aspirations soon intertwine with political agitation. Viewed in this light, the Catholic ascendancy looks as fragile as the Royal family that supports it.

Mary arrived in London in the midst of this confusion, and immediately set about giving reality to the project that had maybe been closest to her heart all her life: opening a network of girls' schools in England. Throwing her health problems to the wind, she organised classes in her own house in London, while looking out for premises in which to set up, as she put it, 'common schools in the great city of London.' For financial back-up she secured the patronage of Queen Henrietta Maria.

But the sand was running out from under her feet. Law and order were disintegrating all around her. Altar rails were being torn down, magistrates were challenged, revolt was in the air, nurtured by a veritable avalanche of publications: 900 in 1640, 2,000 in 1641 and 4,000 in 1642. 'The spring of 1640 to the summer of 1642,' writes David Cressy, 'saw an extraordinary upsurge of hostility to established authority, an outpouring of scorn against magistrates and constables, and an overflow of derisive and abusive language directed against the clergy, nobility and gentry.'[3]

As in Liège, supporters of reform rallied behind parliament, while opponents gathered behind the sovereign. Among the latter, ironically, were the large majority of England's Catholics – the very population which the previous two monarchs had treated as potential traitors.

Eighty-six of Yorkshire's ninety-six Catholic families of rank would commit to the Royalist side, and a quarter of Yorkshire's Royalist colonels would be Catholics.

Galileo's death in January 1642 went unnoticed in a London that was in turmoil. Archbishop Laud had been imprisoned in the Tower of London in 1641. Charles marched into the House of Commons to arrest John Pym and four other MPs, but this clumsy move undermined any vestiges of the king's authority. Five days later Charles fled to York with a paltry escort of thirty-nine gentlemen and seventeen guards, while Queen Henrietta Maria sailed to Holland to pawn the Crown jewels and buy munitions.

At a stroke, then, London's Catholics were bereft of their strongest supporters, and vulnerable to harassment or imprisonment. Mary's house was searched repeatedly, and she was finally forced to abandon her plans and see to her companions' safety. But which way to flee? Flanders offered security, at the price of giving up the English mission. Yorkshire was riskier, but family connections offered a chance of keeping the English mission alive. So in April 1642, Mary, her companions, a priest and a small group of pupils set off north to Newby.

They left London to the news that 4,000 Protestants had allegedly been slaughtered in a Catholic uprising in Ulster, and from behind the curtains of their carriages Mary and her pupils will have seen anti-Catholic demonstrations in town after town as they clattered north. Even Newby was considered unsafe, so in September Mary's little group moved on to Hutton Rudby near Stokesley, where her relations, the Inglebys, lent her a house. Mary and her companions soon fitted out one of its rooms as a chapel.

So Mary had come full circle. Her destiny had led her to European capitals from Brussels to Vienna, from Rome and Naples to Munich and Prague, and now she had returned to a Yorkshire village just 30 miles away from where she had started out. Perhaps, like the medieval monks who built their abbeys deep in the countryside, she savoured the seclusion. We certainly know that Mary made a pilgrimage to the ruins of the Carthusian Mount Grace Abbey, beautifully cradled on a wooded hillside of the North Yorkshire Moors. She climbed the steep track to the

Lady Chapel which at the time was roofless and abandoned, but usefully hidden by trees and foliage so that pilgrims could visit it without being seen. Now restored, the chapel is one of those places where you come maybe as close as anywhere to the spirit of Mary herself.

Peace was not, however, granted to Mary Ward. With both king and parliament raising troops, it was no time for Catholic nuns to be stuck in the sticks, and Mary moved to the safety of York, the de facto royal capital of England. Here she was offered a house by the Thwenges,[4] a family with familiar Catholic credentials: her hostess Anne Thwenge had been imprisoned for sheltering priests, and Thomas, the son of the house, was training to become a priest. Daughters Helen, Catherine and Anne were still at home, though, and they were soon spell-bound by Mary.

The Thwenges' house stood in Heworth, the village just outside York chosen, by coincidence, by Charles to stage a mass rally of Royalist support in June 1642. The event was ambushed by parliament, which sent Sir Thomas Fairfax with a petition for Charles. If the Thwenges were present, they will have seen Fairfax ride up to the king, and Charles angrily turn his horse away. There then followed an unedifying side-stepping across the field, with Fairfax trying to intercept the king, and the king trying to avoid him – until Fairfax got close enough to wedge the petition in a fold in Charles's saddle. Where was Charles's bodyguard? It was not a spectacle that gave much confidence in the king.

Not that the petition had any effect. Both sides continued to raise troops, and later in June a shipload of weapons purchased by Henrietta Maria in Holland arrived in York. War was formally declared in August.

War, then, had caught up once more with Mary Ward. In Royalist York it was, to begin with, a phoney war. The marquess of Newcastle brought the Royalist Northern Army to the city in December 1642, and in March 1643 Queen Henrietta Maria arrived with 500 carts brimming with weapons and munitions. Her cortege crossed Heworth Moor, so Mary may have seized the opportunity to meet her. Early in 1643 the Royalists took Leeds, Bradford and Halifax, leaving only Hull in Parliamentary hands. Nobody felt threatened, and the strengthening of the city's medieval walls was carried out half-heartedly.

But this cosy complacency was shattered overnight when parliament formed an alliance with Scotland in September 1643. Suddenly York found itself in the front line, the prime target of any Scottish army marching south. When, therefore, 16,000 Scottish troops crossed the border in January 1644, the marquess of Newcastle had no option but to head north to thwart their advance – leaving York in the charge of John Bellasis, a prominent Catholic. A Catholic! As recently as 1642 York had been rocked by anti-Catholic demonstrations; now a Catholic was in command of the second city in the kingdom. It was striking evidence of the revolution in attitudes towards Catholicism in the Royalist camp. Not that it stopped the king levying fines on his Catholic supporters. The income had become indispensable for the Royalist cause.

However, the Royalist forces never got the chance to fight the Scots. A Parliamentary force of 5,000 men led by Sir Thomas Fairfax closed in on York from the south, and when John Bellasis failed to halt their advance in Selby, the marquess of Newcastle was forced into an ignominious race back to York before either Fairfax or the Scots got there first. Mary, who had avoided sieges across war-torn Europe, was being sucked into the vortex of the most significant siege of the English Civil War.

By April 1644, York's 13,000 civilians and 4,000 Royalist troops were largely surrounded. Too weak to mount a direct attack on the city, the Parliamentary forces seized strong points outside the walls, like St Nicholas Church, from which they could take pot shots at Royalist soldiers on Walmgate Bar,[5] the chief entrance into York from the east. As St Nicholas Church was only a mile or so from Heworth, Mary and her companions now left their house and joined other refugees within York itself, probably in a half-timbered house, with upper floors jutting out over the street as they still famously do in the Shambles. And yet stone was available in the man-made quarries furnished by the ruins of York's many former abbeys and priories,[6] not to mention the extensive ruins of St Leonard's hospital, once one of the largest medieval hospitals in the north of England. There had been no replacement for St Leonard's, so York would face its siege without the benefit of an established hospital.

For a while, an uneasy status quo was maintained, but the tables turned against the Royalists with the arrival of a further 9,000 Parliamentary soldiers under the earl of Manchester who took up positions in the hitherto unmanned north-east sector. The city was now fully surrounded and under fire from all sides. People shopping at St Sampson's market

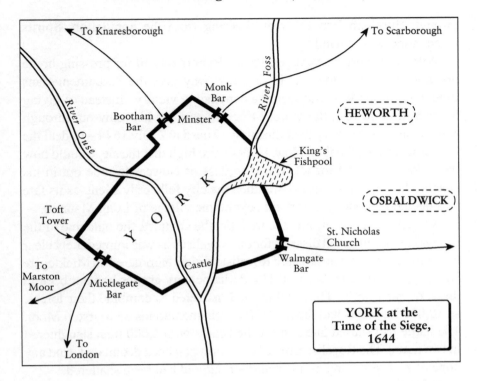

To Knaresborough

To Scarborough

River Foss

Monk
Bar

HEWORTH

Bootham
Bar

Minster

River Ouse

King's
Fishpool

OSBALDWICK

Toft
Tower

Y O R K

St. Nicholas
Church

To
Marston
Moor

Castle

Walmgate
Bar

Micklegate
Bar

YORK at the
Time of the Siege,
1644

To
London

dodged cannon balls; shells crashed through the windows of the minster and other churches where both Anglican and Catholic services were held. Livestock was brought inside the walls, and buildings just outside the city walls were blown up in order to deprive enemy snipers of cover. But still neither side appeared able to make a real breakthrough. Parliamentary soldiers dug a tunnel under the walls near Walmgate Bar, and made a breach in the abbey walls near Bootham Bar, but the defenders were able to repel both these attacks. The Royalists, for their part, tried to break the siege by bursting out of Monk Bar on 24 June, but they too were unsuccessful. All the defenders could now hope for was a Royalist relief force.

They did not have to wait long. In the last week in June there was jubilation for the people trapped within York when they received word that the king's cousin, Prince Rupert, was approaching the city from the south. Soon the Parliamentarian besiegers peeled away from the city walls to try and intercept the relief force, but Prince Rupert and his army outflanked them, and on 1 July Royalist soldiers streamed into the city through Bootham Bar, to great cheering from the population. Spirits lifted, hope was at hand.

With characteristic swagger, Prince Rupert was all for pressing home his advantage. The foe was in disarray: why give the Parliamentarians time to regroup? Why not secure a convincing victory? Instead of giving his men time to rest, therefore, Prince Rupert led his army out through Micklegate Bar the very next morning – Tuesday 2 July 1644 – to deal the Parliamentarians the fatal blow. Hopes were high that the siege could now be broken once and for all. The marquess of Newcastle rode out in his coach. The citizens cheered. And then the city fell eerily silent, as its fate was decided on boggy moorland beyond the village of Long Marston.

No victory, however, was secured. On the contrary, the outcome of the day was an unmitigated disaster for the Royalists, as was immediately clear that same evening when haggard Royalist soldiers hammered on Micklegate Bar, begging to be let back in. The Parliamentary armies had not been in disarray. Far from it. They had instead managed to combine their forces, so 18,000 Royalists had faced 28,000 Parliamentarians on Marston Moor. The battle had started late and finished early, with 6,000 men slaughtered in two hours. The Royalist army of the North had been decimated. And any hope of York surviving as a Royalist stronghold had been shattered.

Indeed there was a real danger now that the remnants of Prince Rupert's army might fall into Parliamentary hands, so the next morning he led his men, more a rabble than an army, out of the city through Monk Bar. The citizens of York looked on in silence, aghast, numb with fear and disbelief. Their helter-skelter from grim resistance to high hopes of victory and to bleakest despair had lasted less than forty-eight hours.

True, the city did not capitulate at once. The siege was renewed. But the defenders' spirit was broken. It was almost a mercy when Toft Tower on the city wall was so seriously damaged on 12 July that the city became technically indefensible. This allowed the marquess of Newcastle to surrender the city with honour. Any remaining Royalist soldiers were allowed to leave, and then the Parliamentary forces finally poured into the city. They sounded the death knell of the Royalist cause in the north of England, and indeed of the role that York had played for some 1,600 years as the northern capital of the nation.

As for Mary Ward, she decided to return to her house outside York. The 1-mile trip to Heworth in July 1644 was her last European journey. Death was just around the corner for her too.

25

Repose: Death and beyond
(1644–1645)

Many refugees never get the chance to go home; those who do face the ordeal of finding their home damaged and desecrated. Mary and her companions were no exceptions: her house, her biography tells us bluntly, was 'full of stinck and vermine.' The 400 Parliamentary soldiers who had been billeted there had defaced the walls, burned the furniture, broken the windows, and stripped the roof of its lead. Corpses lay strewn around the garden. If the 113 skeletons discovered outside the city walls in 2008 are anything to go by, the soldiers are more likely to have died of typhus than of war wounds.

The house that Mary and her companions returned to in July 1644 was therefore a serious health risk. However, there was nothing else for it but to clean the rooms, clear the garden and brace themselves for life under Parliamentary rule.

Changes were not long in coming. The mayor of York and six aldermen were dismissed. Sermons replaced Holy Communion as the central focus in church services. There was less church music, so the organ in York Minster was dismantled. The decree that Wednesday was a day of fasting, largely ignored in Royalist York, was more rigorously enforced. Foolhardy the prophet who would have forecast that the grim toll of executions of Catholic priests would now cease – but in fact fewer Catholic priests were executed under Oliver Cromwell than under Elizabeth, James or Charles.[1]

With York so focussed on its own problems, news of the death of Pope Urban VIII in July 1644 came like tidings from a distant planet. Few people in England could have named him, and Mary Ward and her companions were among the very few people in the whole kingdom who had actually met him. Mary, whose attitude towards Urban was ever one of reverence and obedience, will have prayed for his soul. She will not have known that his lavish spending on castles, wars and countless works of art had made him so unpopular with the people of Rome, who carried the tax burden, that they cheered and defaced his statue when his death was announced.[2]

As normal channels of communication had completely broken down, Mary had no news from Rome and Munich. Were the communities there still surviving? Had they been closed down? She had no means of knowing. So as her own health again deteriorated and autumn drew into winter, Mary asked Winefrid to make the journey to London to see if any letters were waiting for her there. Winefrid! Mary's staunchest friend was herself now 60 years old, but she set out at once. As Royalist support had crumbled across the east of England, she had no battle lines to cross, but she faced the usual dangers posed by marauders, deserters and disbanded soldiers.

With Winefrid gone, the little community in Heworth began to prepare for Christmas – or Christ-Tide, as it was now to be called. As Christ-Tide 1644 happened to fall on a Wednesday, the day of fasting, the authorities put a ban on dancing and excessive drinking and celebrating, and some authorities discouraged the eating of mince pies or the decorating of houses with holly, ivy and rosemary. Parliament set a sober example by listening to long sermons on Christmas Day.

Mary and her companions celebrated Christmas as best they could. They smuggled in a priest and invited local Catholics to Mass. Mary, though very weak, attended Midnight Mass on Christmas Eve and two services on Christmas Day. Of course, Mary had a track record of near-death experiences, but this time she herself conceded that this was 'something more than ordinary.' She was wracked with pain, and it was clear to all that the end was near.

A quietness descended on the house. By day the sisters carried out their duties, then they gathered around Mary's bed where she gently prepared them for life without her. Despite the sadness, there were still attempts at banter. 'If you die,' said one of the companions in an effort to chivvy

Mary, 'we shall take pack in lap and away to the heathen!' And later, when Mary saw the sadness in her companions' eyes, she playfully remonstrated 'Fye, fye, still look sad on it! Come, let us rather sing and praise God joyfully for his infinite loving kindness.' And she led them in song as far as her strength allowed.

Away in Westphalia negotiations to end the Thirty Years' War had begun; closer to home peace talks between Charles and parliament broke down. But the sisters in Heworth were too pre-occupied with Mary to register what was happening in the wider world. Their chief worry was that Mary might die before Winefrid returned with news from London, so great was their joy when Winefrid appeared on 16 January with letters from Winefrid Bedingfield in Munich and Barbara Babthorpe in Rome. Both houses, thank God, were thriving.[3] It was the best news Mary could have received. The two houses, along with the community in Heworth, represented the tangible outcome of her life's work.

Mary now began to prepare more actively for her death and for the survival of her Institute beyond it. The companions, understandably, could hardly conceive of the Institute without Mary at the helm, but Mary had no doubt that the Institute would flourish without her. 'God will assist and help you,' she reassured them, adding, in words of convincing simplicity: 'It is no matter the who, but the what.' And she appointed Barbara Babthorpe to be her successor.

On Monday, 30 January the companions gathered round Mary's bed for the last time. Winefrid Wigmore, Catherine Smith and Mary Poyntz were there from Mary's original companions; Frances Bedingfield and Catherine Dawson represented the younger generation. Mary's thoughts were with all the women who had committed themselves to her venture: 'I would *all* were here,' she said, and prayed for each one of them. She then embraced the women at her bedside, and left them a final command that, characteristically, combined utter commitment with gentle tenderness: 'I commend unto you the practice of your vocation,' she said, 'that it be constant, efficacious and affectionate.'

Affectionate! It was one of her last words. She lay in her bed for four more hours, then breathed her last. Her face, Mary Poyntz later wrote to Barbara Babthorpe, glowed with peace, joy and serenity to the end.

There was, then, no miracle at the eleventh hour, no last minute reprieve, no go-ahead from the new pope. Maligned, impoverished, unacknowledged, Mary died incognito in an obscure village far from the European courts in which she had pressed her case. Her sister Frances died the following year.

To an outside eye, the prospects for Mary's Institute looked bleak indeed. Most of her schools had been closed, the Institute as she had conceived it was still banned by the Catholic Church, and her surviving communities were scattered across three countries. Her successor was 1,300 miles away, unaware of her appointment. Even a Catholic burial was out of the question. The idea that a worldwide movement could arise from such ashes seemed laughable.

To an outside eye, but not to the companions. It would have been beyond them to explain *how* it would be achieved, but Mary's unwavering faith and irresistible charisma had nurtured such confidence in her followers that it never crossed their minds that they could let her down.

Their first job was to bury Mary – not an easy task, for with Parliamentary authorities breathing down their necks, Church of England vicars were wary of burying Catholics. Clearly, a measure of bribery would come in handy, and the fact that they approached the vicar of Osbaldwick shows that the companions had done their homework. For St Thomas's Church in Osbaldwick, a village about 2 miles outside York, was a classic example of the more corrupt practices of the Church of England.

The age-old practice whereby the tithe – the one-tenth of income exacted from parishioners – could be paid to an absentee rector (or priest) continued alive and well in the Church of England and parishes often suffered as a result. For example, absentee rectors often neglected their duty to maintain the chancel, the part of the church around the altar, which rectors were responsible for – and indeed inspections in Osbaldwick in 1575 and in 1596 found the chancel in such a state of advanced decay that services could not be held in the church.[4] Even more scandalously, absentee rectors could pocket the tithe and then pay a vicar or curate a pittance to hold services in their stead – and indeed the vicar's pay in Osbaldwick was so low that in 1638 he was officially classed as a pauper. This played into the hands of the Mary Ward sisters. It is not entirely clear whether the vicar was a Samuel Hollins with a large family to feed on his measly 16 shillings a year, or whether, as a different source suggests, Hollins had been replaced by a stand-in on even lower pay.[5] Either way, the sisters found that they were dealing with a man who, to use Mary Poyntz's delicate choice of words, was 'honest enough to be bribed.' Mary would be buried in Osbaldwick.

The times, we are so often told, were perilous for Catholics, so it does not take much imagination to picture the scene of the burial: by night, in secret, in a far corner of the graveyard, the grave left unmarked so as not to attract the unwanted attention of the Parliamentary authorities...

It comes as a shock, then, to read that on the contrary 'all the people round about eagerly assembled to accompany her body to burial, with much weeping, remembering her rare virtues and qualities.'[6] Interestingly, the crowd included both Catholics and Protestants.

And as for Mary's tombstone! One glance at it is enough to explode any notion that Mary's burial could have been hushed up. It stands almost two metres tall, with Mary's name on it for all to see. The Parliamentarians have a reputation for desecrating monuments, but this stone is whole and its 350-year old lettering remarkably legible.[7]

Having accompanied Mary for so long on her travels, it is moving indeed to enter St Thomas's Church in Osbaldwick and contemplate the stone that forms a tangible link back to her life. But the words on it – attributed to Mary Poyntz – are curious:

> To love the poore
> persever in the same
> live dy and Rise with
> them was all the ayme
> of
> Mary Ward who
> Having lived 60 years
> and 8 days dyed the
> 20 of Jan 1645[8]

No mention of schools, no mention of Mary's Institute on the Jesuit model? And why the repetition in second line of what has been asserted in the first:

> To love the poor
> 'And to persevere in doing this'
> was the aim of Mary Ward

189

But as in all good stories, the epitaph may be a riddle. Could its real meaning lie in the two words at the end of the second line (**the same**)? They are, after all, two of the most important words in the life of Mary Ward, taken from the instruction in Mary's vision: 'Take **the same** of the society.'

I like to believe that the second line has a different meaning: 'To love the poore / persever in **the same** / was the aim of Mary Ward' is a ringing assertion that 'to love the poor' and 'to persevere in her God-given mission to do **the same** for girls as the Jesuits did for boys' was the aim of Mary Ward.

Mary, I believe the epitaph tells us, stuck to her guns. And the clear implication was that her companions intended to do the same.

Rehabilitation: Unfinished business (1645–the present)

It was Mary's companions, then, who ensured the survival of her Institute.

Barbara Babthorpe kept it afloat as a joined-up organisation. Winefrid Wigmore and Catherine Smith opened a school in Paris. Mary Poyntz wrote Mary's biography. Then, after taking over the leadership of the Institute in 1654, she opened a new school in Augsburg – the first of the Institute's schools that has survived to this day. Pupils who alight at the *Englische Fräulein* tram stop today are greeted by a statue of Mary Poyntz in the school yard.[1]

Frances Bedingfield and three other sisters opened a school in London in 1669. One of their sponsors, Sir Thomas Gascoigne, enabled a community to settle in what is now a farmhouse at Dolebank, near Ripley in Yorkshire in 1677. Two sisters came from Germany; the other three were Helen, Catherine and Anne Thwenge, from Heworth. The seeds planted by Mary Ward were still bearing fruit.

It was Sir Thomas Gascoigne, too, who bequeathed Frances Bedingfield £450 to open a convent school in York. To do so, of course, was illegal – but, with all the cheek and bravado of Mary Ward herself, Frances went ahead anyway and set it up not in some hidden side-street, but next to Micklegate Bar, the main gateway into the city from London. Later known as the Bar Convent, it housed a boarding-school for girls, and, from 1699, a free day school too. Mary Ward, buried only a few miles away, will have smiled in her grave.

The Bar Convent sisters faced low-level threats of violence that could, at any moment, escalate into situations of real danger, so for their own protection they were addressed as Mrs (not Sister) and they lived, outwardly, the normal lives of ladies of their rank. But given that the institution was illegal, the Bar Convent enjoyed surprisingly cordial relations with the city authorities, the local Anglican churches and the citizens of York. Their premises were rarely searched for incriminating evidence of Catholic practice, or, if they were, the sisters were alerted in time for evidence to be hidden. When, in 1696, a drunken mob hurled stones and abuse at the Convent's front door, the city authorities offered to post a guard outside to avoid a repeat occurrence. And when a bout of anti-Catholic feeling led to Frances Bedingfield being imprisoned in 1694, she felt able to appeal for help to the archbishop of York, the second highest ranking figure in the Church of England: she was sure, she wrote, that had he been present, the archbishop would have 'prevented the ill-usage [she] met with.'[2]

This is extraordinary, for it was an age in which religious intolerance was raging across Europe. The Revocation of the Edict of Nantes in 1685 condemned thousands of Protestants to exile. The Macdonalds, thought to be Catholic sympathisers, were slaughtered in the Glencoe Massacre of 1692. And the prince-bishop of Salzburg expelled 20,000 Protestants after 1684, forcing many to leave their children behind. Yet Frances clearly knew her man, for Archbishop John Sharp ensured that release was soon granted.

The number of sisters in Hammersmith and York continued to rise, and in the 1760s the Bar Convent was able to commission the beautiful Georgian buildings that have survived in York to this day.[3]

Meanwhile the Mary Ward sisters were still seeking official papal recognition.

A petition sent to Rome in 1699 was supported by the bishops of Munich, Augsburg and Burghausen, who were impressed that the Mary Ward sisters had opened nine more schools in southern Germany and Austria. The petition was rejected.

A second petition in 1703 led to an arcane compromise: Pope Clement XI approved the rules of the Institute, without approving of the Institute as such.

Then, in April 1749 the Vatican came up with one of the most bizarre twists in the whole story: Pope Innocent XIV approved the office of general superior – so long as the sisters denied that their Institute had been founded by Mary Ward.

Anyone who has followed the story of Mary Ward will find it hard to read the last sentence without doing a double-take. Every step of her life screamed the fact that Mary Ward had founded, inspired and directed the Institute. What, then, lay behind the staggering proviso?

Vatican bureaucrats argued that Mary's Institute had been dissolved by Pope Urban VIII, and that the sisters who assembled in Rome after her imprisonment constituted a *different* association (even though they were the same women). And they argued that the rules approved in 1703 had been those submitted by the then superior, Mary Anne Babthorpe, *not* Mary's rules of 1621. More crucially, though, denying the role of Mary Ward gave Innocent XIV the fig-leaf with which to claim that his approval in no way undermined Pope Urban's Bull of 1632. It could be portrayed as applying to a different set of women entirely.

It was a bitter pill to swallow, but as loyal Catholics the sisters understood the pope's dilemma, and they felt sure that Mary would not have flinched from sacrificing herself for the good of the institute.

And so the shabby deal was done. The Vatican airbrushed Mary Ward from its archives. The paintings of the *Painted Life* series were taken down, and the sisters were obliged to destroy any portraits they had of Mary, and to burn any letters or documents in which Mary's name appeared. Books that linked Mary to her Institute were banned. Markus Fridl's biography of the Institute, published in 1732, was put on the index of banned books in 1751 – where it remained till 1928. All new accounts of the Institute toed the new line. John Nicholas Murphy's book of 1876 is a good example. It unabashedly claims: 'Some writers erroneously state that Mrs Mary Ward was the foundress. So far is this from being the case, that Mrs Ward never had any connection with the Institute.'[4]

Never had any connection with the Institute! Who says that fake news began in the twenty-first century?

Did the sisters, in their heart of hearts, believe this twisted version of events? I am, of course, reluctant to believe that they did – and by good fortune there is evidence that they did not. For in the early 1800s an Englishman by the name of John Barrow comes trundling into our story. While travelling through Bavaria, Barrow is surprised to hear talk of an English nunnery in Augsburg and decides to investigate. He is told by the superior that it was founded 'by an English lady by the name of Mary Ward,' and that 'in all Bavaria there are not fewer than eight or nine nunneries established by the same Mary Ward, whose name, at least, must be as well known in that country, as that of the benevolent Mrs. Fry is in England, though ... miss known to ... myself.'[5]

Barrow's disarming frankness about his utter ignorance of Mary Ward is proof of his impartiality, so the record of his chance visit is evidence that the sisters kept Mary's name alive in the belief that Rome would come round to their way of thinking in the end.

It took a while. In 1877 Pope Pius IX approved the Institute as such but still with the proviso that Mary Ward had played no role in her Institute. But a new thirst for truth was abroad, and Mary Chambers' two volume biography of Mary's life, published in 1885, rendered the Vatican line untenable. And finally, on 20 April 1909, Pope Pius X recognised the Institute with Mary as its foundress: 'there is no longer anything against that Institute,' read the decree, '(nor against) being able to acknowledge, in public too, Mary Ward as its foundress.'

It had taken 250 years, but at last the faith of generations of sisters who had never doubted Mary's vision was vindicated. The greatest tribute to them is that when approval came, they had with no help from the Vatican built up their Institute to the point where it could boast of 6,000 sisters working in 200 houses, teaching 70,000 girls.

Papal recognition of Mary Ward was more than just homage to a courageous woman whose vision had been ahead of its time; it signified a new attitude towards the role of women culminating, in the decision at Vatican II (1962–1965) to leave the issue of enclosure to the women themselves. Nuns who wish to live in enclosure can do so, those who wish to relax it or give it up entirely are free to do so.

It all sounds so easy, so sensible. Yet this was the freedom for which Mary Ward had had to struggle.

Today, Mary Ward sisters are active in some forty countries.[6] Many of their schools are for both boys and girls and integrated into the state system,[7] and the sisters have diversified into other activities too – delivering safe baby milk in Zambia, funding shelters for young women in Kenya and Vietnam, housing asylum seekers in Australia, providing meals and medical care in Cuba, Moldavia and Canada – work for which they were awarded United Nations NGO status in 2002.

And Mary Ward still has an uncanny knack of popping up in connection with women's long march towards equality. When in 1993 the University of Augsburg presented its first honorary degree to a woman (after honouring twenty men), the woman was Immolata Wetter, the chief superior of the Institute, and her topic was *Mary Ward: Misunderstandings and Clarifications*. When in 2007 the Yorkshire Society honoured its first woman with a blue plaque (after honouring fifteen Yorkshiremen) the woman was Mary Ward, and her plaque was put up next to the entrance to the Bar Convent.

Remarkably, too, for someone who promoted the Catholic faith during her lifetime, Mary Ward has morphed into a figure of ecumenical reconciliation. With a nod to the ecumenical crowd that attended her funeral in 1645, Catholics and non-Catholics alike commemorate her life each January in the Anglican church of St Thomas in Osbaldwick. A celebration of her life in York Minster in 2009 was the first time the head of the Catholic Church in England had celebrated Mass in this Anglican cathedral since the Reformation. And it somehow seemed appropriate, on my visit to the Bar Convent in 2015, that the voices I heard filling the chapel with song should be those of a Presbyterian choir from Korea.

For all this, Mary Ward's rehabilitation within the Catholic Church itself is still not complete. The process of recognising Mary Ward as a saint has been grinding on for more than a 100 years now, as slowly and as tortuously as did the issue of approval of her Institute. In 2009 Mary moved forward a notch when she was declared venerable.

In one way, of course, this matters not a whit. Mary would probably only smile if she knew that she was still causing the men in the Vatican a head-ache. The Mary Ward sisters take it with a smile too. 'The Church has apologised for its treatment of Galileo and there is a statue of him in Rome,' says Sister Gemma Simmonds, adding: 'We are still waiting ... .'[8]

In any case, the Mary Ward sisters know a saint when they see one, and the website of the Mary Ward school in Kolkata already honours Mary Ward as its patron saint. And why not? Rome has a track record of catching up with them in the end.

We end where we began.

We are in a largely illiterate society with a few schools for boys but none for girls. Men make all the decisions. Wives submit. Girls are married off at a young age, their husbands chosen by their fathers – who receive handsome dowries in return. If the girls refuse, they are punished. It has always been thus.

And then a group of Mary Ward sisters arrives on the scene. They open the first school for girls. The number of pupils grows and the girls realise that their futures can be different. Not all of them will complete their schooling because some will be forcibly married off – but those who make it through to graduation will go out into society and make their mark, each one in her own way.

The description would fit any one of Mary Ward's schools in St Omer, Liège, Cologne, Trier, Rome, Naples, Munich, Vienna and Bratislava. In fact, it describes the first secondary school in the Rumbek region of South Sudan, opened by Mary Ward sisters in 2008. Mary's message that 'there is no such difference between men and women that women may not do great things ... And I hope in God that it will be seen that women in time to come will do much' is as relevant in South Sudan today as it was in Europe in her lifetime.

And not only in South Sudan. Two thirds of the world's 750 million illiterate adults are women.[9] There are more than forty countries in which fewer than 25 per cent of girls attend secondary school. And 54 per cent of the world's 72 million children who have no basic education are girls.[10] So there is still a crying need for Mary's vision of motivating and empowering women to transform their lives and liberate the forces of good in their society.

And yet, of course, we do not end where we began.

Wonderfully, society in most parts of the world has progressed, and women have opportunities to flourish and contribute to society as never before. The example from South Sudan is a reminder that this unlocking of the potential of the female half of humanity has not just 'happened'. It has been fostered, nurtured, furthered by the work and sacrifice of hosts of men and women, for the benefit of both men and women – and one of the many who deserve more recognition for what they achieved is Mary Ward.

Endnotes

Chapter 1

1. The term recusant usually refers to Roman Catholics who refused to conform to the practices of the Anglican Church. Protestants who refused to conform are more commonly referred to as non-conformists.
2. Pursuivants were the men charged with arresting suspected Catholics.
3. Karen Liebreich, *Fallen Order* (New York: Grove Press, 2004) p. 232.
4. Laurence Lux-Sterritt, *Redefining Female Religious Life: French Ursulines and English Ladies in Seventeenth-Century Catholicism* (Aldershot: Ashgate, 2005), pp. 9-27.
5. Patrick Collinson, *Elizabethan Essays* (London: Hambleton Press, 1994), p. 127.
6. The following are the most authoritative biographies of Mary Ward. The authors are all sisters in the order set up by Mary Ward.

   Mary Catherine Chambers, *The Life of Mary Ward in Two Volumes* (London: Burns and Oates, 1882);

   Henriette Peters, *Mary Ward: A World in Contemplation* (Leominster: Gracewing, 1994);

   Margaret Mary Littlehales, *Mary Ward, Pilgrim and Mystic* (London: Burns and Oats, 2001);

   M. Immolata Wetter, *Mary Ward, Under the Shadow of the Inquisition* (Oxford: Way Books, 2006).

   Mary Ward herself wrote two accounts of parts of her life and also wrote a large number of letters. Her most important writings have been collected in *Till God Will*, edited Gillian Orchard Gillian (London: Darton, Longman and Todd Ltd, 1985)

   Mary Poyntz wrote a biography – called *A Briefe Relation* – within a few years of Mary's death.

A further source of information is *The Painted Life:* a remarkable series of fifty paintings depicting the life of Mary Ward that survives in the *Englische Fräulein* school in Augsburg. Some were painted before 1680, so are likely to have been commissioned by sisters who knew Mary Ward during her lifetime. They can be seen online at http://www.congregatiojesu.org/en/maryward_painted_life.asp.

7. Gemma Simmonds, *Mary Ward: A Spiritual Journey*, BBC York and North Yorkshire, Monday, 21 December 2009.

Chapter 2

1. Née Wright. Ursula Dirmeier: *Mary Ward und ihre Gründung, Die Quellentexte bis 1645* (Münster: Aschendorff Verlag, 2007), Vol. 4, p. 270.
2. Selby Abbey was unused and decaying in 1605, but re-established as a parish church in 1618.
3. Probably from the old Latin Vulgate Bible. Contrary to widely-held belief, the Catholic Church produced an English-language Bible, called the Douay-Reims Bible. It was, however, difficult to smuggle it into England.
4. GENUKI, https://www.genuki.org.uk/big/eng/YKS/ERY/Hemingbrough/Hemingbrough92, Original source: *History, Topography & Directory of East Yorkshire* (Preston, T. Bulmer & Co, 1892), p. 631.

   The same hierarchy dictated that non-conforming Protestants were not hanged, but burned at the stake – the fate of Anne Askew, for example, burned at Smithfield in London in 1546.
5. Littlehales, *Mary Ward, Pilgrim and Mystic*, p. 30.
6. *Painted Life* (see Chapter 1, Note 6).

Chapter 3

1. Spink, *The Gunpowder Plot and Lord Mounteagle's Letter* (London: Simpkin Marshall Hamilton Kent & Co Ltd, 1902) p. 71.
2. Ibid.
3. With a population of something over 200,000 London was perhaps the fourth largest city in Europe after Istanbul, Paris and Naples.
4. Stephen Porter, *Shakespeare's London* (Stroud: Amberley Publishing, 2011), p. 13, quoting Jacob Rathgeb, *Wahrhafte*

Beschreibung zweyer Reisen in 1599 (1604), translated by William B. Rye (*England as Seen by Foreigners*) (London: J.R. Smith, 1865).

5. St Martin's in the Fields was indeed in the fields.

6. In some accounts, Richard Holtby's opposition to Mary's desire to become a nun begins in Osgodby. Christina Kenworthy-Browne (ed.), *Mary Ward, 1585–1645: A Briefe Relation, with Autobiographical Fragments and a Selection of Letters* (Woodbridge: Boydell and Brewer for the Catholic Record Society, 2008).

7. Quoted in Mary Catherine Chambers, *The Life of Mary Ward in Two Volumes* (London: Burns and Oates, 1882), p. 93.

8. Littlehales, *Mary Ward, Pilgrim and Mystic*, p. 35, quoting from Mary Poyntz and Winefrid Wigmore, *Briefe Relation*, c. 1650, p.8.

9. After her father's execution, Margaret Roper had retrieved Thomas More's head from London Bridge, and had brought it back to be placed it in the Roper family vault in St Dunstan's Church in Canterbury. Pilgrims to the shrine of Thomas More have flocked through St Dunstan's Church ever since – some maybe pausing for thought in the south aisle at the monument to Claude Rondeau, a Huguenot 'refugee in England for the Protestant religion'.

Chapter 4

1. Winefrid Wigmore's *Italian Life* quoted in Henriette Peters, *Mary Ward: A World in Contemplation* (Leominster: Gracewing, 1994), Foreword.

2. E.S. Bates, *Touring in 1600* (Boston and New York: Houghton Mifflin, 1911) p. 63; touringinastudy00conggoog. OCLC/WorldCat 01290825.

3. Marie-Amélie Le Bourgeois, *Les Ursulines d'Anne de Xainctonge* (1606) (Saint-Etienne: Publications de l'Université de Saint-Etinne, 2003), p. 107; https://books.google.tt/books?id=d-be6kVffXwC&printsec=frontcover&source=gbs_atb#v=onepage&q&f=false.

4. Eileen Power, *Medieval English Nunneries* (New York: Biblo and Tannen, 1964), p. 341. Original in French; https://www.gutenberg.org/files/39537/39537-h/39537-h.htm#Page_341.

5. Jesuits made a point of mastering the local languages, which in St Omer meant Flemish, Picard and Walloon dialects as well as French and Spanish. St Omer's councillors gave their edicts in

Flemish as late as 1507, and villagers in nearby Bourbourg were still speaking Flemish in 1800.
6. Power, *Medieval English Nunneries*, p. 4.
7. The village, now in France, goes by the French name of Esquelbecq.

Chapter 5

1. Jacques Van Wijnendaele, *Promenades insolites dans Bruxelles disparu* (Brussels: Editions Racine, 2008), pp. 58, 72.
2. Jakob Rathgeb, on journey in 1599, quoted in Antje Stannek, *Telemachs Brüder: die höfische Bildungsreise des 17. Jahrhunderts* (Frankfurt/New York: Campus Verlag, 2001), p. 65; https:// books.google.co.uk/books?id=MEx0lSYJHg8C&printsec= frontcover&source=gbs_ge_summary_r&cad= 0#v=onepage&q&f=false.
3. French wiki entry: Couvent des Dames de Berlaymont.
4. Chambers, *Life of Mary Ward*.
5. Quote from Chambers, *Life of Mary Ward*. See also Peter Guilday, *The English Catholic refugees on the Continent 1558–1795* (London: Longmans, Green, 1914), p. 166; https://archive.org/details/ englishcatholicr00guiluoft/page/166/mode/2up?q=Mary+Ward.
6. Henry Kamen, *European Society 1500–1700* (London: Hutchinson, 1984). p. 40.

Chapter 6

1. And this despite the role models of Archduke Isabella and Elizabeth I!
2. 'Mary Ward: Holiness', talk given by Pamela Ellis, first published in *The Tablet*, 24 January 2009.
3. Jerome, *Commentary on the Epistle of the Ephesians, III, 5*, quoted in Karen Armstrong, *The acts of Paul and Thecla,* in *Feminist Theology, A Reader*, edited by Ann Loades (Louisville, Kentucky: Westminster John Knox Press, 1990), p. 87.
4. Michael Kelly (ed.), *This Time in the Church* (Adelaide: ATF Theology, 2015), p. 63.
5. Janet Burton, *The Yorkshire Nunneries in the 12th & 13th Centuries*, Borthwick Papers, no. 56 (1979), p. 2.
6. I Corinthians 14: 34–37.

7. Béguinages existed outside Flanders too: Cologne is said to have had 169 béguinages, with 1,170 resident women, in the fourteenth century. In the Netherlands, béguine communities usually had their own church, cemetery and hospital, with walkways lined with cottages for the younger sisters and pupils, and larger houses for the well-to-do. Béguine communities in Germany and Italy lived by different rules, often in single houses.

8. An example of how pressure was brought to bear is the case of the Haus zum Lämmlein, a béguine community in Solothurn in Switzerland. The pope's nuncio (or ambassador) to Switzerland urged the béguines to 'reform' in the spirit of the Council of Trent; but when the women realised that 'reform' meant enclosure and life-long vows of chastity and obedience, they refused to go along with it. And when the nuncio sent sisters from a nearby convent to impose his reforms, the béguines threw them out. The nuncio and the béguines asked the pope to adjudicate – and he ordained that the existing béguines should be allowed to remain as they were, but without taking on any new sisters, while a new 'reformed' convent with full enclosure was to be established in a new building. The effect of this 'compromise' was of course that in time the béguines were doomed to disappear. Website of the *Frauenkloster Namen Jesu*, Geschichte / 17. Jh. / Gründung: http://www.namenjesu.ch/geschichte/17-jh/gruendung/index.htm.

9. There is some dispute about the age of Mary Poyntz. Gillian Orchard (ed.), *Till God Will* (London: Darton, Longman and Todd Ltd, 1985), p. 28, note 12.

10. Winefrid had three brothers who were Jesuit priests and two sisters who were nuns, Susanna Rookwood's home at Coldham Hall was riddled with priest holes to provide for their escape, and Mary Poyntz's father Edward was on a government list of known recusants.

11. Alum came from the pope's works near Rome, with production from rival works in Yorkshire only starting in 1606.

12. Littlehales, *Mary Ward, Pilgrim and Mystic*, p. 60.

Chapter 7

1. Mary Poyntz and Winefrid Wigmore, *Briefe Relation*, c. 1650 quoted in Orchard, *Till God Will*, p. 29.

2. A hill where pagans had worshipped in the mists of time, it had been appropriated by the Church, and Albert and Isabella had recently raised its profile by having a new chapel built there.
3. Mary Ward letter to Nuncio Albergati.
4. Silvia Evangelisti, *Nuns: A History of Convent Life* (Oxford: Oxford University Press, 2007), p. 214.
5. Mary Ward put this argument at the opening of a letter to Isabella in September 1612 (Papiers *d'Etat et de F Audience at Brussels,* Liasse, 466), quoted in Chambers, *Life of Mary Ward.*

Chapter 8

1. Henry Barrow, John Greenwood and John Penry.
2. Neil MacGregor, *Shakespeare's Restless World* (London: Penguin, 2014), p. 174.
3. Christopher Lee, *1603* (New York: St Martin's Press, 2003), p. 3.
4. Dom Hugh Aveling, *Post Reformation Catholicism in East Yorkshire, 1558–1790* (East Yorkshire Local History Society, 1960).
5. A.P. Baggs, G.H.R. Kent and J.D. Purdy, 'Hemingbrough: Osgodby', in *A History of the County of York East Riding: Volume 3, Ouse and Derwent Wapentake, and Part of Harthill Wapentake*, edited by K.J. Allison (London, 1976), pp. 64-66; *British History Online:* http://www.british-history.ac.uk/vch/yorks/east/vol3/pp64-66.
6. All this paragraph: Jack Binns, *Yorkshire in the 17th Century*, Blackthorn History of Yorkshire, Volume 7 (Pickering: Blackthorn Press, 2007).
7. Lee, *1603*, pp. 223-224.
8. Chambers, *Life of Mary Ward*, p. 44.
9. The Gatehouse Prison, or possibly the Clink Prison next to the bishop of Winchester's palace in Southwark.
10. Caroline Bicks, *Staging the Jesuitess in* 'A Game at Chess', *Studies in English Literature, 1500–1900* (Houston: Rice University, 2009). 'A Game at Chess' is a comic satirical play by Thomas Middleton, first staged in August 1624 by the King's Men at the Globe Theatre, and notable for its political content.
11. The gate was on the site of the street now called *Am Alten Einlass*.
12. Thomas Coryate, *Crudities Hastily Gobbled Up in Five Months* (Whitefish, Montana: Kessinger Publishing, 2007).

Chapter 9

1. And on one of her journeys back to St Omer, Mary brought her sister Elizabeth to join the Institute as a novice.
2. Peter Guilday, *The English Catholic refugees on the Continent 1558–1795* (London: Longmans, Green, 1914), Chapter V1, p. 163; https://archive.org/details/englishcatholicr00guiluoft/page/166/mode/2up?q=Mary+Ward.
3. A son of the former lord treasurer of England and a well-known recusant.
4. Simon Caldwell, 'The First Sister of Feminism', *The Independent,* 11 June 2009.
5. So notorious, indeed, that the English Government tried to reduce its popularity by promoting rival, home-grown spas in Bath, Buxton and Harrogate.

Chapter 10

1. The Spanish branch of the family governed Spain, southern Italy, Milan and the Spanish Netherlands; the Austrian branch ruled the Austrian lands and Hungary. In 1619 Ferdinand of Austria also became the elected emperor of all the German lands.
2. Personal allegiances also crossed the religious divide. Protestants Jan Hoeufft and Barthélemy d'Herwarth financed the armies of Catholic France; Hans de Witte, another Protestant, supplied the wages, weaponry and ammunition Catholic armies in Central Europe. Count Mansfeld, a Catholic, was the commander of Protestant armies.
3. Letter from Father Silisdon to Father Owen, 31 October, 1614, quoted in John Morris and John Gerard, *The Condition of Catholics under James I* (London: Longmans, Green & Co, 1872), p. ccii; https://books.google.co.uk/books?id=obNSAAAAcAAJ&pg=PA161&source=gbs_toc_r&cad=4#v=onepage&q=his%20zeal%20will%2C%20I%20fear%2C%20carry%20him%20too%20far&f=false.
4. Axel Gotthard, *In der Ferne. Die Wahrnehmung des Raums in der Vormoderne* (Frankfurt: Campus Verlag, 2007) p. 17.

Chapter 11

1. Saxony, Brandenburg and the Palatinate were Protestant. The king of Bohemia and the prince-archbishops of Mainz, Trier and Cologne were Catholic.
2. Edwin Burton (ed.), *Douay Diaries*, Vol. I (Catholic Record Society, 1911), p. 397.
3. Matthias replaced Judas Iscariot as one of the twelve.

Chapter 12

1. The Valtellina has access to four Alpine passes: the Bernina, Splügen, Maloja and Stelvio.
2. Daniel Peter, *Riedseltz History, Pages Of History*: http://freepages. genealogy.rootsweb.ancestry.com/~gartner/riedseltz-history.htm.
3. Nick Warlow and Angela Michel, *Freedom to Rome* (Singapore: Skylark Press, prepared and printed by York Publishing Services Ltd, 2013).
4. Venetian ambassador Foscarini in 1613 quoted in Bates, *Touring in 1600*.
5. William Bray, *The Diary of John Evelyn from 1641 to 1705–6*, p. 342.
6. Thomas Coryat, *Coryat's Crudities: Hastily Gobled up in Five Moneth's Travels,* 1611 quoted by Seminar M. Marti, 'British and American Visitors in Switzerland: History of Tourism in Switzerland', Department of English, University of Basel: https://shine.unibas.ch/swisstour.html.
7. Bates, *Touring in 1600*.
8. Isabella had ordered her representative in Rome, Juan Bautista Vives, to organise the meeting.

Chapter 13

1. 'Houses of Benedictine nuns: Priory of St Clement, York' in *A History of the County of York: Volume 3*, edited by William Page (London: Victoria County History, 1974), pp. 129-131; *British History Online*: http://www.british-history.ac.uk/vch/yorks/vol3/pp129-131.
2. Porter, *Shakespeare's London*, p. 155.

3. A measure of its power is that it gave the world a new word: *propaganda*.
4. They included Margaret Genison, Mary Ratcliffe, Elizabeth Cotton, Mary Clayton and Elizabeth Keyes.
5. Peters, *A World in Contemplation*, p. 382.

Chapter 14

1. John Tillotson, *Marrick Priory: A Nunnery in Late Medieval Yorkshire*, *History of the Medieval Monastic Foundation of St Mary's Thicket Priory* (York: Carmelite Monastery, Thicket Priory, 1989).
2. James E. Kelly (ed.), *English Convents in Exile 1600–1800* (Abingdon: Routledge, 2013), p. 17.
3. Dom Basil Whelan, *Historic English Convents of Today* (London: Burns and Oates, 1936), p. 94.
4. John Vasa, Prince-Bishop of Warmia in Poland.
5. Eileen Power, *Medieval English Nunneries c. 1275 to 1535*, p. 345.
6. Ibid, p. 351.
7. Ibid, p. 346, quoting Thiers, De la cloture, preface.
8. Caroline Bicks, *Producing Girls on the English Stage* in *Gender and Early Modern Constructions of Childhood*, edited by Naomi J. Miller and Naomi Yavneh (Farnham: Ashgate Publishing, Ltd., 2011), p. 145;
  https://books.google.co.uk/books?id=9_Qh5CEZKSkC&pg=PA145&lpg=PA145&dq=now+publicly,+now+privately,+now+many+together,+now+alone,+among+men,+seculars,+and+not+seldom+of+bad+morals&source=bl&ots=MT_vnhSvnd&sig=ACfU3U3ww9JmFE5uG-nGkVx2-SPJ7b_sSw&hl=en&sa=X&ved=2ahUKEwjr9Ovj0pvtAhXlrnEKHR1NApIQ6AEwAHoECAEQAg#v=onepage&q=now%20publicly%2C%20now%20privately%2C%20now%20many%20together%2C%20now%20alone%2C%20among%20men%2C%20seculars%2C%20and%20not%20seldom%20of%20bad%20morals-&f=false.
9. Burton, *Douay Diaries*, p. 397.
10. Caroline Bicks, *Staging the Jesuitess in* 'A Game at Chess', in *Studies in English Literature, 1500–1900,* Vol. 49, No. 2, Tudor and Stuart Drama (Houston: Rice University, 2009), p. 464.

Chapter 15

1. We do not know for sure when the plan was formed – maybe during her stay with the Grand Duchess Maria Magdalena at the Palazzo Pitti in Florence. Maria Magdalena's mother-in-law Christina was the sister of Elisabeth Renata of Bavaria, the wife of Duke Maximilian whose ear she wished to bend.
2. The long-distance *Via Spluga* footpath follows this dramatic old road through the gorge.
3. Sales soared to 117,424 gallons of beer in 1605, and in 1607 production moved to the larger *Hofbräuhaus am Platzl*, where it continues to this day.
4. Ulrike Strasser, *State of Virginity: Gender, Religion, and Politics* (Ann Arbor: University of Michigan Press, 2004), p. 18; https://books.google.co.uk/books?id=W09QHQS4yRYC&pg=PA18&lpg=PA18&dq=%22the+first+true+absolutist+ruler+in+the+Holy+Roman+Empire%22&source=bl&ots=KnmrXb-uPl&sig=ACfU3U2RzSj32hqGMr074VSLFBS3L5-asg&hl=en&sa=X&ved=2ahUKEwi6xpyQ2pvtAhUVEcAKHWvEAo8Q6AEwAHoECAEQAg#v=onepage&q=%22the%20first%20true%20absolutist%20ruler%20in%20the%20Holy%20Roman%20Empire%22&f=false.
5. A bridge and a metro station are named after him in Munich today.
6. *Hostienfrevel* (1624) by Peter Candid, now in the store of diocesan paintings in Freising, was shown at the *Stadt Ohne Juden* exhibition in Munich in May 2010.
   http://www.sueddeutsche.de/kultur/muenchen-stadt-ohne-juden-die-finstere-seite-1.690870-2.

Chapter 16

1. The part of Hungary not occupied by the Ottomans.
2. The city was then more usually called Pressburg (in German) or Pozsony (in Hungarian).
3. David P. Daniel, *Lutheranism in the Kingdom of Hungary*, in *Lutheran Ecclesiastical Culture: 1550–1675*, edited by R. Kolb (Leiden: Brill, 2008); https://doi.org/10.1163/ej.9789004166417.i-533, p. 487.
4. Walter Nigg, *Maria Ward, eine Frau gibt nicht auf* (Zürich: Rüffer & Rub Sachbuchverlag, 2012), p. 114. Original in German.

5. As related by the English traveller John Bargrave, in his travels in Rome in the 1640s. John Bargrave, *Pope Alexander the Seventh and the College of Cardinals*, edited by James Craigie Robertson (reprint 2009), pp. 34, 35.
6. Peters, *A World in Contemplation*, p. 456; Littlehales, *Mary Ward, Pilgrim and Mystic*, p. 172.
7. Present day Cheb.

Chapter 17

1. 100,000 soldiers, according to Ciro Paoletti, *A Military History of Italy* (Santa Barbara, California: Praeger, ABC-Clio, 2007), p. 27; https://books.google.co.uk/books?i,d=Uz8eiwzEMHQC&pg=PA23&source=gbs_toc_r&cad=3#v=onepage&q&f=false.
2. Christina Kenworthy-Browne, *A Briefe Relation*.

Chapter 18

1. Augsburg, for example, had more than five times the usual number of deaths in 1628, and its population collapsed from 45,000 to 16,400 between 1618 and 1635.
2. Christine Rogler, '*Die Freisinger Hexenverfolgung von 1590*', *Fink Magazin* (Freising: Fink Media, 28 Oktober 2015): http://www.fink-magazin.de/die-freisinger-hexenverfolgung-von-1590/; Ellwangen city website, https://www.ellwangen.de/index.php?id=65; Katja Auer, *Bambergs dunkle Vergangenheit*, Süddeutsche Zeitung, https://www.sueddeutsche.de/bayern/dokumentation-der-hexenverfolgung-bambergs-dunkle-vergangenheit-1.1822632; Wolfgang Behringer, *Witchcraft Persecutions in Bavaria* (Cambridge: Cambridge University Press, 1997), p. 308.
3. Adam Contzen, for example, defended the persecution of witches in his book *Methodus Civilis* (1628).
4. Decio Carafa was archbishop of Naples when Mary arrived there to set up her school; Carlo Carafa was the nuncio in Prague that the Vatican considered too meek.
5. In 1623 Philipp von Sötern had taken over from Mary's supporter, Lothar von Metternich.
6. Littlehales, *Mary Ward*, Pilgrim and Mystic, p. 197.
7. Sister M. Gregory Kirkus, *The Companions* (Eckbolsheim: Editions du Signe, 2009), p. 21.

8. Henriette Peters, *Mary Ward, A World in Contemplation,* pp. 526-527.
9. Galileo was not shown any written evidence either.
10. Littlehales, *Mary Ward,* Pilgrim and Mystic, p. 213.

Chapter 19

1. *St. Mary's Convent, Micklegate Bar York (1686–1887)* edited by Henry J. Coleridge, (London: Burns and Oates, 1887), p. 103; https://archive.org/stream/stmarysconventm00convgoog/stmarysconventm00convgoog_djvu.txt.
2. Immolata Wetter, *Mary Ward's Apostolic Vocation* (Oxford: The Way, supplement 17, 1972), pp. 70-71, note 4, quoting J. Morey, *Anne de Xainctonge* (Paris/Besançon, 1892), pp. 30-31; https://www.theway.org.uk/back/s017Wetter.pdf.
3. Sioban Nelson, 'The Modern Nurse in 17th Century France', edited by Joan E Lynaugh, *Nursing History Review,* 7 (1999), p. 175; https://epdf.pub/nursing-history-review-volume-7-1999-official-publication-of-the-american-associ.html.
4. Lux-Sterritt, *Redefining Female Religious Life,* p. 54.
5. Liebrich, *Fallen Order,* pp. 69, 116.

Chapter 21

1. Jeffrey S. Gaab, *Munich, Hofbräuhaus and History: Beer, Culture, and Politics* (New York: Peter Lang, 2006), p. 15; https://books.google.co.uk/books?id=-X4jgPG0360C&pg=PA17&source=gbs_toc_r&cad=3#v=onepage&q&f=false.
2. Princes Wilhelm and Bernhard of Saxe-Weimar set an example by stealing valuable books and manuscripts from Maximilian's *Residenz,* returning the compliment on the duke who had plundered Frederick's library in Heidelberg.
3. Stadtarchiv München, *Historischer Verein von Oberbayern*: http://www.muenchen.de/rathaus/Stadtverwaltung/Direktorium/Stadtarchiv/Stadtgeschichte1/Stadtgeschichte.html.

Chapter 22

1. The citizens of Munich blamed the 'dirty' Spaniards for the disease, the Italians blamed the 'dirty' German soldiers who had marched on Mantua: 'Most of these Germans are infected with plague because

of their wantonness and dirtiness,' noted an Italian Public Health officer. Carlo Cipolla, *Christofano and the Plague* (Berkeley: University of California Press, 1973), p. 15.

2. Cipolla, *Christofano and the Plague*, p. 20.
3. Wetter, *Under the Shadow of the Inquisition*, p. 97.
4. Ibid., p. 99.
5. Ibid., p. 163.
6. Kirkus, *The Companions*, pp. 12, 107.
7. Catholic Encyclopaedia, www.newadvent.org.
8. Immolata Wetter, *Under the Shadow of the Inquisition*, p. 142.
9. Ibid., p. 146.
10. Ibid., p. 174.
11. Ibid., p. 179.

Chapter 23

1. Guido Bentivoglio, *A Collection of Letters to Divers Persons of Eminence* (Livorno: Tommaso Masi, 1721), p. 241; https://books.google.co.uk/books?id=w3z3qu7mVssC&pg=PA241&dq=Collection+of+Letters+Written+by+Cardinal+Bentivoglio&hl=en&sa=X&ved=2ahUKEwja7ora_53tAhWFQxUIHTbfDgsQ6AEwAHoECAUQAg#v=onepage&q=Collection%20of%20Letters%20Written%20by%20Cardinal%20Bentivoglio&f=false.
2. The hefty fees charged by the Stockalper family, for example, who controlled the Simplon pass from Italy to Switzerland, paid for their golden-domed castle that still stands in Brig.
3. Kamen, *European Society*, p. 38, quoting *Histoire de Dix Ans de la Franche-Comté de Bourgogne* by Girardot de Nozeroy.
4. Mary was also short of money. She had hoped to tap into funds from England, but as the records of the English Benedictine monastery in Paris put it, 'Mrs Marie Warde, Mrs Marie Poynes and Mrs Whinfrid Wigmore were ... disappointed of moneys.' The monks stepped into the breach, and lent the women the very large sum of £50. The sum was later paid back.
5. Istanbul vied with Beijing for the title of largest city in the world.
6. The Pont Neuf (1607) was the first bridge free of houses and the first fitted with a pavement to allow pedestrians to avoid soiling their shoes with horse muck.

7. A large number of such palaces were going up in the up-and-coming district that we have come to call the Marais.
8. Between Charleville and Dinant.
9. Guilday, *English Catholic Refugees.*
10. Littlehales, *Mary Ward, Pilgrim and Mystic*, p. 198.
11. The meeting with Frances was not the only reunion. Winefrid Wigmore met her sister Helen, and Mary will have chatted with Chrysogona Wakeman, who had worked in the Institute house in Naples. She had joined the English Carmelites when the school in Naples was forced to close.

Chapter 24

1. David Cressy, 'Revolutionary England 1640–1642', *Past and Present*, 181 (Nov. 2003), p. 49.
2. From 6,000,000 in 1603 to almost 8,000,000 in the 1640s.
3. Cressy, 'Revolutionary England 1640–1642', p. 64.
4. Often spelt Thwing.
5. In York, the streets are called gates and the town gates are called bars.
6. Not only the enormous ruins of St Mary's Abbey that still dominate the Museum Gardens, but seven acres of ruins of the former Benedictine abbey in Micklegate, and those of a Franciscan monastery, an Augustinian friary, a Gilbertine Priory, a Dominican monastery, a Carmelite friary and the nunnery of St Clements.

Chapter 25

1. Edward Norman, *Roman Catholicism in England* (Oxford: Oxford University Press, 1985), p. 34.
2. J.N.D. Kelly, *The Oxford Dictionary of Popes* (Oxford: Oxford University Press,1986), pp. 280-81.
3. Littlehales, *Mary Ward,* Pilgrim and Mystic, p. 241. Other sources say that Winefrid returned empty-handed.
4. J.S. Purvis, *The Condition of Yorkshire Church Fabrics 1300–1800* (York: St Anthony's Press, 1958); N.J.G. Pounds, *A History of the English Parish* (Cambridge: Cambridge University Press, 2000).
5. Littlehales, *Mary Ward, Pilgrim and Mystic*, p. 242; Samuel Margerison, *The Registers of the Parish Church of Calverley in the*

West Riding of the County of York (Bradford: G.F. Sewell, Printer, 1883), p. 120.

6. Littlehales, *Mary Ward, pilgrim and mystic*, p. 242; 'Mary Ward: Dangerous Visionary', Marywarddocumentary.com.

7. It was moved inside the church in 1967.

8. 'To love the poor / persevere in the same / live, die and rise with / them was all the aim of / Mary Ward who / Having lived 60 years / and 8 days died the / 20 of Jan 1645.' The confusion in the date of death is explained by the fact that the sisters were using the Gregorian calendar, while England was still using the Julian.

Chapter 26

1. The paintings of the *Painted Life* series that hung in the school corridor while my mother-in-law was a pupil in Augsburg are now displayed in the school's Maria-Ward-Saal.

2. *St. Mary's Convent, Micklegate Bar York (1686–1887)* edited by Henry J. Coleridge, (London: Burns and Oates, 1887), p. 81;
   https://archive.org/stream/stmarysconventm00convgoog/
   stmarysconventm00convgoog_djvu.txt.

3. The new chapel was said to be 'secret' because its domed roof could not be seen from the street, but it is unlikely that the unloading of the chapel building materials (next to York's busiest gateway!) could have been hidden from the public gaze. Its eight exits, to allow priests to escape, became superfluous in 1791 when the law allowed the chapel to apply for a licence and operate legally.

4. John Nicholas Murphy, *Terra Incognita, or the Convents of the United Kingdom* (London: Burns and Oates, 1876), p. 296, note 1;
   https://archive.org/stream/terraincognitaor00murpiala#page/298/
   mode/2up.

5. John Barrow, *Tour in Austrian Lombardy, the Northern Tyrol and Bavaria in 1840* (London: John Murray, 1841), p. 353;
   https://books.google.co.uk/books?id=
   TEILAAAAYAAJ&pg=PA341&source=gbs_toc_r&
   cad=4#v=onepage&q&f=false.

6. Since 2004 Mary Ward's Institute has been known as the *Congregation of Jesus*, and sisters add the letters CJ after their names, in the same way as Jesuits add SJ (Society of Jesus) after theirs.

7. The Bar Convent school in York, for example, has become All Saints R.C. School, a state Catholic comprehensive school for girls and boys.
8. Caldwell, 'First Sister of Feminism'.
9. Fact Sheet Nr 45, September 2017, *Unesco Institute for Statistics*, http://uis.unesco.org.
10. Right to Education: Situation around the world. https://www.humanium.org/en/right-to-education/